—t. Hellie

D0888715

The
Theatre of
Edward Gordon Craig

Of all the theatrical pioneers of the first half of the twentieth century, Edward Gordon Craig remains amongst the most influential. He, more than anyone, created the concept of a totally integrated stage action in which the actor is just one animated element in a powerful combination of sculptural lighting, expressive costumes and ambitiously three-dimensional sets. Craig worked with Stanislavsky in Moscow and found support for his schemes in Italy, France and Germany, though hardly at all in his native Britain. But it is through his writings and his designs that his ideas have had most impact on his own and successive generations of directors, actors, designers and students of the theatre.

Long unobtainable, this book by the French theatre specialist, Denis Bablet, provides a well-documented account of Craig's long life and the evolution of his ideas. It tells of his successes and failures as he strove to put his ideas into practice often with inadequate resources; it describes particularly fully Craig's great creative period from the 1890s to the First World War, including his meeting with Isadora Duncan, his work on the Moscow *Hamlet*, the founding and editing of his own theatre journal, *The Mask*, and the publication of his most influential book, *On the Art of the Theatre*, which still keeps his ideas alive today.

This volume includes thirty-six black and white photographs of productions and scene designs as well as several of Craig's line drawings in the text. The translator is the late Daphne Woodward, herself a member of Craig's circle.

The photograph of Edward Gordon Craig on the front cover was taken in 1920 by Hugh Thomas. It is reproduced by kind permission of Anthony Thomas from an original print loaned by Edward Craig.

The
Theatre of
Edward Gordon Craig

DENIS BABLET

translated by
Daphne Woodward

Eyre Methuen · London

First published in English as *Edward Gordon Craig*
in 1966 by Heinemann Educational Books Ltd

Re-issued in hardback and paperback editions as
The Theatre of Edward Gordon Craig
in 1981 by Eyre Methuen Ltd,
11 New Fetter Lane, London EC4P 4EE

Originally published in French in 1962 by L'Arche Editeur

Copyright © 1962 L'Arche Editeur
Translation copyright © 1966 Heinemann Educational Books Ltd

ISBN 0 413 47870 X (Hardback)
0 413 47880 7 (Paperback)

Printed and bound in Great Britain
at The Pitman Press, Bath

CONTENTS

ILLUSTRATIONS

(appearing between Pages 102 and 103)

FOREWORD

On the first page of his *Private Notebook*, Craig has written: 'My ambition was always to *do* something, not to *be* something.' This book attempts to explain what Craig has done. It may perhaps help to give an idea of what he has been. I have tried to disentangle the facts from the many legends that have grown up around him, disregarding the violent and biased judgements that have been passed on him. In order to do so I had to make persevering investigations into the events of his life, his writings (books, articles, unpublished MSS., annotated copies), his theatrical productions, his scene and costume designs, his numerous unfulfilled projects, and his dealings with other theatre men of his day; and I would like to take this opportunity of thanking the many people who have helped me. This book is intended not as an exhaustive monograph or an essay on Craig's ideas, but as an account of his development and a description of the landmarks in his career. I have purposely omitted the countless anecdotes related about him, amusing and vivid though many of them are, and I have not dealt in any detail with the incidents of his private life, useful as they may be in clarifying his psychology. What concerns us here is the man of the theatre and his contribution to the present-day stage. I have dwelt at some length on Craig's practical achievements, because it is too often forgotten that he was active as a producer before he began to write down his ideas. Hence the motto of his magazine, *The Mask*: 'After the practice, the theory.'

D.B.

I

CHILDHOOD

The latter half of the nineteenth century in England was, of course, dominated by the figure of Queen Victoria. It was a period of great economic and social changes and of a prosperity that reached its climax between 1860 and 1880, when the country was at the height of its power. Between 1837 and 1887 the population more than doubled, and the cities expanded tremendously as a result of unprecedented industrial and commercial development, to the great benefit of the bourgeoisie. That class controlled politics and financed the Empire, the growth of which it had promoted: in 1877 Victoria became Empress of India. The power of the aristocracy was declining, but their polished manners were spreading to the sons of the manufacturing and merchant classes.

Middle-class respectability was the hallmark of the Victorian age, the keynote of its active social life and its fashionable clubs. It was 'the thing' to send one's sons to Oxford or to collect pictures, but etiquette was rather starched, and fashion, to gain approval, must not exceed the limits of good taste. Snobbery was one rule of life, puritanism another, and the accepted code of morals was really a form of discipline.

Industrial expansion, however gratifying to believers in progress – to the positivists, the rationalists, the men of science, who looked upon it as undeniable proof of human powers – was regarded with scepticism, even with repugnance, by those whose minds were more attuned to art and beauty: industry, these declared, had killed art, and art alone could redeem mankind. Man must be helped to rediscover the beauties of nature. Hence the mystical quest for beauty pursued by Ruskin and Walter Pater, William Morris's dream of a golden age based on an aesthetic form of collective economy, and the nostalgic cult of the past which found expression in the Pre-Raphaelite poets and painters, such as Rossetti, Millais and Burne-Jones, of whom Ruskin was the ardent champion. Pragmatism and the ugliness and vulgarity engendered by an industrial civilization were to be offset by the worship of beauty, the cultivation of art for art's sake. A time would soon come when the intellectual youth of England would discover the French 'Parnassian' poets and become devotees of Mallarmé and his Symbolist school.

The English theatre seems to have been little affected by these artistic urges. It reflected the prevailing taste of the day. People expected the drama to entertain them, playwrights avoided delicate subjects, and if they ever made bold to criticize certain defects of the social system they kept within the permissible limits and never sought to propose remedies. At a time when the novelists – Dickens, Thackeray, Meredith – were putting forward astute and often highly critical descriptions of contemporary society, the dramatists were following Sardou along the rut of historical tragedy or imitating Bulwer-Lytton's sentimental moral platitudes. Some of them copied Dickens or Scott, Dumas *père* or Dumas *fils*. Browning and Swinburne wrote philosophical dramas few of which were actable, for they were usually tenebrous, overloaded with aesthetic flourishes or metaphysical subtleties. T. W. Robertson soon began to work the vein of the *pièce à thèse* and the would-be fashionable public flocked to the Prince of Wales Theatre to applaud such pieces as *Caste*, with their 'daring' themes, frequently childish plots and skilful but mechanical construction. The wind of change did not begin to blow through the English theatre until the last years of the century, when Pinero, Wilde, Barrie and Shaw began to write for it.

Nevertheless, theatrical activity was on the increase. In 1851 London had nineteen playhouses; by 1870 there were thirty, and in 1899 the total was sixty-one. People of fashion were venturing in ever-growing numbers into the commercial theatres, and actors, formerly ostracized, were now regarded as socially acceptable. Indeed, by the end of the century, financiers, aristocrats and intellectual leaders were happy to boast of their acquaintance and to be received in their circles. Needless to say, however, there was no question of a National Theatre for England – the State would not condescend to maintain a company of players.

In the course of the nineteenth century the style of theatrical presentation in England developed along much the same lines as in other European countries. There was an increasing tendency towards archaeological exactitude and realism, great importance came to be attributed to the accurate reproduction of details and no effort was spared that might heighten the illusion. This trend continued virtually without interruption from Garrick to Samuel Phelps and Kean and from Kean to Henry Irving, who became the 'leading man' at the Lyceum Theatre in 1871, and proceeded to introduce new methods of production there. Irving soon became the supreme example of the actor-manager, reigning over the English stage in the dual role of chief performer and stage-director.

*

Edward Gordon Craig's father, Edward William Godwin, was an architect with a passion for the theatre. Craig's mother, Ellen Terry, was to become one of England's most celebrated actresses. She and Godwin first met in 1862, when the fifteen-year-old girl was playing at Bristol. In 1864 she married Watts, the painter, and left the stage; but the marriage broke up, and she went to live with Godwin at Harpenden – then a mere village. In 1869 they had a daughter, Edith, and three years later, on 16 January 1872, Edward Gordon was born, at Stevenage in Hertfordshire.

Oscar Wilde wrote of Godwin that he was 'one of the most artistic spirits of the century in England'. (1) He was a fervent admirer of Gothic art, and like many men of his generation had been influenced by Ruskin, whose *Stones of Venice* he read with avidity, and by William Morris. He shared their love of beauty, their repugnance for all that was ugly and vulgar, and their desire to train and improve the taste of the age. An austere, brilliant and refined man, he numbered Whistler and Burne-Jones among his friends. His architectural work, which included a church in Ireland, the Northampton Town Hall and the White House, built for Whistler in Chelsea, illustrates his feeling for proportion, his sense of the balanced composition of forms and surfaces, his logical approach to beauty.

But Godwin did not consider that an artist should be confined to his particular profession, that an architect should think of nothing but plans and buildings. He did not disdain to take an interest in such things as furniture and wallpaper. Beauty, for him, was a matter of harmony. And it was perfectly natural that like the Renaissance architects, Palladio, Serlio, Sabbattini or Inigo Jones, Godwin should turn towards the theatre. He was a cultivated man, and came to it as an enlightened amateur, an expert on scene and costume. He worked both as a designer and as a producer.

In 1857, when he was only twenty-four, Godwin became theatre critic of a Bristol newspaper, and already showed a particular interest in the visual side of the drama. He was an expert on Shakespeare, and made a systematic study of the plays from the producer's point of view, subsequently writing a series of articles, published in *The Architect* in 1875 under the general title 'Architecture and Costume of Shakespeare's Plays', which reveal him as a learned archaeologist and perceptive historian. He wanted each of the plays to be presented with complete truth to history, and went much further than his contemporaries in his pursuit of this aim. These articles constitute methodical, precise studies, and provide a mine of information for producers and for the designers of costumes, scenery and properties.

In 1874, Ellen Terry returned to the stage as Philippa Chester in Charles Reade's *The Wandering Heir* at the Queen's Theatre. The Bancrofts decided to put on *The Merchant of Venice* at the Prince of Wales Theatre, with Ellen as Portia, and entrusted the artistic direction of the production to Godwin. This gave him an opportunity of applying his research and testing his ideas, and the first performance (19 April 1875) was undoubtedly a milestone in the history of the English theatre. 'It was the first production in which the modern spirit of stage-management asserted itself, transporting us . . . into the atmosphere of Venice, into the rarified realms of Shakespearean Comedy.' (2)

Ellen Terry and Godwin thus seemed both to be assured of a reputation based on artistic success. Their collaboration might perhaps have continued regardless of the difference in their ages (Ellen Terry was twenty-eight and Godwin forty-two); but there was a conflict of temperaments, exacerbated now by the intrigues of those around them, and a few months later they parted. Craig, writing his memoirs, yields to the temptation of speculating about what they might have achieved if they had stayed together:

> *Question:* If she had stood firmly by his side – if she had puffed Charles Reade away (or told him to unite with E.W.G. and establish a theatre) and brushed 'fly and gnat aside' and all these silly self-seekers – and had she for a space of time stood FIRM in support of her heart's BELIEF (i.e. her love – and her conscience and her good sense), would he not awhile later have found the very path along which the two could go, and on together? *I don't doubt it for a single moment!* E.W.G., architect, producer of plays in which she, E.T., would act Portia, Rosalind . . . Imogen, Beatrice, Juliet, Perdita and Hermione, Desdemona, Miranda, Viola, Ophelia, Cordelia and Olivia, Kate Hardcastle; in *Everyman* and in the plays of Ford, Ben Jonson, Webster and others; and E.W.G. would have produced them all. Might not that way have proved the very best for her, for him and for the British Theatre? (3)

In 1876, Godwin married Beatrice Philip. In the following year Ellen Terry was married for the second time – to an actor, Charles Kelly. Their admiration for each other remained undiminished however, and at Ellen's request, Godwin advised Irving in the production of *The Cup*, by Tennyson. But their careers took them along separate paths. Ellen Terry appeared in several plays under John Hare's management at the Court Theatre before being engaged by Irving to act Ophelia at the Lyceum (1878). Godwin helped to present several productions, including *Claudian*, by Henry Hermann and W. G. Wills (1883), and *Hamlet* at the Princess's Theatre (1885). In 1884 Lady Archibald Campbell asked him to produce *As You Like It* for open-air performance at Coombe Wood. He also chose the actors and designed the costumes, in tones of brown and green that went well with the delightful setting and drew warm praise from his friend Wilde. (4)

But Godwin's importance as an innovator and pioneer was best revealed in his production of *Helena in Troas*, by John Todhunter (1886), only a few months before his death. He himself adapted the piece, designed the scenes and costumes, selected the actors and directed the rehearsals, thus revealing himself as a producer in the present-day sense of the word. The most original feature of the whole thing was, however, his choice of the place of performance and the use he made of it: twelve years before Lugné-Poe put on *Measure for Measure* at the *Cirque d'Eté* in Paris and twenty-four years before Reinhardt produced *Oedipus* at the Schumann Circus, Godwin transformed Hengler's Circus, in London, into a theatre with the architectural features of a Greek amphitheatre. How he did it is clear from a drawing published in *The Graphic* of 5 June 1886, which shows his combined use of the ring, in the centre of which he placed the altar of Dionysus, and of a narrow stage from which the portal of Paris's house leads off. This was a piece of archaeological reconstruction, but it was also an important contribution to the search for forms of theatrical architecture independent of the Italian stage structure. Godwin's concern with archaeological exactitude relates him to the Meiningen Company, which had presented *Julius Caesar* at Drury Lane in June 1881, while his views on production, as exemplified in *Helena in Troas*, foreshadow the experiments of Craig and Reinhardt.

Does this mean that Godwin had any great influence on his on's work? Craig has often paid tribute to Godwin, reprinting his articles on Shakespeare's Plays in *The Mask* and even writing a study entitled 'A Note on the Work of E. W. Godwin',(5) but he does not seem to have been influenced in his own work by his father, whom indeed he scarcely knew. From Dudley Harbron's book, *The Conscious Stone: the Life of Edward William Godwin*, which appeared in 1949, (6) he learnt much that he had not known before. He notes in his memoirs, 'My voice is my mother's, but maybe I acquired that. I can't recall hearing my papa speak. I can't recall him at all, for I was seldom with him after the age of three.' (7) The effect of this separation from his father was to give him a distressing sense of frustration. Throughout his childhood he was surrounded almost exclusively by women. He went so far as to compare himself to Hamlet, who had also been deprived of his father; and his book on his mother, *Ellen Terry and her Secret Self*, (8) is dedicated to his father. There was thus no direct influence, no more, at the most, than a spiritual heritage and certain points of resemblance which should not be exaggerated. It was no doubt from his father that Craig inherited his feeling for architectural proportions, the relationship of forms, the balance of mass and volume. Godwin took charge of every aspect of the production of *Helena in Troas*, and Craig considered, as we shall see, that the producer must have complete control of the stage presentation. But Godwin approached the theatre as an outsider (he was 'not *of* the Theatre'), (9) whereas Craig was to approach it from within. The son of an actress, he began his career as an actor.

*

In Craig's childhood and boyhood, impressions, feelings and dreams played a more important part than lessons. The unfolding of his sensibilities, with their modifications and fluctuations, can be clearly traced through the *Index to the Story of my Days* (where he has recorded the memories of his youth) and his books on Ellen Terry and Henry Irving.(10) There was nothing conventional about his education, little that conformed to the recognized Victorian pattern.

We read of the school, or rather the schools, he attended, of certain books, certain early enthusiasms, of the plays he saw and of those in which he took part during his early years.

It was not in his nature to submit easily to an official curriculum. About 1880, when he was going to a school in Earl's Court, he was backward in all subjects except drawing, music and Shakespeare. He tells us that at Bradfield College, where he went in 1886:

> I learnt very little Latin, no Greek, and mathematics meant and still mean nothing to me. I much regret this. The whole attempt to push, pump and worry learning into me failed. I was not a credit to my learned tutors. But I picked up easily anything ignorant but funny . . . (11)

He adds:

> Bradfield was all right in a way – but one wasn't exactly trained there – except for the cricket and football and the occasional military drill it was dull and meaningless. Latin, mathematics, history – this for a dull boy as I was was money thrown away. (12)

Was Craig such a dunce as he makes out? He had undoubted abilities, but he was naturally lazy.

In 1887 he was sent to the English College at Heidelberg. There he acquired a smattering of German; but he was more responsive to the romantic charm of the Neckar valley than to the patient efforts of his teachers. One evening he crept out for a cycling expedition – a short-lived escapade that led to his being expelled from the College. The last school he went to was a private one, kept by Mr Gorton, a clergyman, at Denchworth. By this time Craig was seventeen, and Denchworth's chief interest for him was the Shakespeare readings that took place there, in which he delighted.

He was not a very great reader in these early years, but certain books appealed to his imagination. Jules Verne, of course, and a little later a book illustrated by Howard Pyle, *The Adventures of Robin Hood*, a present from Irving. Craig was enthralled by Pyle's drawings, and his admiration went so deep that it in due course influenced even his designs for *Hamlet*. The boy seemed much more sensitive to what he saw than to what he read. He needed to be able to use his eyes, he responded to all visible things – landscape, architecture, illustrations, plays. Another of his favourite authors was Dumas, whose books he still reads for their adventures, their mystery, their intrigues and machinations, their secrets and masks. Craig himself came to resemble a character from Dumas: he was fond of signing articles in his magazine with pseudonyms and has never lost a certain love of mystification.

First and foremost in his reading, however, came Shakespeare. As a small boy he used to act scenes from *As You Like It* with his sister. When he discovered, at Heidelberg College, that the boys were only allowed to read German books, he appealed to his mother to ask if he could keep his 'old Shakespeare' with him. And he was immensely proud when Henry Irving inscribed the second volume of his edition of Shakespeare to him in 1888.

Many of the plays Craig saw in these early years were productions of Shakespeare, though there was also a famous melodrama, *The Corsican Brothers*, in which he saw Irving act for the first time. 'Teddy', then eight years old, watched from the wings, for his mother was afraid he might have a fit of hysterics at the point when the ghost of one brother appeared to the other. The other plays he went to included W. G. Wills's version of *Jane Eyre* at the Globe Theatre (1883), *Claudian*, at the Princess's Theatre (1884), and in 1889, Sarah Bernhardt in *Tosca*. But the performances he enjoyed most and still remembers best were the Shakespearean productions at the Lyceum Theatre, with Ellen Terry and Irving. In 1882 there was *Romeo and Juliet*; he saw this several times, and can still recall the music and some of the scenes. In the same year came *Much Ado About Nothing*, in which his mother 'played Beatrice marvellously well'. Of *Twelfth Night* (1884), he notes: 'I recall much of this production. In it Irving was remarkable in the guise of Malvolio – not playing the buffoon, but solemnly comic, with great distinction, calm and dark.' (13)

Craig was thus always in the atmosphere of the theatre, even when school kept him away from the London playhouses. He was already more than a mere spectator, for he had made his first appearance on the stage at the age of six, in *Olivia*, an adaptation of Goldsmith's *Vicar of Wakefield*, in which his mother was acting at the Court Theatre; Teddy was among the crowd of villagers. At the end of 1884 he joined Ellen Terry and Irving, then on tour in the United States, and walked on in *Hamlet*, *Much Ado About Nothing*, *Twelfth Night* and *Charles I*. And at Chicago, in 1885, he played his first speaking part – as Joey, the gardener's boy, in *Eugene Aram*:

It is because of Teddy, [writes Ellen Terry] that *Eugene Aram* is associated in my mind with one of the most beautiful sights that I ever saw in my life. . . He was so graceful and natural; he spoke his lines with ease and smiled all over his face! 'A born actor!' I said, although Joey was my son. (14)

His eyes are full of sparkle, [was the comment of one American journalist] his smile is a ripple over his face, and his laugh is as cheery and natural as a bird's song. . . . This Joey is Miss Ellen Terry's son, and the apple of her eye. On this Wednesday night, 14 January 1885, he spoke his first lines upon the stage. His mother has high hopes of this child's dramatic future. He has the instinct and the soul of art in him. Already the theatre is his home. His postures and his playfulness with the gardener, his natural and graceful movements, had been the subject of much drilling, of study and of practice. He acquitted himself beautifully and received the wise congratulations of his mother, of Mr Irving, and of the company. (15)

His first part, his first professional experience. Four years later, Edward Gordon Craig took the role of Arthur St Valery in *The Dead Heart*, a melodrama by Watts Phillips, adapted and produced by Irving. He was given an engagement at the Lyceum Theatre. He had become an actor, as the first step in his career.

NOTES

1. Oscar Wilde, 'The Truth of Masks', in *Intentions*, Methuen, London, 1909, p. 238.
2. Herbert Beerbohm Tree in a speech to the Oxford Union Debating Society (1900). Quoted by John Semar in his introduction to E. W. Godwin's article on 'The Architecture and Costume of The Merchant of Venice', *The Mask*, Vol. I, No. 3–4, May–June 1908, p. 75.
3. Edward Gordon Craig, *Index to the Story of my Days*, Hulton Press, London, 1957, p. 21.
4. Oscar Wilde, 'The Truth of Masks', in *Intentions*, pp. 257–8.
5. *The Mask*, Vol. III, No. 4–6, October 1910, pp. 53–6.
6. This book (Latimer House Ltd) is the best source of information on Godwin's life and work.
7. Craig, *Index to the Story of my Days*, p. 11.
8. Edward Gordon Craig, *Ellen Terry and her Secret Self*, Sampson Low, Marston & Co., London, 1931.
9. See Craig, *Index to the Story of my Days*, p. 21.
10. Gordon Craig, *Henry Irving*, J. M. Dent & Sons, London, 1930.
11. Craig, *Index to the Story of my Days*, pp. 72–3.
12. Ibid., p. 75.
13. Ibid., p. 59.
14. Edith Craig and Christopher St John ed., *Ellen Terry's Memoirs*, Victor Gollancz Ltd., London, 1933, p. 138.
15. Ibid., p. 215.

II

APPRENTICESHIP

Craig was sixteen when his mother decided to 'put him on the stage'. He can really be said to have been 'born in the theatre', to have had it 'in his blood', to have been 'an instinctive actor'; but he had had virtually no practical experience of the stage. At that time, as he himself admits, (1) though he knew something about William Blake and Rossetti, he knew nothing of the technique of acting. He had seen the Lyceum productions, he had watched his mother and Irving, England's most famous actors, and he had even made two appearances on the stage himself; but that was not a training.

And now he had suddenly become an actor, with a salary – £5 a week! Flung into the midst of the renowned Lyceum Company, headed by the most admired of actor-managers, he would have to learn by watching the others, listening to their advice – and by acting.

Where could Craig have found a school, with teachers who could direct his natural gifts and instruct him in the rudiments of his craft? The Lyceum was world-famous, but it had no school. In 1894, Irving declared that 'for actors, the advantage of a permanent school would be invaluable', (2) but all his own time was taken up by managing his theatre, rehearsing his company and learning his own parts – a threefold task which left him no time to establish the school whose absence Craig never ceased to regret. It was in part, no doubt, this regret that made him attach so much importance, later on, to the foundation of a real school of the theatre.

For lack of a school, Irving entrusted the budding actor to two teachers. One of these, Walter Lacy, was a picturesque old actor, a veteran of Charles Kean's day. Craig went to him regularly for elocution lessons. He would sit down, he would read a little; and then Lacy would begin to draw upon his fund of amusing stories. . . . The other teacher was the mime and ballet-master, Leon

Espinosa, whose great pride was that he had once walked along the Champs-Elysées with Dumas *père* leaning on his shoulder. A recollection calculated to enthral the young actor, with his passion for *The Three Musketeers*! Craig's lessons with Espinosa took place in the greenroom at the Lyceum Theatre. There he was shown how to carry himself in the role of Arthur St Valery, how a dashing young buck of the late eighteenth century would move and behave. Espinosa gave a splendid performance – but how could Craig learn in three-quarters of an hour what the old gentleman himself had taken many years to acquire and practise?

It was, in fact, on the stage itself that Craig gradually learnt his craft. Ellen Terry's sound advice began with *The Dead Heart* and he listened to it, full of admiration for her. He studied the diction of Squire Bancroft, his partner in the first scene. And then there was Irving, of whom Craig still says, 'I never had a greater master than he was. But Irving never had a more faithful follower than I.' Irving watched over him affectionately, guiding and advising him as he did all the actors who came to him. So Gordon Craig's school was the Lyceum Theatre itself:

> . . . in 1889, Lyceum Theatre and Henry Irving – my real school and my real master . . . I became an actor. And now the mere physical state of being in a theatre – in the best in England with the greatest actor in Europe and with my mother-actress – that was enough. . . . It was a beginning. I did not understand much – I had a receptive organism – only that. (3)

Craig remained at the Lyceum for eight years, acting and observing. He got little help in his training from the repertory, for the Lyceum was not venturesome in its choice of plays – a fact which drew caustic criticism from Bernard Shaw. Shakespeare had to share the honours with 'obsolete tomfooleries like *Robert Macaire*, schoolgirl charades like *Nance Oldfield*, blank verse by Wills, Comyns Carr and Calmour'. (4) This was, however, the general rule in those days; there was an extraordinary shortage of good contemporary plays, so that the only resource was to fall back upon the classics. Goldsmith and Sheridan were seldom performed, Marlowe, Ford, Dekker and Middleton not at all; but fortunately there was always Shakespeare. Craig gained two things from the Lyceum: above all a practical knowledge of stagecraft and the example of Irving, the actor-manager who was at the same time a kind of adopted father for him.

One has to read Craig's books in order to understand his admiration for Irving as an actor – to read *The Artists of the Theatre of the Future*, his own memoirs, his book on Ellen Terry, and most of all his *Henry Irving*. One must look through his *Daybooks* with their

Wood engraving of Henry Irving

scattering of notes on Irving's performances. Irving had not been endowed by nature from the outset with the qualities that ensure an actor's success and give him an authoritative presence. In fact, one day during an American tour, when Ellen Terry asked him what he was thinking about, he replied:

> I was thinking how strange it is that I should have made the reputation I have as an actor, with nothing to help me – with no equipment. My legs, my voice – everything has been against me. For an actor who can't walk, can't talk, and has no face to speak of, I've done pretty well. (5)

But Irving possessed the faculty Craig valued above any other – imagination – and another, complementary to it – self-control.

Everything he did was calculated, measured, deliberate; no gesture, movement, facial expression or intonation of the voice was left to chance. He knew how to control the emotional impulses triggered off by a situation or by the lines of a play. As Craig said later, 'Spontaneity he valued, but seldom indulged in: what he did, he did by design.' (6) Irving was forthright, sure of himself, of the effect he wished to produce, sure of his mask. He was a man who turned to nature for his inspiration, yet in whom everything was 'massively artificial'. (7) His intention was always clear, he never wrapped it up in mystery. As an actor he paid no great attention to other people's criticism, for he was his own most relentless critic.

With such a personality it is small wonder that his influence was so overwhelming. Other actors copied his qualities and his defects indiscriminately, in the belief that by imitating him they could rise to his level; beginners dreamt of one day becoming another Irving. This was only natural at a time when the actor-manager reigned supreme on the stage, attracting all eyes. As for Craig, he was watching his 'master' closely. When he came to describe his ideal, the *Über-marionette*, he declared that Irving had come closest to what he had in mind.

The Lyceum Theatre also stood for a style of performance, a method of work, a relative degree of perfection. And all this – style, method, perfection – was the result of Irving's patient efforts. Later, Craig was to shake off this influence, rejecting a realism which conflicted with his ideal; but he never forgot certain of Irving's working methods, or the persistence with which he strove for perfection.

28 September 1889 saw the first performance of *The Dead Heart* and Edward Gordon Craig's first appearance at the Lyceum. A few months earlier, André Antoine, the great French producer and director of the Théâtre Libre, had been to a performance there when on tour; he had not been enthusiastic about Irving as actor, but Irving as stage director was a different matter. In *Mes Souvenirs sur le Théâtre Libre*, he notes on 10 February 1889:

I let all the others go home and stayed here to see Irving's famous Lyceum at my leisure; I went there yesterday evening. They were giving *Macbeth*, with Miss Ellen Terry and Irving himself. I did not much admire the great actor, who reminded me of Taillade, with less fire; but what was incomparable was his stagecraft, which is something we can hardly conceive of in France. The scene where the castle wakes up, and above all that of the banquet, with the appearance of the ghost, are masterpieces, with lighting effects of which we have no idea as yet. (8)

A few months later, Antoine published the celebrated red-covered brochure in which he summed up the results achieved by the French theatre and formulated his hopes for it:

Our school of scene-painters is the foremost in Europe; no one can can compete with us in the quality of our back-cloths. So we may well wonder how it is that the English and German productions leave those of us who have had occasion to see them with such a profound impression of art, far exceeding what we feel at the sight of the most skilful and magnificent scenery that our Paris theatres have to show.
Every Frenchman who has visited Irving's theatre in London has come home in a state of amazement, having seen things there that he never suspected to exist. All actors and theatre people are unanimous on this point. . . . (9)

And he adds:

Irving manipulated his crowds with patient care and achieved an ensemble that astonishes our travellers. Nearly all English theatres are exceptionally clever in their use of properties, plants and artificial flowers in their settings. (11)

Irving arrived at these results by improved methods of production: he introduced stricter discipline into his theatre and gave more time to rehearsals than was usual in those days – so much so that people wondered how he found the time to learn his own parts. He rehearsed not only the leading actors, but the supers as well, for he set great store by lively crowd scenes that really heightened the dramatic effect. He also held scenery and lighting rehearsals. His technical staff were always at hand, ready to carry out his instructions. He attended to every detail.

Irving was no doubt influenced to some extent by Godwin, who worked with him more than once: for instance, in his production of *The Merchant of Venice* (1879), he took great pains to reconstruct Venetian life, to make it historically convincing. He tried to heighten the illusion. Many of his scenes were three-dimensional. The use of electricity was becoming general in the theatre, and Irving took the greatest care with his lighting, even if, as was often the case, the stage tended to be too shadowy. (11) In his concern for realistic detail, historical accuracy and general effect, Irving resembled the Duke of Saxe-Meiningen; he too thought that the visual aspect of a production was the first to capture the audience, and that the aim should be to give an impression of unity. The style of Craig's productions was poles apart from Irving's realism, but he was equally insistent upon perfect unity of presentation. And one understands how he can say that 'It took me long to break free from the glorious influence, but I always have loved to be Irving's pupil, and I count on his help to this day.' (12)

*

The years from 1889 to 1897 were of decisive importance for Craig. In those eight years he built up the experience from which he was to draw conclusions later on. They were eight years of discoveries and activities that fascinated him but left him unsatisfied. His personality was not yet fully developed, it was awakening, little by little, with each new part he played, stimulated by the books he was reading and the people he met.

In 1890 he appeared as Moses in *Olivia* and as Henry Ashton in *Ravenswood. Much Ado About Nothing* saw him as a messenger and a watchman; his other parts included Alexander Oldworthy in *Nance Oldfield* and Abel Quick in *A Regular Fix*, a farce by Maddison Morton (1891). 'Ted is first rate,' wrote Irving to Ellen Terry, 'He'll be a splendid comedian in time, and a genial one.' (13) In 1892 he acted Cromwell in *Henry VIII* and Oswald in *King Lear*.

In the summer, with Irving's approval, he would join a provincial touring company. This was excellent training for a young actor; it gave him the chance to attempt more important parts, gain varied experience and get used to different audiences. In the summer of 1890 he went on tour with the Haviland-Harvey company, playing parts that were chosen for him by Irving – Biondello in

The Taming of the Shrew, Caleb Deccie in *Two Roses*, Maynard in *The Corsican Brothers* and Sir Almerik in *Iolanthe*. The following summer he joined Sarah Thorne's company, playing the First Gravedigger in *Hamlet* and Charles Surface in *The School for Scandal*. In the summer of 1892 he was back with the same company, appearing as Ford in *The Merry Wives of Windsor* and as Petruchio in *The Taming of the Shrew*.

Craig's horizon was already widening. His work as an actor left him a fair amount of spare time, and Irving gave him advice which contributed to his general education. Up to now he had been content to receive books as presents; it would never have occurred to him to buy any. Irving suggested that he might spend part of his salary on books, and from that time on he was constantly adding to his library, as his tastes and his new discoveries prompted him.

The young man was enthralled by poetry, and now developed a passion for Shelley. Like his father, he admired Rossetti, and he began to read Ruskin, whom he did not fully understand as yet, but whose artistic fervour he could share. Ruskin's anti-realist influence no doubt helped to offset that of the Lyceum. Craig's mother gave him a *Life of Edmund Kean* and a *Life of Mrs Siddons*. He was still reading Dumas, and now he turned to Goethe and Heine. In 1890 the books he bought included G. H. Lewes's *Life of Goethe*, Tolstoy's *Kreutzer Sonata*, Crabb Robinson's *Journal* and Marlowe's *Faust* . . . an ill-assorted mixture of historical novels, studies of actors, philosophy and poetry. Craig was a 'receptive organism', absorbing and digesting pell-mell whatever came along and influenced by whatever he read.

He was beginning to draw, too. He had no real training for this. The few lessons he had been given in his school days were quite inadequate, and later he was to express regret at having never been properly taught. (14) He drew by taste and instinct. During his summer tours he made sketches in the theatre or out in the country. In 1890 he made a number of visits to London museums, noting details of costumes, gloves and hats, sketching pieces of furniture or copying some ornament that caught his attention.

He gained much from these visits to museums. Everything he saw was a spur to his imagination. In the National Gallery he was fascinated – first by the Italian Renaissance painters – Bellini, Crivelli, Piero della Francesca, Piero di Cosimo, Ghirlandajo, Mantegna. He looked at every picture as though it were a meticulously organized stage scene, admiring the attitudes and expressions of the characters and the manner in which they were grouped; noting how the painter had brought his composition to life through the play of light and colour; letting his imagination roam in the backgrounds of the pictures, with their sunny landscapes, winding roads and stylized Italian towns, whose architectural proportions would one day influence his own work. Then came Van Eyck, Canaletto ('To me, it had to be all "theatre" '), (15) Rubens, Titian, Rembrandt, Turner and a host of others. Some twenty years later, when he wrote 'Tuition in Art: a note to the young generation of theatrical students', his visits to the National Gallery were still fresh in his memory, and he advised actors to turn to the works of the great painters in order to study movement and facial expression, saying that they should not try to learn from nature until they had drawn full benefit from an attentive scrutiny of the old masters. (16)

Thus, during his first years at the Lyceum, Craig was waking up, developing his feeling for the stage, becoming increasingly perceptive, training himself as an actor. He had as yet no idea of turning to theatrical production, but he made two designs for scenes. One of these, a small colour-sketch for *Romeo and Juliet* (1891) is carefully preserved in one of his *Daybooks*. (17) It is no more than the record of an idea, and shows the direct influence of the Lyceum style in the choice and arrangement of the scenic elements. The other project, for *Henry IV* (1890), is carried a little further: (18) he has jotted down the chief events in Prince Hal's life, suggested some music that might be used (from Scottish airs to Chopin and Dvořák!) and made a rather clumsy sketch with notes suggesting materials for the scenery, the use of certain parts of the stage, and even the arrangement of the lighting. But this, too, might pass for a copy of some Lyceum scene, as Craig himself readily admits:

> I was working under an actor-manager at the time. I was working in a theatre where the chairs and the tables and other matters of detail played over-important and photographic parts, and, not knowing any better, I had to take all this as a good example. The play of

Henry IV, therefore, consisted to my mind of one excellent part, Prince Hal, and thirty or forty other characters that trotted round this part. There was the usual table with the chairs round it on the right side. There at the back was the usual door, and I thought it rather unique and daring at the time to place this door a little bit off the straight. There was the window with the latches and the bolts and the curtains ruffled up to look as if they had been used for some time, and outside the glimpses of English landscape. There were the great flagons; and, of course, on the curtain rising there was to be a great cluster and fluster of 'scurvy knaves', who ran in and out, and a noise of jovial drinkers in the next room. There was the little piece of jovial music to take up the curtain, that swinging jig tune which we have all grown so familiar with, there were the three girls who pass at the back of the window, laughing. One pops her head in at the window with a laugh and a word to the potman. Then there is the dwindling of the laughter and the sinking to piano of the orchestra as the first speaking character enters, and so on. (19)

*

1893. An important year for young Craig, now aged twenty-one. He was still playing at the Lyceum, his roles including Lorenzo in *The Merchant of Venice* (which earned him a drubbing from the critics) and the Young Templar in Tennyson's *Becket*. He was adding to his collection of books – Whitman, Montaigne (whose Essays have been among his bedside books ever since); he bought reproductions of Holbein's *Dance of Death* and Jacques Callot's *Misères de la Guerre*. Callot's style later influenced his engravings, sketches of stage characters and costume designs, and one of his most famous wood-engravings is entitled 'Hommage à Jacques Callot' (1921). And while his cultural range was thus widening, other events were taking place which helped to determine the course of his career.

At the beginning of the year he rented a little house at Uxbridge, living alone there for a time and going up to London for the Lyceum performances. Shortly after this he married Miss May Gibson. Irving advised him against this step, and Craig himself regarded it later as a youthful error. The marriage ultimately broke up.

But while at Uxbridge, he made the acquaintance of James Pryde (20) and William Nicholson (21), members of the New English Art Movement, launched to counteract the academic banalities of pseudo-realism and the vulgarity current at the time. Pryde was influenced by Hogarth, Piranese, Whistler and Velasquez, and admired Daumier almost to idolatry. Nicholson was a wood-engraver with an incomparable mastery of technique. It was about this time that the pair began to work in partnership, designing posters which they signed 'The Beggarstaff Brothers'. Thanks to them, Craig was introduced to a new branch of art and its technique. Watching Nicholson, he learnt how to set to work on a woodblock. Pryde did not give him any technical hints, but the two of them used to hold long, friendly arguments – for Pryde was passionately devoted to the theatre. From Pryde he learnt style. Craig's earliest woodcuts were so much influenced by these two men that many of them look like imitations. He was learning an art that would not concern itself with reproducing details; he was learning to appreciate line, to enjoy a craft for its own sake, to go straight to essentials, to simplify his design, retaining only dominant forms and elemental masses – to be sparing of his re-sources, building up a decorative composition from the balance of simple but dramatic elements – and he was reverting to a certain stylistic naïveté. Craig's discovery of engraving, its technique and its possibilities, was an outstanding event in his life, not merely because it became one of his principal activities. It was Pryde and Nicholson, no doubt, who revealed to him the value of black, not merely as an outline, but as a colour, covering extensive surfaces and giving expression to a drawing. Playing draughts with Craig one day, I remarked with surprise that he always chose the black pieces. 'It's because black is a favourite colour of mine,' he explained. Much might be said about this predilection of his, the key to which lies perhaps in the quotation from Odilon Redon with which he prefaces *List B* of his woodcuts (1923):

Black is the most essential of colours. It finds its glorification, its life, shall I say, in the direct and deeper springs in Nature. . . . Black should be respected. Nothing can prostitute it.
It does not please the eye nor awaken the sensuality.

It is an agent of the mind far more than the beautiful colours of the palette or prism. . . . In the Louvre the galleries devoted to drawings contain a far greater and purer sum of art than the galleries of paintings. But few visitors are to be seen there, the paintings being far more popular. (22)

For the time being, however, it did not occur to Craig to put his new knowledge of wood-engraving to practical use; he had no intention of becoming a professional wood-engraver:

At that time, [he writes] it did not occur to me that I could do any-thing as a producer of plays, or that I should later put my scrap of experience as a wood-engraver to any practical use. I was quite convinced that acting and make-up and costumes and the words were the be-all and the end-all of the Art of the Theatre; and had you told me at that time that I should some day cease to act, I should have smiled the hearty and forgiving smile of youth at you, and laughed at your prediction. (23)

Meanwhile Craig was studying *Ion*, by Talfourd, and Peer Gynt – a part he longed to play in a London theatre together with Prince Hal in *Henry IV*, Hotspur, Othello and Hamlet. And when he thought of the producer, it was in the shape of the actor-manager of that day, who stood on the stage giving orders to the stage-carpenters, electricians, costumiers and actors. 'Later on,' he writes, 'I came to see that standing in the middle of the stage and making others do the work is not the sole qualification for being a producer.' (24)

But at the end of that year, on 13 and 14 December, the first theatrical production for which he was entirely responsible was presented at the Uxbridge Town Hall. This was Musset's *On ne badine pas avec l'amour*. Craig's preparations for this had lasted two months; he had designed the scenery, helped to build it, painted it and rehearsed the actors – Tom Heslewood, Violet Vanbrugh and Italia Conti (Camille), he himself taking the part of Perdican. We know little about this production; Craig dismisses it as of no real importance, declaring that he was still under the influence of the Lyceum Theatre and its methods. The programme announces that 'the costumes are an exact reproduction of the clothes worn in the fourteenth century, and are made from designs by M. Viollet-le-Duc'. (25) Craig had a lasting respect for the documentary value of Viollet-le-Duc's writings, even after he felt obliged to discard their influence. In *The Artists of the Theatre of the Future*, he writes:

> Better than these that I have mentioned [Racinet, Planchet and Hottenroth] is Viollet-le-Duc. He has much love for the little truths which underlie costume, and is very faithful in his attitude; but even his is more a book for the historical novelist. . . . (26)

When he put on *On ne badine pas avec l'amour*, Craig was still in the grip of the theatre's archaeological mania, the historical realism exemplified by the Meiningen Company. But the experience was no doubt useful in showing him that he could do something else besides acting, and bringing him into contact with the other branches of stagecraft. In any case it shows that Craig, so often accused of being a mere theorist, ignorant of the practical aspects of theatrical activity, had, on the contrary, begun to tackle them by the time he was twenty-one.

*

For the time being this experiment was not followed up; Craig continued his acting career in accordance with circumstances and really had no thought of any other.

In August 1894 he joined W. S. Hardy's small 'Shakespearean Company', tempted by the offer of the parts every young actor dreams of playing – Hamlet, Romeo, Cassio, Gratiano, Richmond. Three days of rehearsals for *Hamlet*, three days for *Romeo*. The work was rushed through somehow, in circumstances which were often farcical. Audiences were occasionally rowdy, too, as the company made its round of large and small towns – Hereford, Wrexham, Wolverhampton, Rugby, Ludlow and Uxbridge among them. The tour came to an end in the middle of December.

From 1895 onwards, Craig seldom appeared at the Lyceum. Dissatisfaction and doubt were stealing over him, and for several years he felt much perplexed: 'I now see what an empty, *idle* life the stage (in England) offered us in those days,' he writes. 'In the old stock-company years much work kept the actors well occupied; in 1890 the actor had days of time on his hands.' (27) One has the impression that he was not sure what he wanted, that he was allowing himself to be carried along by events and guided by his own inclinations. His personality was not yet fully developed.

Engagements were offered to him and he accepted them. At the beginning of 1895 he was acting Cavaradossi in *Tosca*, in a touring company under the management of Hubert Evelyn, which visited Eastbourne, Yarmouth, Norwich, Southampton and Newcastle. On another tour, in the summer, he played Armand in *La Dame aux Camélias*, Claude Melnotte in *The Lady of Lyons*, Hamlet, and other roles.

Such spare time as he had, he spent in drawing. He was drawing the whole time, declares one of his fellow actors. And he began to write music. It wasn't 'great' music, he explained to me; but he felt he knew enough, had enough talent and skill, to compose music for the stage. About this time he set several of Heine's poems to music, and composed a few songs.

As we have seen already, landscape, architecture, pictures and illustrations were immensely important to Craig. He drew feeling and inspiration from everything that met his eyes. This accounts for the zeal with which he collected illustrative material – old maps and plans, reproductions, books with imaginative illustrations, even picture postcards. It also explains his taste for illustrated magazines. In June 1895, an American periodical, *The Century Magazine*, published an article by T. A. Janvier on 'The *Comédie Française* at Orange'. (28) The article itself was naturally interesting to Craig, but he was particularly delighted by its illustrations, drawings by Louis Loeb. From these he not only discovered the Roman theatre at Orange, but it was brought vividly before him by contrasting light and shade, by the proportion of the actors to the simple architectural forms, the vertical lines and clearly-outlined surfaces that combined and contrasted to give a feeling of space, the tremendous wall towering behind the stage, and its centre portal. No written description could have been so eloquent. When, later, he designed his unadorned stage scenes, with their balanced masses of shadow and brilliance, their lines and planes in which the vertical was dominant, he was not copying Orange, he had assimilated a 'vision' he found inspiring, as he notes in his *Daybook* for 1931–1932–1933.

> ... I have seen drawings in an American Magazine of the Roman theatre of Orange – and this glimpse of a Roman theatre has done what a course of lectures and 2 years' study of theatres in London, Paris or Berlin could never have done. That is how it is that a town which is unknown to me has influenced my work so much.
>
> It was after seeing these drawings that I realized the possibilities which are opened by light, space and background to the stage.
>
> In the Opera House, Paris or the C[omédie] F[rançaise] or in London theatres I had never realized this.
>
> I had often when a child felt the value of tall lines – of the big beds of the 17th century which are at Hampton Court Palace: but beds are not theatres – the avenues of trees at H. C. are not theatres either – the aisles of cathedrals – and so I never associated the grandeur of 2 vertical lines with theatres – theatre scenes were always cut off and stumpy when I was a child – and until 1900, when I changed that. (29)

*

'Perilous years, end of 1896 to 1899', (30) Craig notes in his memoirs. Acting and rehearsing were beginning to bore him at times. In 1896 he joined Sarah Thorne's company at the Opera House, Chatham, to play Petruchio, Hamlet and Macbeth. In July, at the Parkhurst Theatre in London, he acted Hamlet and Romeo with his own company. He reappeared at the Lyceum in *Cymbeline* (Arviragus) and *Richard III* (Edward IV). In the following year he played Hamlet again, for eight performances, at the Olympic Theatre in London. The first-night audience included Irving, Ellen Terry, Gilbert Coleridge and William Rothenstein.

Hamlet, for Craig, was the part of parts: he could never shake off its fascination. He thought about it all the time; in later years he made countless designs for it, he produced it at Moscow on Stanislavsky's invitation, he illustrated it with woodcuts. For the moment he was acting it, and was judged as an actor. Opinions were divided. Gilbert Coleridge wrote, many years later, that because of its youth, intellect, faultless elocution and in particular its air of impromptu, Craig's performance of Hamlet was the finest he had ever seen. (31) E. F. Spence recalled: 'My first memory of Craig is of his Hamlet at the Olympic in 1897, when he was an extremely handsome young man of twenty-five. To this day I remember vividly his admirable work in the first act. I think none of the scores of Hamlets seen by me have been so good in that part of the tragedy.' (32) William Rothenstein says in his Memoirs: 'How good an actor he was I don't know. I saw him once act as Hamlet, somewhere in Islington, and never had I seen such a touching and beautiful figure.' (33) The press was not quite so unanimous. The conservative critic of *The People* (34) accused him of being excessively modern, saying that if he wished to leave his mark on the theatre of the future he should keep to the tradition and beware of innovations. One of the most famous and influential critics of the day, Clement Scott, writing in the *Illustrated London News* (35), praised his imaginative interpretation of Romeo and added, 'I was told that his Hamlet was a still more remarkable and promising performance. But the Romeo was good enough, and all that the young actor has to do now is to forget that he has been under the strong acting influence of Sir Henry Irving, so much as to occasionally imitate his style with far too much fidelity.' *The Era*, after mentioning Craig's easy, expressive style and his intelligent rendering of the part, hailed him as the 'diligent student of the new school of acting as opposed to the stilted, ranting delivery and often mechanical methods of the old.' (36)

Thus, despite a few criticisms of his performances, he won general praise for his subtlety and intelligence, and for the way he was reacting against hidebound methods and traditions. He was making constant progress. His mother found him excellent as Edward IV in *Richard III*. (37) He still needed to work and free himself from outside influences, but there seemed to be no doubt that he had the stuff of a great actor in him.

In July 1897, Craig played Young Marlow in Goldsmith's *She Stoops to Conquer*, at the Kingston-on-Thames theatre. At the end of that year he gave up acting, once and for all. Was this the result of some inner crisis – of dissatisfaction – of new ambitions? Why, after playing some forty parts, should he have abandoned, at the age of twenty-five, a craft he had been pursuing for eight years already? There may be several answers to this question. Craig himself has given us the chief and most correct of them.

Ellen Terry wrote later, 'I have good reason to be proud of what he has done since, but I regret the lost actor *always*.' In 1897, her son had decided that he was not a good enough actor. He had the technique at his finger-tips, he knew his job, he was a sound performer; but this was not enough to satisfy his ambition. In his book on his mother he declares:

> I, too, grieved that I could not go on acting. What actor of twenty-five years old, who had played with H. I. and E. T., would not? Besides, I had played some bigger parts in other theatres during the Lyceum vacation months – I had acted Romeo, Petruchio, Charles Surface, Young Marlow, Macbeth and Hamlet.
>
> Acting these, I discovered that I was not a second Irving. Returning to the Lyceum, I discovered why. (38)

Like all the young members of the Lyceum Company, Craig had dreamt of being another Irving. He measured himself against the great Shakespearean parts, and his dream vanished. He felt there was not enough life in his acting, that it did not spring from a deep-seated desire 'to express something', that he was merely using a technique he had learnt from Irving. He could not resign himself to being no more than a pale copy of his master:

> . . . When I watched H. I. in the last act of *The Lyons Mail* and in *The Bells*, I felt that beyond that there was no going, and I told myself that I could either be content for the rest of my life to follow Irving and become a feeble imitation of him, or discover who I was and be that. So I made my choice, and I turned my back on Irving for many a year – occasionally looking over my shoulder to catch one more look at the loved figure. (39)

But this, though the chief reason, was not the only one. Craig's Uxbridge experiment had shown him that he was capable of putting on a play. He was drawing a great deal, he had learnt to make woodcuts. In 1896, 'bitten by the desire to make posters *à la Beggarstaff*', (40) he rented an extra room at Chatham, where he was appearing with Sarah Thorne's company, so that he could work undisturbed. He had become conscious of his talents, was discovering fresh creative activities into which he flung himself ardently, and had silently determined 'to be *some*body and do *some*thing'.

> I looked around me: 'What,' I asked myself, 'What still remains to be done in this world of the Theatre, where all seems to me to be so perfect?'
> This question teased me for several years – for the last two years at the Lyceum and for two years after I had left. (41)

In 1897 he was still hesitating which road to take. But his experience as an actor proved decisive. *The Artists of the Theatre of the Future* reads like a description of his own development. Addressing the future 'artist of the theatre', he tells him to remember that 'When you have studied these [the crafts which go to make up the art of the theatre] thoroughly you will find some which are of value, and you will certainly find that the experience as an actor has been necessary.' (42)

NOTES

1. E. G. Craig, *Henry Irving*, op. cit., p. 14.
2. Quoted by Craig in *Henry Irving*, p. 119.
3. E. G. Craig, *Index to the Story of my Days*, op. cit., p. 103.
4. George Bernard Shaw in the *Saturday Review*, 19 January 1895.
5. Quoted by Craig in *Henry Irving*, p. 69.
6. Ibid., p. 78.
7. Ibid., p. 78.
8. André Antoine, *Mes Souvenirs sur le Théâtre Libre*, Arthème Fayard, Paris, 1921, p. 136.
9. André Antoine, *Le Théâtre Libre*, May 1890, Imprimerie Eugène-Verneau, Paris, p. 102.
10. Ibid., p. 105.
11. In his book on Irving, Craig declares that it was from Irving that he learnt to make his scenes too dark (p. 117).
12. E. G. Craig, *Henry Irving*, p. 118.
13. Quoted by Craig in *Index to the Story of my Days*, p. 125.
14. Particularly in the notes written in Paris in March 1944 which, with a sketch for *Henry IV*, make up the booklet entitled 'A First Attempt, 1890, E. G. C.' (Gordon Craig's private collection).

15. E. G. Craig, *Index to the Story of my Days*, p. 108.
16. See E. G. Craig, *The Theatre Advancing*, Constable, London, 1921. ('Tuition in the Art', first published in *The Mask*, Vol. III, No. 4–6, October 1910, under the pseudonym of 'Felix Urban').
17. A little colour-sketch mounted on a page from a notebook at the beginning of Craig's *Daybook I. November 1908 to March 1910* (Gordon Craig's private collection).
18. The date of this project is uncertain. In 'A First Attempt, 1890' (see note 14, above), Craig attributes it to 1890. In 'The Artists of the Theatre of the Future' he says he made it when he was about twenty-one, viz. in or about 1893.
19. E. G. Craig, 'The Artists of the Theatre of the Future', in *On the Art of the Theatre*, p. 28 first published by Heinemann in 1911. The page numbers given in these notes refer to the reprint issued in 1962 (Mercury Books).
20. On James Pryde, see *James Pryde*, by Derek Hudson, Constable, London, 1949.
21. On William Nicholson, see *William Nicholson*, by Marguerite Steen, Collins, London, 1943.
22. This quotation from Odilon Redon is taken from 'Pour une conférence faite en Hollande à l'occasion d'une exposition de ses œuvres', printed (pp. 119–20) in his book, *A soi-même. Journal (1867–1915). Notes sur la vie, l'art et les artistes*. Introduction de Jacques Morland. Paris, H. Floury, 1922.
23. E. G. Craig, *Woodcuts and some Words*, Introduction by Campbell Dodgson, C.B.E., J. M. Dent & Sons Ltd., London and Toronto, 1924, p. 10.
24. Ibid., p. 13.
25. Quoted by Enid Rose, *Gordon Craig and the Theatre. A Record and an Interpretation*, Sampson Low, Marston & Co. Ltd., London, 1931, p. 21.
26. E. G. Craig, *On the Art of the Theatre*, p. 32.
27. E. G. Craig, *Index to the Story of my Days*, p. 167.
28. *The Century Magazine*, Vol. I, No. 2, pp. 165–81. One of the most interesting illustrations appears on page 170 with the caption: 'Mademoiselle Bréval singing the Hymn to Pallas Athene'. Craig may well have been impressed by the massive wall shown in this drawing, with its huge vertical sides, the contrast between deep shadow and a kind of veiled light, the imposing doorway beneath a mysterious, shadowy recess, and the relationship between the tremendous architectural structure and the two human figures which, far from being dwarfed by it, gain in tragic intensity.
In an article in *The Mask* (Vol. VII, No. 2, May 1915, pp. 163–4), signed with the pseudonym 'Louis Madrid' and entitled 'In Defence of the Scene of vast proportions', Craig quotes long passages from this article by T. A. Janvier.
29. E. G. Craig, *Daybook*, E.G.C. (1931–1932–1933), p. 26 (Gordon Craig's private collection).
30. E. G. Craig, *Index to the Story of my Days*, p. 182.
31. *Sunday Times*, 19 August 1923.

32. Edward F. Spence, *Bar and Buskin; being memories of life, law and the theatre*, Elkin Mathews & Marrot Ltd., London, 1930, p. 251.
33. William Rothenstein, *Men and Memories*, Vol. I, Faber & Faber Ltd., London, 1931, p. 276.
34. 26 July 1896.
35. 1 August 1896.
36. 25 July 1896.
37. See *Ellen Terry's Memoirs*, op. cit., pp. 255-6.
38. E. G. Craig, *Ellen Terry and her Secret Self*, op. cit., p. 121.
39. Ibid., p. 122.
40. E. G. Craig, *Index to the Story of my Days*, p. 179.
41. E. G. Craig, *Ellen Terry and her Secret Self*, pp. 121-2.
42. E. G. Craig, *On the Art of the Theatre*, p. 7.

III

INTERLUDE

By giving up acting, Craig shook off the obsessive dread of becoming a mere feeble imitation of Irving, and won his independence. But it was a bitter freedom that he gained. He felt more at a loss than ever, to the point of losing confidence in everything – his friends, the theatre, himself. For the next three years he may have seemed to be adrift, with no sense of direction. But although he was no longer acting, his mind was still concentrated on the theatre. This was an interlude during which he grew to maturity, judging the theatre from the outside, polishing his technique in drawing and engraving, and reading widely. Soon he was faced with another, more mundane problem, that of earning a living in his new circumstances.

As we have seen already, books played a prominent part in his imaginative life. Books that Irving or Ellen Terry had given him, books he had bought for himself – poetry, plays, historical novels, essays, biographies of actors. So far he seems to have paid little attention to theoretical writings. There was Ruskin, of course – but had Craig really grasped the teaching of that aristocrat among aesthetes? Once he stopped acting, Craig plunged into a whole series of critical works touching upon art and the theatre. In addition to Ruskin, he began to read Goethe, Tolstoy, Wagner, Nietzsche and Coleridge. Sometimes he felt indignant, being influenced by the actor's traditional hostility to the literary point of view – but soon he began to take their judgements very seriously indeed. Each of them brought him some new idea, some of them even set him an example to follow. With the help of what he read, he was gradually working out his own aesthetic principles.

He had already been fascinated by Blake's symbolism. Pryde and Nicholson, following on the Italian Renaissance painters, had already convinced him that art could not be mere imitation, that it was and must be a form of re-creation. Now he learnt from

Goethe that the function of art was to express the inexpressible and that the truly theatrical must be visually symbolical. (1) Tolstoy strengthened his conviction that realistic reproduction was the negation of art. (2) Before very long, he learnt from Nietzsche that all aesthetic activity or perception implies a state of ecstasy.(3) And thus, little by little, there grew within him a mystical attitude towards Art, a yearning for ideal Beauty, characteristic of the aesthetic idealism of the eighteen-nineties.

Art, he perceived, must be the outcome of conscious effort, of voluntary submission to certain canons. Freedom is the life of art, but anarchy is fatal to it. Art requires the strict discipline advocated by Nietzsche. (4) There can be no creation without discipline.

Did the theatre of the eighteen-nineties satisfy these requirements? In the first place, it was a commercial theatre. And according to Ruskin, people must get rid of the illusion that the theatre can be at one and the same time a money-making business and a medium of culture. No one tries to make money out of a church or a college, and the same should apply to theatres. (5)

The late nineteenth-century theatre was based on the 'star system' and relied largely on scenic effect. It fell far below the standards of true art.

Craig's development, and the progress of his ideas, cannot be explained solely in terms of the influences to which he was subjected. But neither must we underestimate the effect of his reading, which undoubtedly helped to guide him and shape his personality.

Craig's work in the theatre was never the mere reflection of what he had found in Nietzsche, Ruskin, Goethe or Tolstoy; but it was in their company, absorbing their views and sometimes giving a fresh interpretation of them, that he came to realize the nature of art, the importance of imagination and of discipline, the emptiness of conventional realism, the futility of overloading a work with decorative or descriptive details, and the value of forms of art where suggestion takes the place of reproduction and an idea is more important than the way in which it is expressed. And this led him away from the style of performance for which the Lyceum Theatre stood. In a certain sense, as he himself remarks in his book on Ellen Terry, (6) Craig was self-educated: his teachers were not college professors, but the writers with whom he felt an affinity which grew stronger as time went on and he discovered how much he had in common with them, despite their manifest differences. He then came to regard Ruskin, Nietzsche, Leonardo, Blake, Flaubert and others as 'rebels', men who preferred a dangerous life to a safe one. (7) And he felt that he too was a 'rebel'.

Among his masters, Wagner took a curious place. Craig remembers that when he was a small boy, aged nine, he once watched as Irving showed Ellen Terry a big book of scenes from the Opera House at Bayreuth. Whether or not he understood Wagner's dramas, he loved their music. But what chiefly interested him was Wagner's basic theories, his idea of a 'music drama of the future', based on an alliance between poetry, music, painting and acting and requiring a new type of theatrical architecture; in other words, a new way of seeing things and showing them to others. At much the same time he was told that Godwin, his father, had transformed a circus into a Greek theatre and devised a new type of stage. Craig began to feel that it was possible and necessary to go further than anything hitherto done and seen, and to search for new ideas. About 1898 he began to think about a change of front, a complete change, and he was seized by a desire to re-interpret Shakespeare's plays, to bring them to fresh life on the stage. Two projects have survived from a number of others to show that this was a real change of attitude, though Craig did not give it practical expression just yet.

One of these, in a manuscript dating from 1897, (8) shows a new shape of theatre. There are no boxes and no circles; the floor of the auditorium slopes gently down towards the stage without a break. There is a mobile proscenium. In the majority of cases, particularly when a tragedy is to be performed, there will be no curtain – changes of scene will be covered by darkness, a veil, or some kind of mist. Another technical innovation – now become common – is that the man in charge of the performance is to direct it from a cabin at the back of the auditorium: this will give him a full view of the stage and enable him to keep an eye on all aspects of the performance (scenery, lighting, music, etc.). Craig even plans a system of speaking-tubes and bells to enable the director to communicate with the stage and give his orders. This project is interesting not only because of its revolutionary character but because it shows that Craig was not satisfied with 'having ideas', but went into technical problems in detail and made suggestions for solving them.

Another significant indication is to be found in a water-colour sketch for Act III, Scene 4 of *Hamlet*, usually attributed to the year 1899 (Plate 14A). This shows not the faintest trace of Lyceum influence, there is not a single archaeological detail or 'historically correct' decorative motif. It is a harmony in grey-blue and bistre, a composition of bare walls, vertical lines, vaguely-indicated hangings, patches of light and shadow; on the prompt side the figure of the Ghost can just be perceived with its back to the light. All the lighting comes from above or from the side, casting bright patches on the stage; Craig makes no provision for lighting from below, he has no footlights. (9) This design already reveals his predilection for rectangular surfaces, vertical parallel lines, and the expressive play of light.

*

This sketch also shows that Craig had now acquired sufficient technical skill to express his intentions in drawing, water-colour or wash, with no danger of distorting or misrepresenting them. This was the result of the three-year 'interlude' during which he had been constantly drawing and engraving. Indeed, at this time his friends and acquaintances regarded him as first and foremost a draughtsman and wood-engraver; those were the forms in which he was expressing himself, and the means by which he was making a living.

Though he had left the stage, he still spent much of his time in theatres, where he liked to sketch the actors. Some of these sketches, and of the woodcuts he made from a few of them, were published in newspapers and magazines, including the *Daily Mail* (a sketch of Henry Irving and his son Laurence, made at the dress-rehearsal of *Robespierre* in April 1899), the *Tatler*, the *Sphere* (which bought one of the sketches he made of Sarah Bernhardt in July 1899, when she appeared as Hamlet at the Adelphi Theatre), the *Lady's Pictorial*, the *Sketch*, the *Anglo-Saxon* and others.

Finding black and white more and more exciting, he became a

prolific wood-engraver, cutting between one hundred and fifty and two hundred blocks in 1899 and 1900, eighty-seven of them in 1899 alone. Many of these still show the influence of James Pryde, but as his skill developed that gradually declined.

He now had the idea of earning a little money with these wood-cuts, by publishing them in a pamphlet, a book or a regular magazine. He began to make bookplates, which, he declared later, brought in about £2 a week. (10) He published a small collection of these in two editions, an ordinary one in small format on white paper and a *de luxe* on grey paper. The booklet contained a short, humorous introduction, ten plates, including those of Christopher St John, Ellen Terry and James Pryde, and a concluding note addressed 'To collectors of ex-libris and others'. (11)

He also published *Gordon Craig's Book of Penny Toys*, with twenty wood-engravings made from children's toys of the period, stylized and simple – which he coloured by hand – each with an appropriate rhyme and a small tail-piece. (12)

But his most important publication in these years was un-doubtedly *The Page*, a magazine of which he was both manager and editor. This was launched as a monthly in January 1898, became a quarterly after the first year, and continued until September 1901. *The Page* was not a theatrical journal, it did not fight for a cause, nor did its contents foreshadow those of *The Mask*. Craig had written nothing about the theatre as yet; he was still asking himself questions rather than proposing answers to them, so he felt no urge to formulate a doctrine or stand up for an idea. *The Page* simply provided him with a new means of displaying his activity, expressing himself as a wood-engraver, and indulging his own tastes through the choice of the illustrations he printed in addition to his own, and the literary material he selected. There were a great many reproductions and comparatively little letter-press. Craig made something like two hundred and thirty woodcuts specially for *The Page*, some bearing his own name, others signed with a pseudonym, 'Oliver Bath'. (13) A number of them were illustrations to Dumas' novels, a few were portraits of actors, including Irving; there were two or three designs for backcloths; and of course there were bookplates. The printed matter included quotations from Marcus Aurelius and La Bruyère, Whitman,

Emerson and Carlyle. The reproductions include the facsimile of the manuscript of a poem by Whitman and works by members of the New English Art Club, James Pryde, Rothenstein and Max Beerbohm. There is a costume design by Burne-Jones, two pen drawings by Bastien-Lepage – of Henry Irving and Sarah Bernhardt respectively – and even a sketch by Irving. There are a few bars of music, by Joseph Moorat, A. C. Mackenzie and Craig's friend Martin Shaw. The little magazine upholds no particular views, and makes no claim to do so.

*

The last number of *The Page* for 1899 announced an important event – the foundation of the Purcell Operatic Society, which intended to stage the long-neglected works of Purcell, Handel, Gluck, etc. The first opera, to be presented in the spring of 1900, would be Purcell's *Dido and Aeneas*. 'No pains will be spared to make these performances complete in every way.' Musical director, Martin Fallas Shaw. Stage director, Edward Gordon Craig.

The former member of the Lyceum Company was entering upon a new phase of his career: Craig was becoming a 'theatrical producer'.

NOTES

1. See quotation from Goethe in *The Mask*, Vol. I, No. 5, July 1908, p. 95.
2. See quotation from Tolstoy (a passage from *What is Art?*) in *The Mask*, Vol. III, No. 4–6, October 1910, p. 85.
3. See quotation from Nietzsche in *The Mask*, Vol. IV, No. 1, July 1911, p. 24.
4. See the quotation from Nietzsche at the head of Ernest Marriott's article, 'The School at Florence', in *A Living Theatre*, Florence, 1913, p. 43.
5. Craig quotes Ruskin's opinion in 'In Defence of *The Mask* and Mr Huntly Carter', *The Manchester Playgoer*, Vol. I, No. 4, November 1913.
6. E. G. Craig, *Ellen Terry and her Secret Self*, op. cit., p. 123.
7. See 'In Defence of *The Mask* and Mr Huntley Carter', p. 130.
8. This manuscript, which has no title, is in the Gordon Craig Collection, Bibliothèque de l'Arsenal, Paris (temporarily housed at the Bibliothèque Nationale, Paris).

9. This sketch is among the Craig items in the Theatre Collection at the Nationalbibliothek, Vienna. With it are some notes by Craig, describing the characters' movements. In *Index to the Story of my Days*, where it is reproduced (opp. p. 208), it is dated *c*. 1899, but Craig tells me he thinks it probably belongs to 1900.

10. See the introduction to Gordon Craig's book, *Nothing, or the Bookplate, with a handlist by E. Carrick*, Chatto & Windus, London, 1924.

11. *Bookplates designed and cut on wood by Gordon Craig*. At the Sign of the Rose, Hackbridge, Surrey, 1900.

12. *Gordon Craig's Book of Penny Toys*. At the Sign of the Rose, Hackbridge, Surrey, 1899.

13. For instance, Vol. II, No. 1 of *The Page* contains a woodcut, 'Le Duc d'Anjou' and some tailpieces, signed Oliver Bath. In No. 2 of the same volume, the woodcuts 'Thoughts Apt, Hands Black' and 'For what we are about to receive', attributed to Oliver Bath, are again by Craig himself. Another pseudonym he used in *The Page* was Edward Arden. Edward Arden was a composer. Vol. II, No. 2 prints 'his' song, 'My Johnnie was a Shoe-maker', written by Craig in October 1895, and a note on 'Edward Arden and the Music of the Future', signed 'Samuel Drayton'. This use of pseudonyms enabled Craig to give the impression that the magazine had more contributors than it actually possessed, and that his own position was not absolutely predominant. It also satisfied his love of acting, mystery and adventure.

IV

PRODUCTIONS

1900. The 'Belle Époque'. The Universal Exhibition in Paris. The triumph of stucco and 'staff'. Official art ranged from academic realism to mawkish languors and convoluted ornamentation. For Craig, this was the year when he 'woke up in his mind' (1) and the year when he met Elena Meo, the woman who was to give him the staunchest and most practical help and act as a source of inspiration to him. It was also the beginning of a new phase in his development, the year of *Dido and Aeneas*.

He had put on plays before now – *On ne badine pas avec l'amour* at Uxbridge, *Hamlet* and *Romeo and Juliet* at the Parkhurst Theatre. But he is disinclined nowadays to include these in the list of his productions. They were influenced by the Lyceum, and the work had been rushed, even by the standards of that period. He himself had not been conscious of any seeds or principles of new art in them, and no one else is likely to have perceived any such thing.

The Purcell Operatic Society presented *Dido and Aeneas* on 17, 18 and 19 May 1900. Why was this production so particularly important? It was the first of the seven staged by Craig between 1900 and 1903, and the first opera he had produced (the next three productions were also musical pieces). But the chief importance of *Dido and Aeneas* was that it marked 'the first step of a new movement which is destined to revolutionize the production of the poetic drama'. (2)

*

Craig had made the acquaintance of Martin Shaw, the composer, pianist and organist, in April 1897, while he himself was still on the stage. The two men took to each other at once. Before long they were helping James Pryde to put on a variety performance in a pub at Southwold – a programme of songs, sketches, monologues and piano solos which gave rise to some unexpected and amusing incidents. Reading Craig's and Martin Shaw's memoirs, one realizes the importance of this friendship, which enriched both of them and led to considerable work in common. Craig has always been generous in his acknowledgement of what he has received from other people, and Martin Shaw introduced him to Purcell, Handel and even Bach – or at least to Bach's *St Matthew Passion*, which he played to him on the piano one day in June 1900. Craig later devised for the *Matthew Passion* a detailed *mise en scène*, complete with models, which, though never carried out, ranks among his finest work; and one of his most important books, *Scene*, is dedicated 'To old Bach'.

It was sufficiently daring to think of putting on Purcell's *Dido and Aeneas* in 1899, when Covent Garden audiences were entirely set upon the Italian, German and French operas. Shaw's original idea had been to present the work as an oratorio, with an orchestra, soloists and a chorus, in some concert hall. But Craig soon persuaded him that it would be better to make it a theatrical production, and the musician and producer set to work. They had no theatre and no money, so there could be no question of engaging professional opera singers or chorus. Undaunted, Craig and Shaw embarked upon a quest for a suitable hall and for voluntary helpers.

They decided in favour of the Hampstead Conservatoire, (3) a concert hall with a large podium composed of a front platform and a series of smaller platforms rising in tiers to form the traditional orchestra seating. Craig was responsible for turning this arrangement into a stage and for creating a system of lighting with which which he could carry out his ideas for the production:

> On this front platform [he writes] I erected a long proscenium, built of eight immensely tall scaffolding-poles – and from 4A to 4B I threw six or eight more scaffolding-poles, forming a deep frame, thus, of a rather unusual shape as prosceniums went in those days. I did not set out to force it into any unusual proportions – the proportions of the platforms as I found them told me what I had to do. I used the front platform for most of the scenes – there were four or five platforms. For a scene packed with witches I used all five platforms, and they were useful. (4)

The proscenium was a warm shade of grey, which helped to

bring out the stage picture. The stage was wide for its height; this of course was due to the shape of the premises, but Craig found it memorable and in later years he often made illustrations and scene designs, and even constructed models (for instance, some for the Moscow *Hamlet*) in this oblong form, which was later to be that of 'cinemascope'.

Craig arranged his lights, too, in a way that had never been thought of before. There was no side-lighting from the wings, and no footlights; all the light came from overhead. Craig arranged the lamps to light the stage and backcloth on a 'bridge' above the stage (it must be remembered that the 'lighting bridge' was not introduced in Germany, whence it spread to other countries, until several years after this). Another of Craig's innovations was to put two projectors at the back of the auditorium, so that their light could be trained straight on the actors, above the heads of the audience.

Craig and Martin Shaw also had to form their company, to find the necessary soloists and about seventy members of the chorus. Only the two principals, Dido and Aeneas, were professionals. The others were amateurs, with or without experience, recruited as the need arose. Few of them had trained voices, and most of them had never acted before. The difficulty of working with such a company was formidable, but the idea appealed to Craig, who already had a strong dislike for the 'star system'. His amateurs were ready and willing to do whatever he asked, but he must be careful not to make too great demands on their skill. So while he might call upon them to crawl, jump, swing or run, (5) he avoided complex movements and elaborate dances. For the greater part of the time, indeed, there was very little movement on the stage. (6)

The Purcell Operatic Society's programme sums up the plot of *Dido and Aeneas* as follows: (7)

The Morning breaks. Dido, Queen of Carthage, filled with a Presentiment that her Love for Aeneas will end in Disaster, refuses to be comforted by her Handmaidens. Aeneas enters, and his Words revive her. They leave for 'the Hills and the Vales. . . to the musical Groves and the cool shady Fountains,' accompanied by their Train. Meantime the Sorceress and her sisters plot the Destruction of these Lovers. They sing –

> 'Harm's our delight
> And Mischief all our skill',

and it is agreed to send a Messenger in the shape of a God to summon Aeneas away. This has the desired effect; the Witches exult, and Dido is left Alone to mourn her loss. Her heart breaks, and she dies singing a most glorious Song.

The story, in Craig's opinion, 'straggles'. (8) But it was the music, not the words, that inspired him. He set himself to give it visual expression, or rather to create, through the eye, feelings in harmony with those created by the music for the ear, so that each sense should heighten the impression made on the other, the stage movement being adapted to the music and the scenes and costumes to the music and the movement. The preparations lasted six months, something unknown in the theatre at that time. Craig was already revealing his insistence on thoroughness, his rejection of makeshift solutions, his determination to attend to every detail, though never for a moment losing sight of the general effect. There were endless rehearsals, the amateur company was tireless in its enthusiasm, and most important of all, there was perfect under-standing between the musical director and conductor, Martin Shaw, and the producer, Gordon Craig: 'The fact that I worked in absolute harmony with Shaw and his view of the Purcell opera went far towards getting it all of a piece. On the music we were entirely in agreement – so that what he felt I felt.' (9) This perfect agreement gave unity to the whole thing.

The most striking feature of the production was its avoidance of all attempt at descriptive realism or historical reconstruction, its rejection of the archaeological approach and of tricks to deceive the eye. The programme itself was a war-cry raised against the Lyceum style and the pretensions of the naturalistic school. Craig's art was an art of suggestion, of evocation, which gave free play to the audience's imagination. Nowhere was this more clearly evidenced than in the first scene of Act I, which takes place in Queen Dido's palace. A long trellis, with flowers and green creepers rambling over it, ran across the stage from side to side, with an opening in the middle where the Queen's throne stood, heaped with scarlet cushions and surmounted by a canopy supported by four slender pillars. The backcloth bore no resemblance to the traditional perspective views in which skilful scene-painters took such pride: it was simply a great purple-blue sky-cloth, descending from invisible heights. Craig used no borders and no wings; he closed the stage at either end with a curtain of the same colour as the backcloth, hung at right-angles to the proscenium. This gave an impression of spaciousness never conveyed by the usual clutter of painted canvas, furniture and properties.

But Craig's great service to the stage lay not so much in his introduction of an entirely new type of scenery, reduced to a few essential elements and fundamental colours, as in his completely original manner of presentation, by which the expressive harmony of the stage picture, composed of colour, line, movement and light, was uninterruptedly maintained. Each scene was built up like a picture, its components inseparably combined, and interpreted the dramatic atmosphere of the moment in association with the music. The costumes, based on simple colour-combinations, consisted chiefly of draped robes and veils, and made their own contribution to the visual effect. Mabel Cox, writing in *The Artist*, noted that '. . . there was a distinct artistic intention of the inseparableness of the dresses from their surroundings; they were essentially part of the design of each scene and this gave a harmonious completeness which is rare on the stage; managers are apt to forget that a number of isolated dresses, however beautiful, do not make a beautiful picture'. (10)

Two elements – colour and light – were of prime importance, their effects combining and supplementing one another. Mabel Cox writes that the play of colour is 'more fashionable than beautiful', particularly in the first act (11) – that the contrasts of green, purple, blue and scarlet reflect the modern artists' penchant for deliberate colour-clashes and transplant to the stage the effects aimed at by the members of the New English Art Club. But she goes on to say that in the last act Craig makes a complete change in his colour-scheme and creates an extremely beautiful picture, by projecting a yellowish light on to the stage: 'Under the play of this light the background becomes a deep shimmering blue, apparently almost translucent, upon which the green and purple make a harmony of great richness. . . .' (12) At that time Craig's palette was undoubtedly very similar to that of the painters who had formed the New English Art Club. But the important point was that he was introducing these bright colour-combinations on the stage instead of the insipid, drab, expressionless tones used in conventional scene-painting. Mabel Cox's second remark is even more important – Craig was already painting with light, using it to transform the stage picture.

Thus, Craig did not think of light and colour as means towards naturalistic description, but as contributions to the dramatic expression, to be used in their own right to act on the sensibilities of the spectator and help to convey the central idea of the piece. To some extent he made a symbolic use of colour in his scenes and costumes. It was by no mere accident that the cushions on the throne, which were scarlet in the first act, should have been black in the final scene, where Dido laments the loss of Aeneas and sings her death-song. The contrast between light and shadow was used to the full, while the dramatic intensity of the witches' scenes was tremendously enhanced by plunging the stage into deep shadow. This helps us to understand Craig's remark about his work on *Dido and Aeneas:* 'The instrument I worked with was a company – 60 men and women – line and colour – in movement, sound and scene.' (13) All the elements of the production were indissociable – actors, colour, music, movement. Each one of them was *mitspielend*, played in with the rest, as the German Expressionists were to put it later on.

This unity of expression, this interaction of the stage elements, is made clear in the critics' reviews – those of 1900 and those published in 1901, after a further series of performances of *Dido and Aeneas*, at the Coronet Theatre, for which Craig made a few changes in his presentation without altering anything essential. (14) Particularly valuable in this respect is an article entitled 'Some Thoughts on the Art of Gordon Craig', written for *The Studio* by Haldane Macfall, who describes the principal scenes in the production. Here are some extracts from that article:

The note of tragedy was sustained throughout the piece with consummate mastery in the colour as in the music. The stage, for all its simplicity, was always filled. No posturing actor took the limelight in order to show off his personality or advertise his necessity. The main scheme of the play was the main thing – it was never anything but the main thing.

In the opening scene, when the love-sick Dido, weighed down by the premonition that evil will come of her love for Aeneas, refusing to be comforted by her maidens, seats herself on the scarlet cushions of her throne, a broad green belt of ivy-clad wall flanking the throne to right and left, the note of doom is struck. Her figure at once gives the dignity of her despair, where she reclines miserably at the foot of the great lilac heavens, bowing her head to her destiny – and the sense of doom seems to grow vast as the heavens at the foot of which she bows in queenly shame.

That was a splendidly composed scene in which, amidst the mysteries of the night, against a background of moonlight, the Sorceress stands high above her sea-devils, who crawl about her feet, and flout and rise and fall, like clouts of raggy seaweed that flap against the rocks at the incoming of the treacherous tide, as she evilly plots the destruction of the lovers, and plans to send a messenger in the guise of a god to summon Aeneas away. It was in this scene that Gordon Craig's fine artistic feeling for black and white did him yeoman service. The dim figures, seen in half-light, compelled the imagination. (15)

It is in the final scene that the noblest triumph is achieved. Attended by her kneeling maidens, the woe-begone figure of Dido, wrapped in her black robes, reclines amidst the sombre black cushions of her throne. The disconsolate woman appears with rare dignity at the base of the great lilac background that springs in one vast broad expanse straight upwards to the heavens, large and majestic as the heavens themselves. (16)

The footlights being absent, and the illuminations coming from above, there was flung down upon Dido's face a gentle light, which made tragic darks hover below the finely wrought and massive brows, casting a mysterious gloom about the eye-pits, and holding the lower part of the features in shadow that swept into the blackness of her robe, as she uttered the exquisite death-song, The dignity and beauty of this scene, the gracefully poised figure in the midst of the sternly tragic picture, and ultimately the majesty of the dead queen as she lay, fallen back, with upturned face towards the vast sweep of the heavens, made one of the noblest death scenes the stage has yielded. (17)

.   .   .   .   .

Macfall's appreciation was by no means exceptional, for the Press was almost unanimous in its praise. The critics of *The Times*, the *Musical Courier*, the *Daily Chronicle*, the *Daily Graphic*, the *Musical Standard* and *The Lady* were among those who hailed the birth of a new art, the substitution of imaginative suggestion for realism, the rejection of trivial and wastefully lavish display, and the harmonious beauty of the whole production. The theatre critic of *The Review of the Week* hoped that Covent Garden would invite Craig to put on an opera during the coming season. But Craig was never to make a production at Covent Garden. . . .

The venture was thus a great artistic success, and many people considered that this new style of acting, staging and scenic decoration should not be confined to musical drama – that it provided an ideal solution to the problems of Shakespearean production. This opinion was put forward, for example, by the critic of *The Review of the Week*, who objected equally to the pedantic reconstructions attempted by the Elizabethan Stage Society and to the Lyceum's accumulation of superfluous details. (19) Haldane Macfall expressed the same view, declaring that *Dido and Aeneas* '. . . gave abundant promise that the poetic drama of Shakespeare may be rendered with something of its innate intensity, instead of being the somewhat tedious thing it has become – to those of us who are honest in the frank society of our conscience. . . .' (20)

So did W. B. Yeats, who declared that the scenery of *Dido and Aeneas* was the only good thing of its kind that he had ever seen. (21) Writing to Frank Fay on 21 April 1902, he said: '. . . Two years ago I was in the same stage about scenery that I now am in about acting. I knew the right principles but I did not know the right practice because I had never seen it. I have now however learnt a great deal from Gordon Craig.' (22) And in *The Speaker* for 11 May 1901, he wrote:

. . . Naturalistic scene-painting is not an art, but a trade, because it is, at best, an attempt to copy the more obvious effects of Nature by the methods of the ordinary landscape-painter, and by his methods made coarse and summary. It is but flashy landscape painting and lowers the taste it appeals to, for the taste it appeals to has been formed by a more delicate art. Decorative scene-painting would be, on the other hand, as inseparable from the movements as from the robes of the players and from the falling of the light; and being in itself a grave and quiet thing it would mingle with the tones of the voices and with the sentiment of the play, without overwhelming them under an alien interest. . . . Mr Gordon Craig used scenery of this kind at the Purcell Society performance the other day, and despite some marring of his effects by the half-round shape of the theatre, it was the first beautiful scenery our stage has seen. He created an ideal country where everything was possible, even speaking in verse, or speaking to music, or the expression of the whole of life in a dance, and I would like to see Stratford-on-Avon decorate its Shakespeare with like scenery. As we cannot, it seems, go back to the platform and the curtain, and the argument for doing so is not without weight, we can only get rid of the sense of unreality which most of us feel when we listen to the conventional speech of Shakespeare, by making scenery as conventional. . . . (23)

Craig was now making designs for *Hamlet* and for *Peer Gynt*; but more than ten years went by before he produced *Hamlet*, and then it was at the Moscow Arts Theatre.

After the three performances in 1900, Craig and Shaw made up their accounts. Expenditure, £379 2s. 0d; receipts, approximately £377. The chorus and most of the actors had given their services for nothing, and neither Craig nor Shaw had taken a penny.

*

With *Dido and Aeneas* Craig revealed his gifts as a producer in the fullest sense of the word. He directed the performers' movements and their style of acting, designed the scenes, costumes and lighting, and achieved an artistic success, quite apart from the actual manner of presentation, through the harmony he established among the various elements in the performance. He achieved his aim because – with the entire approval of Martin Shaw – he was given a completely free hand; because he was using tractable 'materials' – colour, light, movement, and amateur performers who were more disposed to respond to his demands and follow his instructions than any professional would-be stars; and because he was able to give a long time to planning his production. His first success was founded on thorough preparation and strict discipline, and he was never to forget the fact.

In July 1900, two months after *Dido and Aeneas*, Craig and Shaw began work on a new production – *The Masque of Love*, from Purcell's opera *Dioclesian*. Betterton had adapted the libretto from a play by Beaumont and Fletcher, *The Prophetess, or the History of Dioclesian*.

On 26 March 1901, after eight months' hard work, the curtain of the Coronet Theatre, London, rose on a new series of performances by the Purcell Operatic Society (24) – *The Masque of Love* and a revival of *Dido and Aeneas*. To give publicity to this second venture and help to attract larger audiences, Ellen Terry came with some fellow-actors to perform *Nance Oldfield* as a curtain-raiser.

The artistic success was as great as before, and brought Craig letters of congratulation from Walter Crane and W. B. Yeats.(25) This time the producer had been curiously restrained in his use of movement, line and colour. Once again he had used symbolism rather than description, allusion in preference to imitation. Every performer, even in the smallest role, had something definite to do and this, far from distracting the spectators' attention, helped to create an impression that was all of a piece. The scenery followed the same principles as in *Dido and Aeneas*, and was extraordinarily simple. 'In *The Masque of Love*,' Craig writes, 'I had only three large cloths (back and two sides), one large floorcloth and one cut cloth in front, and all these were painted a uniform grey, flat tone.' (26) The rest was done by the lighting and by the colours of the costumes, a harmony of grey, green and white with an occasional touch of red. The costumes were made of the most inexpensive material – hessian, the appearance of which was transformed by the lighting.

The critic of the *Daily Graphic* wrote of this performance (27 March 1901): '. . . Mr Craig has wisely avoided anything like the realism of modern scenery, which would consort but ill with the conventionality of seventeenth-century opera. He seems to have sought his inspiration in Japanese art. A vast background of pure colour and an austerely simple scheme of decoration are the prevailing notes of his system.' It seems hardly likely that Craig had really 'sought his inspiration in Japanese art'. Some time was to elapse before he discovered the oriental theatre, its manner of presenting plays, its actors, marionettes and masks. He was certainly acquainted with Japanese painting, but it was not until three years later that he bought some portfolios of Chinese and Japanese reproductions. If *The Masque of Love* really showed any Japanese influence, it was due to the fact that Craig belonged to the movement in modern art whose chief exponents – Whistler and Wilde in England, Lautrec and the 'Nabis' in France – had already discovered and been influenced by Japanese art.

Yeats was enthusiastic, and a year later, when the *Saturday Review* gave its readers to understand that the Purcell Operatic Society performances were not worth a visit, he promptly sent a letter to that journal in which he said:

> Last year I saw *Dido and Aeneas* and *The Masque of Love*, which is to be given again this year, and they gave me more perfect pleasure than I have met with in any theatre this ten years. I saw the only admirable stage scenery of our time, for Mr Gordon Craig has discovered how to decorate a play with severe, beautiful, simple effects of colour, that leave the imagination free to follow all the suggestions of the play. Realistic scenery takes the imagination captive and is at best but bad landscape painting, but Mr Gordon Craig's scenery is a new and distinct art. It is something that can only exist in the theatre. It cannot even be separated from the figures that move before it. The staging of *Dido and Aeneas* and of *The Masque of Love* will some day, I am persuaded, be remembered among the important events of our time. (27)

For Craig, too, *The Masque of Love* was a new experience. He was quite aware of the value of his innovations, but a technical problem had arisen to cause him some perplexity. The audiences had been enthusiastic, but their patience had been put to the test by the long time required for scene-changes. Craig realized that the 'old-fashioned' stage machinery was only suitable for 'old-fashioned' scenery. The new theatre must have new machinery – not only to deal with his original type of scenery, but because of his whole new conception of stage production, acting and presentation. Craig began to reflect on possible solutions for this problem. (28)

During the eight months he gave to preparing *The Masque of Love*, Craig kept up his other activities as well, particularly his drawing. He was working at what might be called 'interpretations', selecting a play and then devising settings for it. Examples of this include the designs for *The Masque of Love* and for *Henry V* (the latter including 'The Tents', of 1901). Then there were the sketches he made for 'stage visions', unconnected with any specific play – such as 'Enter the Army' (1900), 'The Lights of London' and 'The Arrival' (1901). Some of these were reproduced, with notes written subsequently, in Craig's book *Towards a New Theatre*. Of 'The Arrival', he writes:

> This is for no particular play, but it is for what I believe to be true drama. The name explains the drama. The first picture in this volume ('Enter the Army') is a stage direction; so is 'The Arrival' a kind of stage direction. It tells us of something which is being done, and not of something which is being said, and the fact that we do not know who is arriving and why they are arriving, or what they will look like when they appear, makes it, to my mind, dramatic. (29)

Although written retrospectively, these words make clear what Craig intended when he drew 'The Arrival'. He had already begun his quest for an art that should be more than mere interpretation, a return to the 'purely dramatic', where action and movement are more important than the written and spoken words. His feeling was still only a presentiment, but certain of the principles laid down in *On the Art of the Theatre* were already germinating in his mind – certain of the ideas which a few years later were to find expression in his 'Studies for Movement' and in that dramatic sequence, *The Steps*.

*

The Purcell Operatic Society pushed on with its programme. After *Dido and Aeneas* and *The Masque of Love*, Craig and Martin Shaw began – amid the same difficulties as before – to prepare *Acis and Galatea*, Handel's 'pastoral' opera in two acts, with words by John Gay. Again the preparations lasted eight months, and on 10 March 1902 they opened at the Great Queen Street Theatre, with a revival of *The Masque of Love* in the same programme.

Craig and Shaw hoped for fifteen performances. They had tried in vain to obtain financial support, appealing in all kinds of directions for the five or six hundred pounds that would have made their venture secure. The only outside help they received was from a painter who gave them ten pounds. The reviews were favourable, but the public was not interested, and the run had to be stopped after six performances, although the artistic success of *Acis and Galatea* was as complete as that of *Dido and Aeneas* and *The Masque*. (30)

The opera is set in a pastoral landscape at the foot of Mount Etna, and its plot relates a simple mythological story. The nymph Galatea loves and is loved by Acis, a young shepherd; she is mourning his absence and refuses to join the chorus of other nymphs and shepherds who are singing their delight in the beauties of nature. Acis returns, and the pair resolve never to part again. The chorus warns them of the approach of the giant Polyphemus, who has been seized by a fierce passion for Galatea. Polyphemus kills Acis. The gods, moved by Galatea's grief, change her dead lover into a living spring, whose softly-murmured song of love will float through the valley for ever.

Craig had to decide whether to abide by the principles usually followed in staging a 'mythological' piece and try to design an idyllically bucolic 'Sicilian' landscape, or to give free play to his imagination and follow where the music led him. He chose the second course, making it his aim to render the poetical atmosphere of the piece by the play of line, colour in movement, and light.

In the opening scene, Galatea's melancholy contrasts with the joy of the nymphs and shepherds. Craig gave no hint of a traditional landscape – no meadow, not so much as a patch of sky. The scenery was completely stylized, consisting of a 'white tent' made of long white ribbons – strips of upholsterer's webbing – which hung down from the flies against a pale yellow background. The floating strips formed a kind of linear ballet, to which the movements of costumes responded and contributed. Craig used ribbons for the costumes too – particularly for those of the nymphs and of Galatea and Damon – and, as the performers moved, these fluttered in shifting arabesques against their robes and tunics. The young shepherds were dressed in white, with little hats of brown straw that had nothing classical about them; and at one point a cluster of children's balloons was released in a pink and white cloud. This was a true modern equivalent of the pastoral spirit, with the interplay of all these bright, moving colours that harmonized with the music, giving material expression to the innocent happiness of the scene:' . . . you feel the actual sensation of a pastoral scene, of country joy, of the spring and the open air, as no trickle of real water in a trough, no sheaves of real corn among painted trees, no imitation of a flushed sky on canvas, could trick you into feeling it'. (31)

In the next scene, the chorus warns the 'wretched lovers' that the 'monster Polypheme' is approaching. In the programme this scene is called 'The Shadow', a mysterious title which is explained when we see Craig's design (Plate 3A): the lovers are clinging together in the middle of the stage, while the huge shadow of Polyphemus hovers threateningly, about to descend on them and extinguish their happiness. Craig made full use of the power of light and shadow, so that Polyphemus became, as Max Beerbohm put it, 'a real giant – the one and only real and impressive giant ever seen on any stage.' (32) Some interesting further particulars are supplied in a drawing by Percy F. S. Spence, reproduced in *The Sphere* in March 1902, together with the accompanying caption: 'The background consists of a great dark-blue cloth; the lovers, Acis and Galatea, are seen in the centre of the stage, which is in darkness save for a red light turned upon them. Later, when the chorus adjures them to "contemplate the monster", the picture of an imposing castle outlined in gold is projected onto the backcloth.' The lovers are thus isolated by the light from a dusky, hostile background where the massed chorus can be dimly seen.

Then comes the tragic moment when Acis is killed, and Craig's presentation of this climax moved Yeats to write: 'Surely that second Polyphemus scene, the scene where he kills Acis, belongs to an art which has lain hid under the roots of the Pyramids for ten thousand years. . . .' (33) (Plate 3B).

In the last scene, Craig replaced the 'white tent' of the opening scene by a 'grey tent', to express Galatea's grief. How was he to convey the metamorphosis of Acis after his death, without resorting to the clumsy artifice of stage machinery, its shoddy realism making the whole thing absurd? Instead of a real spring, Craig used a symbol, *suggesting* the fall of water by a decorative, stylized design of curved, dotted lines on the backcloth. This was a typical example of his aesthetic approach at this period, a combination of out-and-out convention and decorative symbolism. It was *Acis and Galatea* that Arthur Symons had in mind when he declared that a new art of the stage had been born:

> Mr Craig aims at taking us beyond reality; he replaces the pattern of the thing itself by the pattern which that thing evokes in his mind . . . The eye loses itself among these severe, precise and yet mysterious lines and surfaces; the mind is easily at home in them; it accepts them as readily as it accepts the convention by which, in a poetical play, men speak in verse rather than in prose. (34)

*

In July 1902, Martin Shaw and Craig drew up a prospectus announcing their next idea – for a 'travelling' production, to be entitled *The Harvest-Home*. (35) This was to be a 'Masque' based on a description by Hentzner, who had travelled through England towards the close of the sixteenth century, embellished with dances and with music – consisting of folk-songs, some of them little known, and two pieces by Purcell – and presented by about forty performers. It would last for three-quarters of an hour, 'or longer if desired'. Unfortunately this project was never carried out, for the Purcell Operatic Society could still obtain no financial help, and had to be disbanded.

Acis and Galatea was not, however, the last production on which Craig and Shaw worked together. Laurence Housman, who had seen all their joint ventures and conceived a great admiration for Craig's style, had written a nativity play, *Bethlehem*, with music by Joseph Moorat. He asked Craig to produce this, and offered to pay the expenses. Craig agreed, with the proviso that he should be free to work 'in his own way', without interference from author or composer. Housman asked Martin Shaw to rehearse the singers and conduct the orchestra. (36)

Craig thought the piece was not good, except for a few pretty verses, that the subject was difficult and the music feeble. He made cuts in the script, reducing the Virgin's part to two lines, and kept only a few passages from Moorat's music, replacing the rest – with the somewhat grudging consent of the composer – by extracts from Palestrina, Sweelinck, Tenaglia, Bach and Beethoven. In thus completely overhauling his material, Craig discovered the role a producer might play in relation to the author of a dramatic work. Confronted with a written text or a musical score, it was incumbent upon the producer, he felt, to suggest or even insist upon whatever changes might be needed in the interests of theatrical effectiveness; and his subsequent views were influenced by this realization. (37)

Bethlehem was presented in December 1902, in the large hall of the Imperial Institute, South Kensington. Craig adapted the auditorium and the stage, as he had done when staging *Dido and Aeneas* at the Hampstead Conservatoire. He divided the hall into a stage thirty-eight feet deep, occupying nearly half its total length, and an auditorium with twenty-three rows of fifteen seats. (38) As at Hampstead, there was an oblong proscenium, a lighting bridge, no flies and no footlights, But a serious technical problem now arose – the acoustics were bad. Craig thought of a remedy for this – to drape the walls of the hall. Laurence Housman bought six or seven hundred yards of cotton stuff in a shade of blue to tone with the stage picture, and the auditorium was transformed into a huge tent. Experience proved that this was the right method, for the acoustics gave no more trouble.

The company was composed largely of amateurs who had already worked with Shaw and Craig.

Bethlehem is generally regarded as one of Craig's minor productions. He himself, however, thinks it was better than the next two he undertook, (39) and it was undoubtedly important in several respects.

The first scene (40) gave an impression of profound tranquillity. A group of shepherds, dressed in rough garments (made of hessian) and sheepskins, and holding long crooks, sat under a lean-to, almost motionless until the angel appeared to them. A few hurdles were placed about the stage and the ground was strewn with vague shapes covered with sacking, to give the impression of sheep lying huddled together (Plates 4 and 5). The scene was a harmony of neutral tones, backed by a vast sweep of dark grey-blue sky with a few stars twinkling in it.

The second scene showed a hill running right across the horizon, with a purple sky above, heralding the Three Wise Men. First

Costume for *Bethlehem*.

came a motley procession of pilgrims, rich and poor, strong and weak. Then the three Magi arrived, one dressed in black, the second in grey and the third in white. They were followed by three groups, the first and second of which brought a burst of rich colours – black, white and purple; black, purple, green and white – while the third was a harmony of greys, this being the train of the wretched and destitute, the sick and the wicked. There were lepers, imbeciles, a murderer with bloodstained head and beard, beggars, a musician and a puppet showman. All this provided a striking example of the symbolical use of colour. Craig never regarded colour harmonies as an end in themselves, texture and colour were not to be used simply for decorative purposes, they must play a real part in building up the dramatic effect.

The last scene of *Bethlehem* was perhaps the most instructive of all. Craig did not attempt to reconstruct the stable, he suggested the divine presence by the use of ethereal lighting. The stage was arranged as an amphitheatre, (41) with the shepherds grouped around the Virgin and the crib. When Mary drew the coverings from the cradle, there was no doll inside to represent the Child, but light streamed up from its depths into the faces of those gathered round it. The divine presence was indicated by the radiant faces of the shepherds gazing at the Child. Light had never before been used like this in a performance.

Bethlehem was Craig's last production of a musical play. Later he worked on Bach's *St Matthew Passion*, but he was never given an opportunity to carry out that project. This first series of experiments had taught him a great deal. Though always responsive to music, he had never before been brought into such close contact with its laws, perceived its beauties and its powers of suggestion so clearly. He was now discovering classical music, works where expressive effect was more important than analysed meaning, and which demanded complete unity of presentation. It was by no chance that he later took as the 'motto' for the French edition of his book, *On the Art of the Theatre*, Walter Pater's well-known dictum, 'All art constantly aspires towards the condition of music.' The art of the theatre, he felt, must now aspire towards the perfect order that prevailed in music.

Bethlehem was also the last production in which Craig worked with a company most of whom were amateurs. His ideas about the actor's manner of work and the role of the stage director had been shaped to a great extent by their open-mindedness, their willing response to suggestions, and the fact that they were neither slaves to outdated shibboleths nor eager for personal publicity. From now on he would have to deal with the commercial theatre or with national theatre companies.

*

Craig's first attempt to work with the professional theatre was of no very great importance. It was a production in which he was not given an entirely free hand. On 31 January 1903, his uncle, Fred Terry, put on a play called *For Sword or Song*, by R. G. Legge, at the Shaftesbury Theatre. He had asked Craig to stage Act I, scene I of this, and the whole of the last act, and Craig had designed three scenes. The critics, on the whole, were favourable. But difficulties were already making their appearance, as is evident from a comment by Martin Shaw: 'This play had a supernatural scene which Craig was asked to do, and did. But the scene as he invented it and the scene as the public beheld it were two different things. The management and other actors did some editing and the result, despite some fine acting by Fred Terry and Julia Neilson, was a strange hotchpotch with little bits of genius shining through.' (42) In the margin of his copy of *Up to Now*, Martin Shaw's volume of memoirs, Craig has written: 'This is why I want 100 per cent liberty when at work in a theatre.' He discovered that his ideals were at loggerheads with current theatrical practice and tradition. He must first of all impose his own views, overcome resistance. He must be absolute master of the stage. His earlier productions had shown him the advantages of that situation, and *For Sword or Song* confirmed the opinion he had already formed.

Ellen Terry decided to take a theatre and present a series of plays with a company of her own. Her son would produce them and her daughter, Edith Craig, would make the costumes from his designs. After considering a number of plays, she finally took her son's advice and decided upon Ibsen's *The Vikings of Helgeland*, which opened at the Imperial theatre on 15 April 1903. Realizing the exceptional quality of Craig's previous productions and his great and original talent, Ellen Terry hoped to make his work known to a wider public and give him a chance to gain a footing in the professional theatre; she would meet the entire cost of the season at the Imperial, and give him the valuable support of her own celebrity as an actress. She may also have had an inkling that the Lyceum style had had its day, that the theatre was now moving in a new direction and that she owed it to herself to move with it. Few passages in her memoirs are more touching than the one in which she speaks of this venture:

At the Imperial Theatre . . . I gave my son a free hand. I hope it will be remembered, when I am spoken of after my death as a 'Victorian' actress, lacking in enterprise, an actress belonging to the 'old school' that I produced a spectacular play of Ibsen's in a manner which possibly anticipated the scenic ideas of the future by a century, of which at any rate the orthodox theatre managers of the present age would not have dreamed. (43)

The Vikings was a four-act tragedy, little known and seldom performed. Ibsen was twenty-nine years old in 1857, when it was staged for the first time, at the theatre at Christiania (now Oslo). He had taken as his theme the Norse mythology, the quarrels and adventures of Siegfried, Brunhilde, Kriemhild and Gunther. But instead of seeking his characters in the German *Nibelungen* legends, like Wagner, he turned to the Icelandic sagas, and tried to transpose the plot to the human level. The heroes of *The Vikings* are not demi-gods but men belonging to Scandinavia's earliest history. Ibsen says in his introduction: 'The idealized and somewhat impersonal figures of the legends are less than ever suited to stage representation. My main intention was to show our life as it was lived in ancient times, not the universe of our legends.'

So the tragedy is romantic in its events and in the contrast between the characters involved in them, and realistic in its attempt to draw a picture of Scandinavia in ancient times. Ibsen made a transposition, an interpretation of the legend, changing the characters (Brunhilde becomes Hjördis, and this is more than a mere change of name), the incidents and the settings (the famous castle in its circle of flame becomes a room guarded by a terrible white bear), and uses the plot to illustrate the first emergence of a new system. Hjördis is still pagan, whereas Sigurd has been converted to Christianity, and espouses its philosophy of renunciation. The tragedy thus has symbolical implications above and beyond its rather vague plot; it belongs to a world where the human figures are simply the incarnation of different passions.

The first night at the Imperial Theatre was a considerable success. Without wishing to detract from the importance of the Purcell Operatic Society's productions, Martin Shaw, who had composed incidental music for *The Vikings*, looked back on it later as the 'real beginning' of Craig's work. William Rothenstein, indignant at finding no mention of the piece in the *Saturday Review*, wrote to that paper to express his conviction that Craig's production would undoubtedly influence the development of the theatre in Europe, (45) and in a letter to Ellen Terry, on 8 May 1903, he expressed his deep admiration for its 'unique beauty':

> ... never before had we seen such perfect marriage of dramatic suggestions in the foreground, background and grouping of the figures, and the actual delivery and gesture, which resulted in a perfectly noble expression of the tragedy of men's and women's lives. ... Everything seemed terribly but simply inevitable, from the black sky, to the checked gowns of the heroes. . .

Referring to Craig, Rothenstein adds:

> I am sure that in a very short time he will have won that foremost place in the modern theatre he already has shown his right to.

Yet in preparing this production, Craig had been faced with a number of difficulties. Hjördis was not a part that came naturally to Ellen Terry. Moreover, the thirty-one-year-old producer had to cope with senior members of the company who were shocked by the slightest attempt at novelty. Some of them declared they could not fight in single combat on the steep slope of the stage, and most of them protested against the lighting – no doubt considering that the producer's job is first and foremost to concentrate attention on the performers' faces. For Craig, however, the actor was far from being the only element in a stage presentation, and he often plunged the scene into semi-darkness in order to intensify the tragic aspect of *The Vikings* and emphasize its symbolism. This forced him into a new battle – against the *egotism* of the actor, and in due course he drew certain conclusions from the experience.

In one of the opening pages of his *Private Notebook*, Craig says that if someone wants to become a *useful* producer, it is *useful* to have a thorough knowledge of all theatrical techniques and be able to exercise them. In *On the Art of the Theatre*, he says that the 'artist of the theatre' must be capable of carrying out his own designs, stage arrangements and lighting, and of directing the movements of the actors. If he is obliged to ask others to do this for him, he will never be more than a brilliant amateur. The story of Craig's work on *The Vikings* makes it clear that his description of 'the artist of the theatre' is prompted by his own experience, and this is confirmed by a study of his working copy of the play, which is full of notes about the production and lists of costumes and properties. He even made drawings for a lantern, a bundle, a lance-head or a cushion. Nothing escaped his attention, and he designed everything, down to the smallest 'prop'. He arranged the music, plotted the lighting, and of course directed every movement of the actors. The written play was Ibsen's, but the finished production was the work of Craig. Inspired by the subject of the tragedy and the impressions he gained from it, Craig had translated it into visual form. A play presented on the stage was not, for him, a succession of lines repeated by the actors, but a pattern built up from visual elements (movements, colours, lights, actors) and auditory elements (sounds, and the spoken words), each of which must have its effect on the spectator. For the play to make its full impact the various means of stage expression must be harmonized and brought to effect by careful planning.

This gives the producer a certain freedom in interpreting the text of the play and the dramatist's stage directions. Ibsen introduces each act of *The Vikings* by a description of the scene, but in so doing he shows himself to be still in the grip of the romantic imagination. Craig sought inspiration in the tragedy itself rather than in the playwright's over-specific descriptions. He did not design an objective setting for each act, a scene existing, as it were, before the events of the tragedy took place, a space independent of the people present in it: he created for each successive phase of the struggle a scenic vision in which actor and setting were inseparably associated because, since both were interpreting the same work, both must help to give expression to it. Craig's aim was to arrange and light his material in such a way as to create a place where the tragedy would be played out, to express its tensions and explain its symbolism. Not that he omitted all reference to the ancient Scandinavian community imagined by Ibsen; but he refused to present a 'photograph' of it. Instead, he suggested it, using the shapes and the rough materials of the costumes in Act I, for instance, to give the feeling of a primitive, barbarous world.

By refraining, as in his previous productions, from any attempt at archaeological reconstruction, he struck a balance between the realism of the play and its symbolism.

Ibsen gives a very detailed description of the setting for Act I. There is a seashore with a background of towering cliffs. On the left is a wooden hut, on the right are mountains covered with larch trees. The masts of two ships can be seen on one side of the bay. The sea is very rough. 'A cold winter's day with snow driving before the wind.' Craig simplified all this to the utmost, building a great platform of rock that sloped down towards the front of the stage, with the cliffs rising against a dark, undefined background. The tilt of the stage is shown clearly in a drawing by Fred Pegram, reproduced on page 51 of *The Sphere* for 18 April 1903. Craig spread out his actors, bringing the chief characters into prominence, and brought the action as close as possible to the audience, accentuating the impression of tragic dignity. The stage was plunged into a semi-darkness that drew protests from Bernard Shaw. (47) Craig had, it is true, a tendency to darken his scenes; but in this case the dim light was in keeping with the atmosphere of the play and helped to emphasize the strange remoteness of its primitive setting.

In the second act, Craig demonstrated his gift for imaginative stylization; this was a forerunner of some of his later work. Ibsen's description of the setting is as follows:

Gunnar's banqueting-hall. In the back wall is the main doorway, with smaller doors to right and left. In the left foreground is the seat of honour; facing it is another, lower one. A brushwood fire is burning on a stone hearth in the middle of the room. Long tables with benches are ranged between the two seats and the walls. Outside is pitch darkness; the hall is brightly lit by the fire on the hearth.

Craig altered all this completely, basing his design on the use of vertical lines and of the circle. There was a semi-circular backcloth of grey hangings which descended from an invisible height and parted in the middle to reveal a single imposing doorway. On a round platform stood a circular table for the guests, with the two seats of honour in the centre background; above it hung an immense wrought-iron circle, bearing lights. (48) The impression was one of solemnity, of a feudal world, with the candelabrum suggesting a huge iron crown (Plate 6A). There is an obvious resemblance between this scene and Wagner's immense round table for the Temple of the Graal in *Parsifal*. Craig had no doubt seen photographs of *Parsifal*, which had been staged at Bayreuth at the end of the previous century. But in *Parsifal* the round table was only one of many decorative elements, lost among a clutter of pillars and arches in what was alleged to be the Romanesque style; whereas in *The Vikings* it was the essential feature, standing out against a vague background which helped to give it prominence and enhance its symbolic value. In fact, the scene of which Craig's design reminds us most strongly is that in the new production of *Parsifal* staged at Bayreuth a few years ago by Wagner's grandson, Wieland Wagner, where a huge round table stands out against a dark, undefined background. (49) Craig's production of *The Vikings* undoubtedly presaged the 'New Bayreuth' that was to emerge some fifty years later – as Arthur Symons seems to have foreseen when he wrote in 1906:

> I am not sure that [Craig] would not reconcile those who prefer Wagner in the concert-room to this new kind of performance on the stage. He would give us the mind's attractive symbols of all these crude German pictures; he would strike away the footlights from before these vast German singers, and bring a ghostly light to creep down about their hoods and untightened drapings; he would bring, I think, the atmosphere of the music for the first time upon the stage. (50)

Craig's design for Act IV of *The Vikings* also makes us think of the 'New Bayreuth'. Ibsen explains that 'The scene takes place on the seashore at nightfall. From time to time the moon is glimpsed among dark, wind-torn clouds. In the background is a dark-coloured burial-mound, the soil of which seems to have been fresh-turned'. What did Craig devise? A vast, unbroken black background, a space for death (the death of Hjördis); and in the front of the stage a steep slope towards the footlights, rounded at its upper edge – a kind of naked hillock where the stark drama would be played out. That was all. In Craig's drawing (Plate 6B), a solitary figure suggests the dramatic tension; the lighting is cold and impersonal. Anyone who remembers the celebrated round, sloping stage of the 'New Bayreuth' will realize that Craig did pioneer work in *The Vikings* as much as in *Dido and Aeneas* or *Bethlehem*.

The Vikings having proved to be an artistic success, Craig hoped that it would be commercially successful too. Unfortunately it was nothing of the kind. The public stayed away. The theatre was not in the West End, the business manager was incompetent and there was not enough advertising. If only they could have held on for a few weeks . . . but Ellen Terry could not afford it. On 9 May, less than a month after it was first performed, *The Vikings* was taken off, even though the next production was not yet ready. For Craig the experience had been useful in more ways than one. It was the first time he had produced a play by Ibsen, whose work was to take an important place in his career, for he afterwards designed scenes for *Rosmersholm* for Duse, and in 1926 he made designs for *The Pretenders* and produced it, in collaboration with Johannes Poulsen, at the Royal State Theatre, Copenhagen.

*

On 23 May, when the Imperial Theatre had been closed for a fortnight, it reopened with Ellen Terry and her company in *Much Ado About Nothing*. Craig was not used to preparing a production so rapidly, but time was short and the Imperial Theatre season must be kept going. So *Much Ado* was planned and produced in twenty-five days. Again Craig had to fight the actors, who wanted scenery in the Alma-Tadema style, historically accurate costumes, and the kind of action to be found in every London stage. And again he carried the day, with the support of his mother; Beatrice was one of her favourite roles.

In his memoirs Craig describes, not without humour, the spirit in which his production and designs were prepared:

> When I did the play, this scene and all the others were what was called 'simplified'. We didn't reproduce the interior of a Palace in Messina, because that would have been a very costly affair; we should have had to travel to Messina to measure the place up and bring back the plans

of part of it, and then struggle to get it on to the stage, and so forth. This sort of labour was beginning to strike some of us in the theatre as rather ridiculous. It was very pleasant to come and see the interior of a Cathedral at Messina, almost in facsimile, and to hear a lovely organ booming or purring out the beautiful sounds which sacred music can breathe forth. But somehow all this made the younger people of 1902–3 – and I was one of them – a little impatient. (51)

Craig's way of dealing with the crucial church scene was typical of his style at this time. Count Kessler tells us that in that scene, '. . . except for the curtains there was only one strong ray of sunlight, falling on the stage in a thousand colours through an invisible stained-glass window'. (52) This bears out the impression conveyed by Craig's sketch, which shows a symmetrical arrangement of neutral-coloured hangings and very little else – a harmony of vertical lines. It was the lighting that transformed this setting, brought it to life and created the atmosphere. This lighting was not simply switched on and left at that, but used to reveal the dramatic setting by degrees, as we see from the following description by *Modern Society*'s theatre critic:

> Stage and auditorium are in utter darkness at first. The music of an organ swells out from the gloom of the stage. Then a shaft of light suddenly illuminates the jewelled patriarchal cross on the altar just beyond the centre of the scene; a mysterious blueness, vague, translucent, like the blue of atmospheric space, grows out of the darkness beyond the altar; a warmer glow suffuses the whole stage; dim forms of worshippers take shape and colour; arched mosaic columns spring up on either side; and so, little by little, with the cross, the altar, the priest, and Claudio and Hero for the central group there grows out of darkness a scene of Byzantine splendour. It is as though one were within the walls of a vast cathedral with a vista beyond the altar that seems to soar outward and upward into illimitable space. That scene is a triumph of which Mr Craig might well be proud. (53)

Yet again Craig's work was favourably received in many directions. Even George Bernard Shaw wrote to Ellen Terry: 'As usual Ted has the best of it. I have never seen the church scene go before – didn't think it *could* go, in fact. He should have done something better with the monument scene or else left it alone altogether;

but still, when all is said, nothing quite like it has been done before . . .' (54)

But it was no use. Like *The Vikings*, *Much Ado* was a commercial failure. This brought the season at the Imperial Theatre to an end, and in June Ellen Terry set off on tour to restore her depleted finances.

Much Ado About Nothing was Craig's last production in England and his last work with his mother. 'When I worked with him I found him far from unpractical,' she wrote later. 'It was the modern theatre that was unpractical when he was in it.' (55)

NOTES

1. E. Gordon Graig, *Index to the Story of my Days*, op. cit., p. 211.
2. Haldane Macfall, 'Some Thoughts on the Art of Gordon Craig', in *The Studio*, Vol. XXIII, no. 102, September 1901, Supplement no: 36, p.82.
3. This later became the Embassy Theatre.
4. E. Gordon Craig, *Index to the Story of my Days*, p. 228.
5. See Martin Shaw, *Up to Now*, Oxford University Press, London, 1929, p. 26.
6. See E. Gordon Craig, *Towards a New Theatre*, J. M. Dent & Sons, London and Toronto, 1913, p. 57.
7. Programme designed by Craig.
8. E. Gordon Craig, *Index to the Story of my Days*, p. 226.
9. Manuscript shown to me by Gordon Craig: *Notes, 1904–6. A note for a book of one's Memoirs* (1904), p. 15.
10. Mabel Cox, 'Dress', in *The Artist, an illustrated monthly record of arts, crafts and industries*, July 1900, p. 131.
11. Ibid., p. 131.
12. Ibid.
13. *Notes 1904–6*, op. cit., p. 13.
14. See *Dido (and Aeneas) G.C. 1900*, in the Edward Gordon Craig Collection, Bibliothèque de l'Arsenal, Paris, opp. pp. 3, 4 and 7. This gives a plan showing the arrangement of the scenery and the basic positions of the actors for Act I, a list of stage properties, a note by Craig on the changes he wished to make in his production for the second series of performances (in 1901), and a list of the lighting apparatus: four blues and purples trained on the backcloth from above, three ambers lighting the stage from above, two ambers lighting the actors from the back of the auditorium.
15. This refers to Act I, scene 2.
16. Haldane Macfall is speaking here of the performances at the Coronet

Theatre in 1901. At the Hampstead Conservatoire there were no footlights and no borders.

17. Haldane Macfall, 'Some Thoughts on the Art of Gordon Craig', p. 83.
18. 29 March 1901.
19. *The Review of the Week*, 11 August 1900.
20. Haldane Macfall, 'Some Thoughts on the Art of Gordon Craig', p. 83.
21. Letter from Yeats to Gordon Craig, quoted by Craig in *Index to the Story of my Days*, p. 239.
22. *The Letters of W. B. Yeats*, edited by Allan Wade, Rupert Hart-Davies, London, 1954, p. 371.
23. This article by Yeats is reprinted in his *Essays and Introductions*, Macmillan & Co., London, 1961, where this extract will be found on pp. 100-1
24. There were six performances. The spectators included Lord Howard de Walden and Count Harry Kessler, both of whom were to play important parts in Craig's career.
25. E. Gordon Craig, *Index to the Story of my Days*, pp. 238-9.
26. Ibid., p. 238.
27. In a letter of 5 March 1902. See *The Letters of W. B. Yeats*, p. 366.
28. See the MS already quoted, *Notes 1904-6*, pp. 16-19.
29. E. Gordon Craig, *Towards a New Theatre*, p. 23. The designs entitled 'Henry V - the Tents', 'The Lights of London', 'Enter the Army' and 'The Arrival' are reproduced in this volume.
30. Photographs of this production are reproduced in the Souvenir of *Acis and Galatea, illustrated by Gordon Craig*, (London, 1902); in an article by Max Osborn, 'Edward Gordon Craig, Berlin', published in *Deutsche Kunst und Dekoration*, Vol. VIII, 1904-5, July, pp. 589-95, and as illustrations to an article by Dion Clayton Calthrop which appeared in *The Artist* (1902). Books of press-cuttings relating to Craig's early productions may be seen in the Gordon Craig Collection, Bibliothèque de l'Arsenal, Paris.
31. Arthur Symons, *Studies in Seven Arts*, Constable & Co., London, 1906, p. 354.
32. Max Beerbohm, 'Mr Craig's Experiment', *Saturday Review*, 5 April 1902.
33. Letter from W. B. Yeats to Gordon Craig, quoted by Craig in *Index to the Story of my Days*, p. 242.
34. Arthur Symons, *Studies in Seven Arts*, pp. 352-3.
35. This prospectus - 'A Masque. The Harvest-Home, designed and arranged by Martin Shaw and E. G. Craig' - includes among its contents a reference to Hentzner's work on which the idea was based, and a summary of the proposed libretto.
36. An account of this association between Craig and Housman is given in the latter's book, *The Unexpected Years*, Jonathan Cape, London, 1937, pp. 185 et seq.
37. See the Gordon Craig MS already quoted, *Notes 1904-6*, pp. 22-4.
38. A cross-section of the hall, drawn by Craig, is to be seen in his notebook on the production of *Bethlehem* (Gordon Craig Collection, Bibliothèque de

l'Arsenal, Paris), which also includes sketches of scenes for the piece and notes on the costumes, scenery and lighting.

39. Gordon Craig expresses this preference in his MS *Notes 1904-6*, op. cit., p. 22. Moreover, according to Housman (*The Unexpected Ideas*, p. 192), Craig asked for the right to supervise any future performances of *Bethlehem*, which further evidences his interest in the piece. Finally, in a letter to Edward Hutton, dated 14 October 1907, Craig says he would like to take the production, after revision, to Italy and Germany. (Craig's original letters to Hutton are in the Gordon Craig Collection presented to the British Institute, Florence, by Dorothy Nevile Lees.)

40. I have been able to build up a description of the successive scenes in this production with the help of Laurence Housman's account, and of Christopher St John's review published in *The Critic*, which was shown to me by Gordon Craig. The penthouse roof under which the shepherds are sitting in Scene 1 is not shown in the photograph taken at rehearsal; but it is to be seen in Craig's drawings for that scene (see note 39), and Christopher St John mentions it in his article.

41. It was in 1902 that Craig bought Sebastiano Serlio's books on architecture and began to study them. The curved stage structure used in the last scene of *Bethlehem* may have been suggested by one of Serlio's designs.

42. Martin Shaw, *Up to Now*, p. 37.

43. Ellen Terry, *The Story of my Life. Recollections and Reflections*, Hutchinson, London, 1908, p. 326.

44. Martin Shaw, *Up to Now*, p. 36.

45. This letter was printed in *Saturday Review* for 9 May, the day when *The Vikings* had its last performance.

46. Letter quoted in *Ellen Terry's Memoirs*, p. 267.

47. See Ellen Terry, *The Story of my Life*, p. 327.

48. Gordon Craig thought of using this design again in Act IV, Scene 1 of Ibsen's *Pretenders* in 1926.

49. *Parsifal*, by Richard Wagner, produced by Wieland Wagner, Bayreuth Festival, 1956.

50. Arthur Symons, *Studies in Seven Arts*, p. 359.

51. E. Gordon Craig, *Index to the Story of my Days*, p. 249.

52. Quoted by Janet Leeper, *Edward Gordon Craig, Designs for the Theatre*, Penguin Books, Harmondsworth, 1948, p. 8.

53. See *Modern Society*, 30 May 1903, p. 950.

54. This letter, dated 3 June 1903, is given in *Ellen Terry and Bernard Shaw. A Correspondence*, edited by Christopher St John, Constable, London, 1931.

55. Ellen Terry, *The Story of my Life*, p. 327.

V

EXILE

After this commercial failure, Craig had some idea of joining forces with Martin Shaw again to give open-air performances of *The Masque of Love*. A few exhibitions of his scene and costume designs were held; after being shown at the Imperial Theatre they went to Edinburgh, Glasgow and Liverpool, and he sold a few drawings, which kept his head above water. In May 1904 he announced his intention of opening a School for the Art of the Theatre where the forgotten laws of the theatre would be sought out, relearnt and tested by experiment, so that it could be restored to its former dignity as an art. But nobody was interested in this idea, and Craig had to wait another ten years before he could put it into operation.

He worked. He studied his recently-purchased volumes of Serlio's *Architettura*. Their illustrations – plans, elevations, perspective views – stimulated his imagination. On page 10 of the first Book there were some designs of pillars which he had used for *Much Ado About Nothing*. Henceforth he gained considerable inspiration from Serlio and often referred to these books.

He was also devising mime plays and making designs for them. Already, about 1899–1900, he had written the outline of a piece which had Pierrot as its central character and planned a 'Judas play', the first act of which was set in a vineyard belonging to a Roman general, the second in Mary Magdalene's house, while the third opened in the Temple and then moved to the Mount of Olives.

Since 1902 he had been preparing a number of *Masques*, more or less symbolical in character, with dances and music and the play of line, light and colour. These included *The Masque of London*, which he mentions several times in *Towards a New Theatre*, (1) *The Masque of Lunatics*, and the most important of the series, *The Masque of Hunger*, on which he was still working in 1904.

This was an allegorical drama with a humanitarian purpose, the spirit of which Craig himself defined thus:

> I once wrote, or rather constructed, a Drama called 'Hunger', making for it many designs. I hope to complete this Drama when I have my school and workmen to help me. For to finish a thing for the stage in the study is a mistake I ought not to be guilty of.
>
> And then I hope to give performances of it before a small and select audience.
>
> Not that I believe the theatre is for the 'few' – but there are some plays and some shows which are not for 'the many'. Nothing would make me alter or destroy this Drama – but nothing would persuade me that it would be right to show it to a large and mixed audience.
>
> For it is wrong for the poor and hungry to be *shown* a vision of themselves and their misery – but it is not entirely wrong to show it to a few people who might, if they once *saw*, do something to make Hunger less general.
>
> No amount of preaching in a theatre is of any more use to humanity than preaching in the streets. For words never explain. But to *see* a thing, and how sad some things are and how terrible other things are, is quite a different matter. Argument is silenced. In my Drama the Hunger of the Poor and the Hunger of the Rich were placed side by side. And the king or man of God stood apart – and no one could tell what he felt – as it always was and always will be. (2)

Craig's intention was no doubt to weld all the different means of theatrical expression into one consistent performance in these masques, in a transposition of Wagner's concept of the *Gesamtkunstwerk* (the combined work of art). At the same time he was reviving an ancient British tradition, that of the Renaissance Masques, which in Shakespeare's time had been, he considered, really 'made for the theatre' (3) (together with the pageants), since they were composed in order to be performed, not written by poets or men of letters and then adapted for the stage. What Craig was asserting in these Masques was the existence of an art in its own right, owing nothing to literature, or at any rate not deriving from it. The Masques were his first announcement of the principles he was to develop before long in *The Art of the Theatre*.

But none of these projects was actually carried out. They all remained at the paper stage. Craig seemed fated to work in isolation. No help was proffered to him in his own country.

*

The performances of *The Masque of Love* and *The Vikings* had been seen, however, by a foreigner, a certain Count Kessler, a patron of art and literature who was attached to the Court of Weimar. William Rothenstein, who was acquainted with Kessler and shared his enthusiasm for *The Vikings* (as he had shown by his letter to *The Saturday Review*), now put him in touch with Craig.

In 1903, Kessler invited Craig to come to Weimar and produce a play at the Grand Ducal Theatre. Craig set forth his conditions and confided to Rothenstein:

I've had a long charming letter from Count Kessler – & I don't seem to be able at all to show him that I feel certain that my visit to Weimar would merely end in my returning after a very pleasant waste of time.

I can do nothing talking to Dukes and Grand Duchesses & Poets with a court actress or two thrown in –

I have had so much experience of these *discussions* about a production. If only he or the duke would make me a definite offer I would then make a definite answer.

As I have told him I can do nothing without first reading the play – secondly I can do nothing unless he can assure me that absolute power will be given me over *play, actors & actresses*, scenery, costume & every detail in the production.

You see, my dear Will, it is the only way to do the work & probably the Grand Dook will see me to 'ell before he'll give me full powers. His poets, & actors AND *actresses* and even horses would all be up in arms against the idea – there would be mutterings of resignation & Weimar's actors would all leave in a body for Berlin. . . (4)

Nothing came of this Weimar idea. But Kessler spoke of Craig to Otto Brahm, the manager of the Lessing Theater, Berlin, and after a meeting in that city, Brahm asked Craig to come and work in his theatre.

In August of the following year Craig said good-bye to London and left for Germany, visiting Berlin and going on to Weimar, where he was Count Kessler's guest. After this his visits to his own country were few and far between.

Kessler, the mentor of taste at Weimar and 'one of the men who has done most for the German Theatre', (5) was now to do more than anyone else to make Craig's work known in Germany and help him to carry out and propagate his ideas. Craig always remained deeply grateful to the man of whom he gives the following description: '. . . My friend was immensely energetic. All the time he went unceasingly here and there, placing sums of money in one branch of art after another. Wood-engraving – Painting – the Stage – Publishing – Printing – Type-cutting – Paper-making – Literature – Sculpture – Music – there was nothing in the Arts that he missed.'(6)

For Craig, Weimar meant in the first place an atmosphere, an artistic circle. It also meant a warm welcome and a sympathetic hearing, not merely for the son of Ellen Terry and the pupil of Irving, but for the artist who had made this or that admired design for *Hamlet*, for the man of the theatre who would have no truck with the theatre's sham traditions and its hollow pretensions to realism. It meant new friendships too, and interesting meetings with such men as Henry van de Velde and Joseph Hoffmann, the two pioneers of twentieth-century architecture. The former then held the post of artistic adviser to the Grand Duke of Weimar, and had been director of the Institute of Decorative Arts since 1902, while the latter – who had studied under Otto Wagner, one of the earliest advocates of a functional art stripped of ornamental accretions – had just founded the 'Wiener Werkstätte'; in 1905 he was to design the Palais Stoclet at Brussels, embodying the new architectural features – tall marble columns, lamps with geometrical shapes, clear-cut lines. Both men were reacting against 'art nouveau', with its flourishes, arabesques and writhing coils, and trying to replace these by plane surfaces and cubic volume – at the very moment when Craig was freeing the stage from its decorative clutter. Both were striving to establish perfect harmony between architecture, furniture and decoration, at the very moment when Craig was basing the unity of stage production on a complete harmony between all its components. Thus, in their professional activities, Van de Velde, Hoffmann and Craig had a number of guiding principles in common, the principles underlying the aesthetic revolutions that marked the early years of the present century. Hoffmann and Van de Velde undoubtedly drew Craig's attention to the power of suggestion inherent in an architectural composition confined to simple geometrical elements. Whether or not he was directly influenced by them, the fact remains that from this time forth his scene designs were characterized by increasing geometrical simplicity. Stage decoration, in his hands, was to become a form of architecture.

There was much discussion; ideas were eagerly exchanged; in Weimar Craig could give his views on his own art and describe to a young architect, who agreed with them, some of his principles, Such as, that the art of the theatre should be made up of three-quarters action and one-quarter words, or that the painter, the poet, the musician or the architect could do nothing to help the theatre, which could only be saved by the men of the theatre themselves.

Craig now went to Berlin to work on Otway's *Venice Preserved*, which had been adapted by the Austrian poet-dramatist, Hugo von Hofmannsthal. He saw many plays – Gorki's *Lower Depths*, Hofmannsthal's *Elektra*, Schiller's *Kabale und Liebe*, Nestroy's dialect comedy *Einen Jux will er sich machen*, Wilde's *Salome*, Ibsen's *Lady from the Sea*, Calderon's *Alcalde de Zalamea* – which convinced him of the vitality of the German theatre and the high standard of its repertory, the latter a point he was fond of mentioning as an example in other connections. (7)

He did a considerable amount of preparatory work on *Venice Preserved*, as can be seen from the marginal notes and sketches in his own copy of the play; (8) he made a number of scene and costume designs (Plate 7), and on 29 November he even went to visit Hofmannsthal, who lived near Vienna. The poet made some changes in his adaptation, and in order to give its production every prospect of success he gave *carte blanche* to Craig, whose talents he had heard highly praised.

All would thus have been well, but for the fact that Brahm and Craig were worlds apart in mentality and outlook. Brahm had begun his career as a literary critic. After Antoine founded the Théâtre Libre in Paris, Brahm imitated him by opening the Freie Bühne in Berlin (1889), for the sole purpose of staging realistic dramas. He was incapable of understanding a form of theatrical art which employed symbolism instead of aiming at photographic exactitude. Craig wanted a different theatre: 'Impossible'; some different apparatus: 'Impossible'; he wanted to make some changes in the upper part of the stage: 'Impossible.' When shown a design for a scene which would usually include a door, Brahm exclaimed in astonishment, for there was no door to be seen. 'There is a way in and a way out,' Craig rejoined. 'Yes,' said Brahm, 'but I see no door handle nor lock. You cannot have a door without a handle.' To make him happy, Craig declared that he had copied this scene, line for line, from an old Italian manuscript. 'I did not want this nice old gentleman to imagine a door, but I wanted him through his imagination to see that no door was necessary, and I only succeeded when I assured him that it was a replica of an actuality.' (9)

For Craig, Otway's Venice could not be a mere copy of a historical and geographical city, it was the setting imagined by a poet for his drama. But Brahm, with his passion for realism, called in a German scene-painter, who made alterations in the scenery. Regarding this as an insult and a betrayal, Craig sent a letter of protest and explanation to the Press, and it was published simultaneously in Berlin, Munich, Hamburg, Frankfurt, Cologne, Leipzig, Weimar, Dresden, Magdeburg, Nuremberg and Breslau. The English draft of this letter has vanished and we have only the German translation, probably made with the help of Count Kessler, which runs as follows:

I should be grateful if you would allow me some space in your columns, as I should like to correct some slight misunderstandings which have arisen with regard to my relations with the management of the Lessing Theater.

In the first place it is being said that I came to Germany to reform the German stage in general and the Berlin theatre in particular. But although the hardest work is always the kind I enjoy most, I can assure anyone who may be offended by this idea that it is far from my intentions. I consider that if Germany makes mistakes it produces its own reformers. Indeed, I can name one such reformer among my Berlin friends, so I need say no more about that.

Secondly, it is supposed that I came over here in order to work with Dr Brahm, of the Lessing Theater, for an indefinite period. I wish to make it clear that my contract with Dr Brahm expired on 31 December 1904. It is indeed true that I came over from England at Dr Brahm's invitation, and it was agreed that I was to produce *Hamlet*. I believe *Hamlet* has been crowded out by a play by a well-known modern writer. Shakespeare is in his grave, and cannot feel the blow; let us hope that he at any rate appreciates the humour of it.

Thirdly, it is generally supposed that I am to stage Dr von Hofmannsthal's play, *Venice Preserved*. This is not quite correct either; for although – at Herr von Hofmannsthal's express wish – I was expecting to conduct rehearsals of this play, as I have always done in England with plays for which I have made designs, it was preferred at the last moment to put on a performance that was all shreds and patches, presumably on the grounds that this was more in line with the artistic principles of the Lessing Theater.

Now a performance composed of shreds and patches is a performance arranged according to the views of five or six people instead of one, and it has certain advantages over a performance designed by one man and intended to give an impression of unity. It makes the work easier for the one man and more profitable for the others. It makes the performance more expensive for the management, of course, but that is no business of ours.

Only two scenes in this play are to be carried out from my designs, and I am not sure that if I were to attend a performance I should recognize these. A scene-design is not finished when the drawings and the model are handed over, but only when the artist who designed the scene lights it himself and directs the movements of the figures and groups appearing on the stage, which only too often spoil the picture. Unfortunately, however, the artistic principles of the manager of the Lessing Theater are not the same as those followed by the Greeks, the Egyptians, the Japanese and a few of the best European theatres of the present day, and so it has been made impossible for me to complete the work I had begun.

But it is my intention to produce Shakespeare's *Hamlet* in German within the next six months, and I hope later on to stage a number of masterpieces of the Elizabethan period – plays by Shakespeare, Marlowe, Fletcher, Chapman, Massinger and Ford – in the English language.

I come from a country where, since Henry Irving has practically retired from the stage, nearly all London theatres have degenerated into counting-houses. I am now in a country where so far I have found only one example of that hateful disease, and I hope I shall soon be able to describe how wonderfully Germany has preserved its old theatre and what an exceptional young theatre it is creating for itself in our own day.

Yours, etc.,

Ed. Gordon Craig.

The pseudo-collaboration with Brahm, though disappointing, was instructive. Despite the way in which his work had been changed and mutilated, the German artists and public were now discovering Craig as an artist. This cutting letter informed them of his attitude and of his views about the theatre, and his ideas began to spread. For him, however, it was a painful lesson, and it no doubt made him more mistrustful, increased his fear of being swindled, of having his projects misrepresented or pulled to pieces. From now on he became more and more intransigent, laying down his conditions, refusing to make concessions, and preferring to withdraw rather than yield to the temptation of compromising.

*

The reason why Craig has inspired so many artists, producers and designers, been so frequently imitated and even plagiarised, is because his writings have been widely read and his designs attentively studied. Exhibitions did much to spread his ideas. His first exhibition in Germany opened in Friedmann & Weber's gallery in Berlin on 3 December 1904. It comprised sixty items, including designs for *Acis and Galatea*, *The Masque of London*, *Much Ado About Nothing*, *Henry V*, *The Vikings*, *The Masque of Love*, etc., some English landscape sketches, and a number of portraits and illustrations. The very important introduction to the catalogue is signed 'Harry Graf Kessler'. For it was Kessler who had had the idea of arranging an exhibition, and he sponsored it himself. In thus introducing Craig, he defines the position of the artist in the modern theatre, outlining the views expressed a few months later in *The Art of the Theatre*, and concludes by saying:

Craig declares categorically that he looks to the theatre of the coming century to play an entirely new role. He does not despise the dramatist, but he protests against the manner in which all theatre people – managers, actors, designers – rely on the dramatist. He wishes to restore the theatre as an independent art. He has clearly recognized what conditions are required for the pure theatrical art that so many people wish for, and he seems to combine them in his own person. The *Gesamtkunstwerk* that Wagner thought to found on the basis of music and poetry will soon, perhaps, be re-created by Craig or under his influence, from painting, dance and gesture. (10)

Whether this conclusion exactly corresponded to Craig's views was not definitely established until several months afterwards. But in these early days of December 1904, a curious emphasis began to be placed on one of the words used by Kessler – 'dance'; not the classical ballet, with its classified steps and brilliant technique. In his preface to Craig's catalogue, Kessler mentions two dancers whose work seemed to hold out the possibility of a stage art based on the power of the imagination. These were Loie Fuller, adored by the Symbolists, and the Japanese dancer Sada Yacco. However, a few days after the opening of the exhibition an event took place which decisively influenced the lives and careers of two great artists and which stands out in the annals of the European theatre. Craig met Isadora Duncan. (11) Isadora, who had just opened her school of dance at Grünewald, was already a legendary figure, she attracted and intrigued everyone who met her. When Craig first saw her she was giving a 'Chopin recital' in a Berlin concert-hall, and in her dancing he recognized an art closely related to his own, an ideal he shared. The stage was backed by a few grey curtains hung between short pillars; there was a grey carpet, a piano – and the figure of the dancer, standing absolutely still until, swept into the rhythm of the music as though running after it, she broke into movement that was no mere display of brilliant 'steps' or conventional figures. Craig was fascinated, seeing what he recognized as pure movement, one of the essential components of the art of the theatre as he envisaged it.

This was the beginning of a love affair in which both of them found inspiration. Lugné-Poe, after discovering Isadora Duncan, notes in his memoirs that 'Gordon Craig had undoubtedly passed through her life and left on her the indelible mark of his own originality and vigorous strength'; (12) and Craig himself writes in his *Index*, under the date 1905, 'This year and 1906 saw me designing a number of scenes for plays, and a few of these came to be reproduced in *Towards a New Theatre*. To the friendship and inspiration of Isadora I owe some of the best designs of these two years.' (13)

Craig accompanied Isadora on a number of her tours, going with her to Dresden, Hamburg, Moscow, Frankfurt, Brussels, Antwerp, Zurich and Amsterdam in 1905, to Munich and Amsterdam in 1906, and so forth. He made many drawings and sketches of her, some of which were published in 1906 by the Insel Verlag in a portfolio entitled 'Isadora Duncan. Six Movement Designs', with an accompanying text, also by Craig.

All this time his fame was being extended and his ideas for the theatre made known by a series of exhibitions. In March 1905 his work was shown at Düsseldorf; in April, at Cologne; in May, at Dresden (at the Galerie Ernst Arnold); in June, at Munich (at the Kunstverein) and in London; in October, in Vienna (at the Galerie H.O. Miethke). His art and his principles were beginning to influence the European theatre.

*

When he published his first theoretical writings, Craig was thirty-three years old. He had considerable experience behind him. He had been an actor and a producer, he had wrestled with the conditions prevailing in the commercial theatre, he had been obliged to fight for the views he held so uncompromisingly. Inside the theatre, he struggled to put fresh life into it. From outside, he criticized it, explained what was wrong with it, suggested ways of putting it to rights, and then turned his eyes away from the present situation to look into the future – towards the 'theatre of the future' of which he constituted himself the prophet.

Craig notes in his *Index* that in September 1902, about three months before *Bethlehem* was put on; 'Wanting to WRITE of the Theatre, ideas crowding in my head, I asked E.T. how on earth to learn how to write. She couldn't say, but suggested "begin to write".' (14) And Craig soon did begin to sort out his ideas and commit them to paper as they came into his head. From that time on he has never stopped making notes and writing articles and memoranda; they fill notebooks, loose pages, and thick volumes specially bound for him, and at intervals he rereads them, making corrections, adding to or revising them.

In 1904 a German magazine, *Kunst und Künstler*, printed an article by Craig with the title '*Über Bühnenausstattung*' ('On Stage Decoration'). In this he made a violent onslaught upon realistic scenery and then went on to discuss the question of scenes for Shakespeare's plays. (15) The year 1905 was an outstandingly important one; in it Craig published *The Art of the Theatre*, began to meditate and make notes on the *über-marionette*, and made his first plans for a periodical that would help to spread his ideas and lead the campaign for transforming the theatre. The German and Austrian art galleries were eagerly exhibiting his drawings, while he himself was travelling round Europe with Isadora Duncan and at the same time designing some of his most important stage projects, musing about his art, and considering how best to make his views known and help to put fresh life into the theatre. He took only a week (27 April to 4 May 1905, when he was in Berlin) to write a little book which was destined to have a widespread influence – *The Art of the Theatre*, an imaginary conversation between a stage director and playgoer, cast in a form resembling the Platonic dialogue. On 2 August a German translation of this was published by Hermann Seemann, with Kessler's introduction to the Friedmann & Weber catalogue as its preface. An English edition, with a foreword by Graham Robertson, appeared next (Foulis, 1905) and was soon followed by a Dutch translation (S. L. Van Looy, 1906) with three prefaces – one by the actor J. C. de Vos, one by the painter Jan C. Van Looy, and one by the painter and engraver M. A. J. Baur. A Russian version, *Szenischeskoe Iskusstvo*, appeared about the same time (Suvorin, 1906). Thus, the book reached a considerable public in Europe, though French readers had to wait until 1920, when it was published as part of the larger volume, *De l'Art du Théâtre*. (16)

In this, his first book, Craig began by correcting various widespread misapprehensions about the theatre. There was, he pointed out, a frequent tendency to confuse dramatic poetry with **drama**:

the art of the theatre could not consist of the play, for that was a work of literature; nor of the acting, which was simply one of the elements: '. . .the Art of the Theatre is neither acting nor the play, it is not scene nor dance, but it consists of all the elements of which these things are composed; action, which is the very spirit of acting; words, which are the body of the play; line and colour, which are the very heart of the scene; rhythm, which is the very essence of dance.' (17) This definition became celebrated and has been repeatedly quoted and discussed. It shows how close, yet how far was Craig's viewpoint from that of Wagner. Close inasmuch as, like Wagner, Craig regarded unity as vital to a stage performance; far because Craig, unlike Wagner, was not dreaming of some supreme art resulting from the active union and mutual support of several different arts. Nothing was further from Craig's thoughts than the idea of any kind of fusion of the arts. (18) He speaks of line and colour, not of 'painting'; of 'words', not of poetry. Action, words, line, colour and so on are simply *materials*, they have no independent artistic existence. If one of them is more valuable than the rest it is perhaps action, for the art of the theatre 'has sprung from action – movement – dance' and not, as commonly supposed, from speech, literature or poetry. These words are characteristic of the inventor of the *Masques*.

A piece for the theatre is meant to be *seen*, rather than heard. It is not complete until it is presented on the stage. Hence, any work that seems complete when we read it is not, strictly speaking, a piece for the theatre, for it belongs to literature.

PLAYGOER: Then do you mean to say *Hamlet* should never be performed?

STAGE DIRECTOR: To what purpose would it be if I replied 'Yes'? *Hamlet* will go on being performed for some time yet, and the duty of the interpreters is to put their best work at its service. But, as I have said, the theatre must not forever rely upon having a play to perform, but must in time perform pieces of its own art. (19)

When that time comes, the stage director will rise from being a craftsman to being an artist, and 'our art will then be self-reliant'. (20)

In order to understand what Craig was aiming at, we must realize that *The Art of the Theatre* embodied two entirely separate ideas. In the first place, the desire for an immediate and quite feasible improvement in the artistic standards of theatrical production – an improvement to which the stage director can make a considerable contribution in his role of *interpreter* (Craig never for a moment suggested – as he has so often been accused of doing – that stage production could be an art in itself); and in the second place, the vision of a theatrical art that still lay in the distant future. These two ideas are inseparably connected: there can be no theatrical renaissance until the status of the stage director has improved.

This naturally leads Craig to describe the ideal stage director, to define his function, powers and duties. And the portrait he draws is that of the producer of *Dido and Aeneas* and *The Vikings*.

This stage director is something quite different from the actor-manager. He must not be the best actor in the company, because then he cannot take an overall view of the performance and will be in danger of building up his own role, perhaps unconsciously, until the balance is destroyed. Nor must he be a painter. But he must have all the branches of theatre technique at his fingertips, so that he can effectively supervise the carrying out of his ideas and give any advice that is needed. He is the master-craftsman in charge of his workmen, the foreman, the 'ship's captain' who must be implicitly obeyed: 'Without discipline no supreme achievement can be accomplished.' The stage director's ideas for colour, rhythm and action will come to him as he reads and rereads the play. He will not be obsessed by the playwright's stage directions, which are only useful to readers; the play alone is to inspire him and tell him what to do. He must not leave it to anyone else, any artist or scene-painter to design the scenery, for such an intrusion would destroy the unity of the performance. He himself must design the scenes and costumes, avoiding fussy realism and choosing a colour-scheme in keeping with the spirit of the play. He must plan the lighting and make the necessary arrangements for it:

PLAYGOER: . . . in what way does he set to work? What guides him in his task of lighting the scene and costumes which we are speaking about?

STAGE DIRECTOR: What guides him? Why, the scene and the costumes, and the verse and the prose, and the sense of the play. All these things, as I told you, have now been brought into harmony, the one with the other – all goes smoothly – what simpler, then, that it should so continue, and that the manager should be the only one to know how to preserve this harmony which he has commenced to create? (21)

Last, but by no means least, he must be in firm control of the acting, instructing the players on their every movement. This, too, is necessary in the interests of unity, and the more cultivated and intelligent the actors, the easier it will be.

Unity was Craig's foremost requirement. That was why he declared that one man must be responsible for every aspect of the production and why he maintained that the reformation of the theatre could not be partial, limited to this or that technical aspect, but must be complete. It would not be enough to make changes in the scenery, in the acting, or in the architecture. Every aspect must be dealt with simultaneously, and the different innovations must add up to 'the reform of the theatre as an instrument'. (22) After that, the stage-manager will be in control and can become an 'artist of the theatre'. Then, says Craig prophetically, the Art of the Theatre will regain its true place and 'stand self-reliant as a creative art, and no longer as an interpretative craft'. (23) And he concludes by saying:

> . . . I am now going to tell you out of what material an artist of the theatre of the future will create his masterpieces. Out of ACTION, SCENE, and VOICE. Is it not very simple?
> And when I say *action*, I mean both gesture and dancing, the prose and poetry of action.
> When I say *scene*, I mean all which comes before the eye, such as the lighting, costume, as well as the scenery.
> When I say *voice*, I mean the spoken word or the word which is sung, in contradiction to the word which is read, for the word written to be spoken and the word written to be read are two entirely different things. (24)

This blunt statement not unnaturally shocked a great many

theatre people, but Craig was trying to free the theatre from the tyrannous grip of literature. *The Art of the Theatre* opened the era of the theatrical producer. There would perhaps not be many men with the ability to direct the actors and design the scenes as well; but the producer would be a guarantee of unity in all that happened on the stage. He would be responsible for the whole performance. There is nothing illogical about Craig's views on the theatre of the future, unless they are misconstrued as meaning that the playwright will have no share in it. They seem perfectly reasonable when we realize his guiding principle – that the theatre must rely on the combined action of all the elements of stage work. We then perceive that Craig is foreshadowing the most varied of the modern theatre's experiments, from expressionism to the epic by way of the 'abstract'. Craig was writing with his eyes on the theatre as it then was, with its crafts divided among a host of technicians, its general disorganization, and the unbalanced impression created by the struggle for supremacy between the actor, the designer and the playwright. He calls for the artist of the theatre because only such a man can get things into order again. The fact that one man is to be responsible for the final result does not mean that there will be no more team-work. In fact, paradoxical though this may seem, it is a guarantee of team-work. (25)

Thus, the year 1905 was a period of reflection during which Craig took stock of the situation. Having laid down his principles in *The Art of the Theatre*, he found himself standing midway between the present-day theatre, where he could and should play the part of an interpreter, and the ideal theatre of the future whose advent must be speeded. He never ceased to work as an interpreter and on some occasions he returned to the theatre; but he refused a great many offers to do so, and concentrated more and more on the future theatre of which he had a premonition. Some people, failing to understand his attitude, were to accuse him of being a mere dreamer.

As we have seen, Craig considered that if the theatre were to become an art again, all its elements must be brought into harmony. So what about the actor? He too must obey the will of the producer, the master of the stage work. *The Art of the Theatre* contains a curious passage on this subject:

PLAYGOER: But are you not asking these intelligent actors almost to become puppets?

STAGE DIRECTOR: A sensitive question, which one would expect from an actor who felt uncertain about his powers! A puppet is at present only a doll, delightful enough for a puppet show. But for a theatre we need more than a doll. Yet that is the feeling which some actors have about their relationship with the stage-manager. They feel they are having their strings pulled, and resent it, and show they feel hurt – insulted. (26)

Craig had been an actor; he had worked under one of the greatest actors of his generation, Henry Irving; he remembered his own productions for the Purcell Operatic Society and how readily the amateur company had followed his instructions; and he remembered the battles he had had to fight when producing *The Vikings*. He had given it as his opinion that all the necessary reforms must be made simultaneously; so now the position and function of the actor had to be defined. Before long he was to give his views on this subject in *The Actor and the Über-marionette*; but various unpublished manuscripts exist to show that that essay was the outcome of several years' reflection. In one of Craig's notebooks there is an entry of about nine pages, dated 21 March 1905, which deals with marionettes, their possibilities, and their superiority to human beings, those creatures of flesh, blood – and nerves. (27) They are 'extraordinary things', these marionettes, indifferent to applause and unaffected by the ebb and flow of emotion; they are not alive, but they *represent*. Craig already mistrusted the purely emotional side of art, holding emotion to be merely a superficial aspect of life, unconnected with its deeper truths. He was outlining his principles, glimpsing certain ideas. . . . In another manuscript, (28) dated Berlin 1905–1906, Craig considers the possibility of establishing a theatre of 'super-marionettes'. But he had not yet formulated his doctrine on the subject, which was to take shape gradually until the day when *The Mask* published his famous essay and some careless readers formed the impression that Craig wanted to banish actors from the theatre for ever.

The Art of the Theatre revealed Craig as the theorist of an art he wished to renovate. Hailed by some people as a work of genius, regarded by others as utopian or dangerous, it was his first serious writing on the theory of stagecraft. Exhibitions had already made known the style of his own work, and now publications would enable him to spread his views and give the impetus for a complete transformation of the theatre. It was by no mere coincidence that in the very year that witnessed the publication of *The Art of the Theatre* he conceived a new project, the founding of a magazine through which he could influence the theatre and those who worked in it – a weapon that would help him to transform play-writing, acting, scenery, even stage architecture. For the time being, no one seemed interested in the suggestion; it was dismissed as the latest whim of an 'impossible' genius. Early in 1906 Craig began the hunt for support and for an established publisher, but it was hopeless, nobody would put money into a scheme that seemed to offer no hope of a profit. Craig himself had no funds, but he did not lose heart. He drew up his plans. His magazine would be devoted to the art of the theatre, it would be a periodical for producers, actors and actresses, designers and lovers of the stage. It ought to be printed on fine paper. He was already considering what type should be used, and deciding that each (monthly) issue should contain up to sixty illustrations. What subjects would it deal with? The theatre of the future, of course, Bayreuth, marion-ettes, the Greek theatre, and so on. Who would contribute? He himself, naturally, and perhaps Coquelin, Max Beerbohm, F. R. Benson. (29) Was he going to wait until he could find a publisher or a wealthy patron? No, he would be his own publisher. And in 1908 *The Mask* began its long career as the greatest theatre magazine of the century.

*

Craig did not rest content with preparing his first theoretical writings; while doing so he kept up all his other activities, and his graphic work, engravings and scene-designs mirror the ideas he was putting on paper, while his written work is illustrated by his drawings. So it is no wonder that in 1905–1906 he made a number of projects for the stage, some of which reflect his views on the theatre of the future, while others show him in his role of inter-preter. *The Steps* (1905) belongs to the first category; his proposed collaboration with Reinhardt and the work he did for Eleonora Duse, to the second.

When reproductions of *The Steps* were shown in an exhibition of his designs and models at Manchester in 1912, Craig described them in the catalogue as:

> Four designs for a drama I created called *The Steps*. I call it a drama because acts are performed upon these steps – not because something is *said* upon them. Let a person relate in the most perfect words how someone walked up steps, and no drama is either created or performed. The distinction between literature and drama is as simple as it is profound. (30)

The Steps expresses an outright rejection of literature, or of any form of words. In *Towards a New Theatre*, which was published a year later, Craig describes the origin, components and phases of what he calls a *silent drama* (in opposition to the spoken drama). (31) The four designs (Plates 8 and 9) show a flight of steps, running right across the stage between two high walls, and leading up to a distant platform. On the steps are human figures, differently placed in each design, and areas of light and shade. None of the scenes is descriptive, each constitutes a 'mood' (they are called 'first mood', 'second mood', etc.) created by the presence or meeting of different people – small children, girls and boys, a man and a woman. But the central character, the real hero of the drama, which foreshadows the experiments of the 'abstract' theatre, is the flight of steps itself, which is a dramatic element in its own right and not simply a scenic element (as it is in many of Craig's designs, and as were the steps used by Jessner in his famous 'Craigish' production of *William Tell*, which was based entirely on a staircase.)

> But although the man and woman interest me to some extent, [writes Craig of the 'Third Mood'] it is the steps on which they move which move me. The figures dominate the steps for a time, but the steps are for all time. I believe that some day I shall get nearer to the secret of these things, and I may tell you that it is very exciting approaching such mysteries. If they were dead, how dull they would be, but they are trembling with a great life, more so than that of man – than that of woman. (32)

Thus, the drawings for *The Steps* form a sequel in Craig's career to the design of *The Arrival* and are the forerunners of certain studies in movement that he made in 1906 and of those of 1907, etched and reproduced in *Scene*, which he declared to go beyond the art of the theatre. (33) But they illustrate only one of the many directions in which he was searching; they reflect his desire to make the scene play an active part in the drama, to give it expressive 'life'.

Craig's exhibitions and publications were carrying his fame all over Germany. Among Berlin theatre men there was one who soon came under his influence and began to assimilate his ideas. This was Max Reinhardt, whom he had met through Kessler. Reinhardt cannot be associated with any particular style or trend. In the history of twentieth-century stagecraft he is the exponent of eclecticism, passing from realism to stylization, from the small theatre to the arena, from the traditional Italian shape of stage to the Schumann Circus or the Cathedral Square at Salzburg. He was receptive, eager for experience, ready to try anything once and to accept any suggestion; one of the most active experimenters of his day. As an actor he owed his training to Brahm, from whose realism he later gradually released himself. When *The Art of the Theatre* was published he had just taken over the management of the Deutsches Theater, and he came with his assistants to visit Craig in the latter's Berlin studio. He asked questions, he used his eyes; and his future work bore the stamp of the influence thus absorbed. His *Winter's Tale* and *King Lear* were among the first of what were rightly called 'Craigische Vorstellungen' (Craigish productions), with their simplification of the visual element, the three-dimensional architecture of their scenery, and their use of lighting to stimulate the imagination. Though he was not his own designer, Reinhardt as stage-manager came fairly close to Craig's concept of the theatrical producer. He followed the German theatrical tradition and was the successor of the Meiningen company, although he departed from the type of stagecraft they exemplified.

In 1905, Reinhardt invited Craig to produce several plays in his theatre – Shakespeare's *Tempest* and *Macbeth*, and Shaw's *Caesar and Cleopatra*. Craig made many designs for the scenes, but was always asked to change them. In the end he gave up. This was the beginning of the long history of his abstentions and refusals. At the beginning of 1906 he returned the draft contract Reinhardt had given him; and an unpublished manuscript of the same period contains a fresh analysis of his views concerning the medium appropriate to the theatrical art, and emphasizes that there can be no work of art without unity. (34) He felt that the proposed production of *The Tempest* or of *Macbeth* would inevitably fail to reflect his intentions, since he would not have the necessary free hand. What he needed was a theatre of his own, with his own company – as he said years later in his introduction to *The Theatre Advancing*:

> I was five or six times asked by Reinhardt to enter his admirable theatre and produce a play as I wished to see it produced. I did not do so – and I will do no such thing. 'What, you won't produce a play as you wish to see it produced!' I seem to hear the scream. Calmly, please. I never said any such bosh. I said I will not enter another man's theatre and do it. I will do it only in my own theatre. Is that clear? Do you know the old song beginning 'Will you walk into my parlour . . .'? (35)

Moreover, Craig was just then designing *The Steps*, and he may have felt that producing Shakespeare or Shaw would put him out of key with the ideal theatre of the future towards which all his efforts were for the time being directed.

Yet he agreed to work for Eleonora Duse, whom he had seen acting in London during his own days on the stage, when he was eighteen or nineteen. In 1904–1905, at Kessler's suggestion, she sent to ask him to design the scenes for Hofmannsthal's adaptation of Sophocles' *Elektra*. Craig made several designs (Plates 10 and 11A), reflecting more than one approach to the subject. They were never carried out, however, though some of them have frequently been reproduced and made no small contribution to his fame. The most celebrated of them all shows an immense doorway, re-sembling the centre portico of the Theatre of Orange, towering above a platform connected by shallow steps with the front of the stage. Light is used to give expression to the architecture through the juxtaposition of bright and shadowy surfaces, and the vastly enlarged shadows of two of the characters on the stage are thrown against the back wall. Craig comments on this:

> A vast and forbidding doorway, I often think, still remains the best background for any tragedy – yet when I am told by the archaeologist, who enjoys himself in the dry and dusty days which are gone, that vastness and nobility of line are unimportant, and that a nice little wooden stage and some tasteful hangings about eight to ten feet high will serve, I am so ready to agree that I sometimes wonder whether these vast doors and open spaces, these shadows and these bursts of light are not out of place.
>
> Of course, it all depends whether you come to the theatre for drama or literature.
>
> If you come for drama, then let the whole thing live – not alone to the brain, but through the eye and the ear.
>
> If you come for a literary treat – best catch the first train home and own up to having made a blunder. (36)

In 1906, Isadora Duncan brought Craig and Duse together, and it was decided that he should design the scenes for Ibsen's *Rosmersholm*, which Duse was to present at the Teatro della Pergola in Florence. Isadora – a skilful and tactful interpreter – has left an account of the discussions between the actress and the artist. (37) Ibsen's description of the setting as a comfortably furnished, old-fashioned drawing-room did not appeal to Craig. Duse was anxious to have 'a little window'. Determined to work undisturbed, Craig shut himself up in the Teatro della Pergola with his pots of paint and some old Italian women whom he put to sewing pieces of sackcloth together. Duse was not to set foot in the place until the work was finished. At last the day came when she was admitted to a box and saw the curtain rise on the scene in which she was to play Rebecca West:

> Oh, how can I describe what appeared before our astonished, enraptured eyes? Did I speak of an Egyptian temple? No Egyptian temple has ever revealed such beauty. No Gothic cathedral, no Athenian palace. Never have I seen such a vision of loveliness. Through vast blue spaces, celestial harmonies, mounting lines, colossal heights, one's soul was drawn toward the light of this great window which showed beyond, no little avenue, but the infinite universe. . . . Was

this the living-room of Rosmersholm? I do not know what Ibsen
would have thought. Probably he would have been as we were –
speechless, carried away. (38)

Duse made an enthusiastic speech to the actors:

> It is my destiny to have found this great genius, Gordon Craig. I now
> intend to spend the rest of my career (*sempre, sempre*) devoting myself
> only to showing the world his great work. . . . Only through Gordon
> Craig . . . will we poor actors find release from this monstrosity, this
> charnel-house, which is the theatre of today! (39)

Craig's design was bound to seem extraordinary to those who
felt that *Rosmersholm*, despite its symbolical character, demanded
a realistic setting. Anticipating their protests, he wrote in the
programme:

> Ibsen's marked detestation for Realism is nowhere more apparent
> than in the two plays *Rosmersholm* and *Ghosts*.
> The words are the words of actuality, but the drift of the words,
> something beyond this. There is the powerful impression of unseen
> forces closing in upon the place: we hear continually the long drawn
> out note of the horn of death.
> It is heard at the commencement, it mingles with the cries towards
> the end.
> Here and there hurries the figure of Life, not merely a little photo-
> graphic figure of Rebecca West – not even a woman – but the very
> figure of Life itself – and all the while we hear the soft crescendo of
> the Death Horn as its player approaches. Therefore those who prepare
> to serve Ibsen, to help in the setting forth of his play, must come to the
> work in no photographic mood, all must approach as artists.
> Realism has long ago proclaimed itself as a contemptible means of
> hinting at things of life and death, the two subjects of the masters.
> Realism is only Exposure, whereas art is Revelation; and therefore in
> the mounting of this play I have tried to avoid all Realism.
> We are not in a house of the 19th or 20th century built by Architect
> this or Master Builder that, and filled with furniture of Scandinavian
> design. That is not the state of mind Ibsen demands we shall be in.
> Let us leave period and accuracy of detail to the museums and to
> curiosity shops.
> Let our common sense be left in the cloakroom with our umbrellas

and hats. We need here our finer senses only, the living part of us. We are in Rosmersholm, a house of shadows.

Then consider the unimportance of custom and clothes – remember only the colour which flows through the veins of life – red or grey as the sun or the moon will it, dark or fair as we will.

So look upon what is before you, with your eyes – not through pin holes nor opera glasses, for then you will see nothing.

Then you will not see the stately and inspiring figure which passes before you; you will not feel the fire of the life-giving strength which stands in front of you; you will not be in the least aware of what the whole thing exists for. But cease to be curious – throw away all concern, enter into the observance of this as though you were at some ancient religious ceremony, and then perhaps you will be aware of the value of the spirit which moves before you as Rebecca West.

Do you think you see a sad and gloomy picture before you? Look again. You will find an amazingly joyous vision.

You will see Life as represented by Rebecca West, the will to do, free until the end.

That in itself is inspiration without limit.

You will see fools surrounding this figure of Life, fools who are either cowards or knaves – that is to say maimed examples of live beings, but not alive creatures. You will hear these fools, knaves and cowards talking, hoping to entrap Life, to bind it, to control it – and you will see Life triumphant and folly destroyed.

I do not know where except in Ibsen we can today find such faithfulness to the old creed or such an advocate for the individuality of Flame.

Ibsen can be so acted and staged as to be made insignificant and mean. Therefore we must ever remember our artistry and forget our propensity towards photography, we must for this new poet re-form a new Theatre.

And this is the easiest thing in the world – for the reasons are manifold and the will to remould is indestructible.

It is therefore possible now to announce that the birth of the new Theatre, and its new Art, has begun. (40)

The first-night audience was enthusiastic, and the great Italian actor Salvini was among those who led the applause. Duse and Craig, in their joint excitement, announced their intention of working together again. 'You must do me new scenes for *The*

Lady from the Sea, Borkmann, Cleopatra, Dame aux Camelias, all my repertoire.' (41) And Craig began work on *The Lady from the Sea*. But one day he received a telegram: 'Giving *Rosmersholm* at Nice, scene unsuitable. Come at once.' When he arrived it was to find that because the stage of the Casino at Nice was too small his scenes had been cut down, destroying the proportions to which they owed their dramatic power. He burst into a fury, and all idea of further collaboration with Duse was at an end. She replied to his anger with a note: 'What they have done to your scene, they have been doing for years to my art.' (42)

In 1906, when the Italian theatre was stuck fast in academic realism, *Rosmersholm* certainly represented an exceptional achievement; but after the Nice episode Craig was inclined to couple it with what had happened over *Venice Preserved*. He felt he had been betrayed again, his work ruined, his art insulted. *Rosmersholm* served as one more argument in support of his conviction that he must have sole control over any production he might undertake.

*

Nevertheless, his work at the Pergola was much more than a brief episode in Craig's artistic career. For it revealed Italy to him, the Italy he knew only from the pictures in the National Gallery. He saw Renaissance architecture with his own eyes as it really was, instead of depicted in stylized miniature, and the limpid Tuscan sky above it. He had had little chance of absorbing the Florentine atmosphere, for his time had been spent in the theatre, working feverishly on the *Rosmersholm* scenery. But in February 1907 he returned to Florence, the city where every building had its history, every street its traditions, every shop was a stage – a town after his own heart, where the division between theatre and real life seemed non-existent. It is at this point that Craig breaks off his unfinished memoirs:

10th February. Florence. Alone.
  Alone, and warming his five wits
  The white owl in the belfry sits. (43)

NOTES

1. See *Towards a New Theatre*, op. cit., pp. 19 and 28.
2. *On the Art of the Theatre*, note on plate facing p. 262 (Not in the Mercury Books edition).
3. *On the Art of the Theatre*, p. 143.
4. Quoted by William Rothenstein, *Men and Memories*, op. cit., vol. 2, p. 55.
5. *On the Art of the Theatre*, face p. 136. Extract from a note on the design for *Hamlet*, Act I, scene 4, which Craig took with him to Germany in 1904, when he paid his first visit to Weimar, at the invitation of Count Kessler (Not in the Mercury Books edition).
6. *Woodcuts and some Words*, op. cit., p. 37.
7. See *The Mask*, Vol. I, no. 2, April 1908, pp. 17–20 : 'The Energy of the German Theatre'. This article is signed 'George Norman', one of Craig's pseudonyms.
8. This material is in the Gordon Craig Collection at the Bibliothèque de l'Arsenal, Paris.
9. See *Towards a New Theatre*, pp. 29–31.
10. Harry Kessler, 'Edward Gordon Craig's Entwürfe für Theater-Dekorationen und Kostüme', in *Katalog über verschied. Entwürfe fur Scenen und Kostüme für das Theater und einige Zeichnungen englischer Landscenen von Edward Gordon Craig* (Friedmann und Weber, Berlin W., December 1904).
11. Isadora Duncan's version of their meeting is given in *My Life*, Gollancz, London, 1928, pp. 193–211. Craig denies the accuracy of this account and even questions whether it was actually written by Isadora (the book appeared a short time after her tragic death). On the subject of the meeting, see *Index to the Story of my Days*, op. cit., pp. 256 et seq., and Craig's article, 'Memories of Isadora Duncan', in *The Listener*, 5 June 1952, pp. 913–14.
12. Lugné-Poe, *La Parade III, Sous les étoiles, souvenirs de théâtre* (1902–1912), Gallimard, Paris, 1933, p. 239.
13. *Index to the Story of my Days*, op. cit., p. 268.
14. Ibid., p. 242.
15. 'Uber Bühnenausstattung', in *Kunst und Künstler*, Jahrgang III, Heft II, Verlag Bruno Cassirer, Berlin 1904.
16. It may be advisable at this point, since mistakes are often made on the subject, to explain that *The Art of the Theatre* and *On the Art of the Theatre* are two different books. *The Art of the Theatre* is the title of the 'First Dialogue', published in 1905, and of the 'Second Dialogue' which was first printed in *The Mask*, Vol. II, No. 7–9, January 1910, pp. 105–26.
    On the Art of the Theatre, first published in London in 1911, is an important collection of essays including, in addition to the two above-mentioned dialogues, a number of articles reprinted from *The Mask*.
17. *On the Art of the Theatre*, op. cit., p. 138.

18. Two years later, in *The Actor and the Über-marionette*, Craig takes a resolute stand against the *Gesamtkunstwerk*, saying: 'How can all arts combine and make one art? It can only make one joke – one Theatre . . . You cannot commingle [the arts] and cry out that you have created a new art.' (*On the Art of the Theatre*, p. 73.)

19. *On the Art of the Theatre*, p. 144.

20. Ibid., p. 148.

21. Ibid., p. 161.

22. Ibid., p. 176.

23. Ibid., p. 178.

24. Ibid., 180–1.

25. I have already had occasion to mention 'The Art of the Theatre, The Second Dialogue', written by Craig in 1909 and printed in *The Mask* in 1910. This is different in character to the 'First Dialogue', being concerned more especially with the practical aspects of the theatre. In particular, Craig describes the organization of Stanislavsky's theatre and expresses the view that England should have a real National Theatre, not 'a society theatre', and above all, a 'college' for the art of the theatre, containing two theatres, one open-air and one roofed-in – an experimental laboratory where 'every theory shall be tested and records made of the results'. This, he said, should receive 'practical support from the State'. (See *On the Art of the Theatre*, pp. 217, 239–40, 245.) 239–40, 245.)

26. *On the Art of the Theatre*, p. 168.

27. Manuscript: '1904, Germany, Berlin, Weimar, 1905 Weimar' – Gordon Craig's private collection.

28. Manuscript: 'Über-Marions. – Berlin 1905–1906'. Gordon Craig Collection, Bibliothèque de l'Arsenal, Paris.

29. See the MS quoted above.

30. *Catalogue of an Exhibition of Drawings and Models for Hamlet, Macbeth, The Vikings and other plays: by Edward Gordon Graig* – City of Manchester Art Gallery, November 1912, No. 162. Design for a stage scene and movement, *The Steps* (reproduction), p. 21.

31. See *Towards a New Theatre*, pp. 41–7, where the four designs for *The Steps* are reproduced.

32. *Towards a New Theatre*, p. 45.

33. See *Catalogue of Etchings, being Designs for Motion, by Gordon Craig*, Florence, 1908, p. 10.

34. MS notes dates 24 January 1906, in '1904 Germany, Berlin, Weimar, 1905 Weimar', in Gordon Craig's private collection.

35. *The Theatre Advancing*, Constable, London, 1921, p. lxxxiv.

36. *On the Art of the Theatre*, caption to plate facing p. xiv, 1911 edition (Not in the Mercury Books edition).

37. See Isadora Duncan, *My Life*, pp. 212ff.

38. Ibid., p. 217.

39. Ibid., p. 218.

40. Programme for *Rosmersholm*, Teatro della Pergola, Firenze. The first performance took place on 5 December 1906.

41. Quoted by Craig in his article 'On Signora Duse', in *Life and Letters*, London, September, 1928.

42. Note sent to Craig at the Hôtel du Rhin, Nice (1907). Gordon Craig Collection, Bibliothèque de l'Arsenal, Paris.

43. E. Gordon Craig, *Index to the Story of my Days*, p. 300.

VI

THE MASK AND THE *ÜBER-MARIONETTE*

In describing Craig's career and his work, one must beware of drawing a set portrait of him. Craig was never a man of hard-and-fast theories. It is true that once he had shaken off the Lyceum influence he kept up a relentless onslaught on stage realism, a ceaseless attack on everything that degraded the art of the theatre. But he was concerned above all with certain aspirations, with research and with experiment. His work was directed towards achieving his aspirations and was guided by his research, even if he sometimes appeared to be indulging in dreams. He was always projecting his thoughts into the future, because his work took the form of projects. He never tried to force his concepts into an existing framework, because that would have meant distorting or mutilating them. He simply tried to devise means of giving effect to them.

From 1907 to 1914 he advanced steadily on all fronts – in his practical research, his testing of theories, his experimental work and the application and diffusion of his ideas. His base was Italy; though he was sometimes to be found in London, Paris or Moscow, Florence remained his headquarters. It was there that he wrote *The Actor and the Über-marionette*, designed his screens, experimented with his model stages, published *The Mask* and made his designs for *Hamlet*; and it was there that he opened his School. As early as September 1908 he took the lease of an ideal 'studio', the Arena Goldoni, an open-air theatre in the Roman style, which had been built at the beginning of the nineteenth century on the site of a former convent. This became not only his studio but his workshop and *The Mask* offices, and in due course the premises of his School.

This was one of the most productive periods of his career,

though one would not think so on the strength of the work he made public. During these seven years he produced only one play, the Moscow Arts Theatre *Hamlet* – and this, important as it undoubtedly was, aroused fierce argument and met with considerable misunderstanding. Not that he had once and for all resolved to turn down every offer; and not that offers were lacking. His influence was steadily increasing, his ideas were spreading throughout Europe, and a whole book could be written on the subject of the plans that came to nothing – the negotiations that were opened only to be broken off, the contracts that were torn up, the work that was interrupted or refused – all of which helped to make him a legendary figure. The importance of such things should not be over-estimated, but neither should they be overlooked, for they help to build up a picture of the man.

In 1907 Craig was working on the idea of a ballet, *Psyche*, for which he made a number of drawings, some of them now in the Nationalbibliothek, Vienna (Plate 11B). They show great hangings, wide spaces swept by changing light and shadow, and human figures caught, as it were, in the instant of movement. These are not, strictly speaking, scene designs, but rather stage pictures, sketches for the producer and choreographer. Count Kessler showed the project to Diaghilev, who found it too daring; Craig's spacious visions were something quite different from the picture-book art of Bakst and Benois and the dramatic movements he had in mind bore no relation to the choreographic style of the Russian ballet-masters. Craig's art was at the opposite pole from the decorative ventures of the Russian Ballet.

In 1908 Reinhardt approached him again, with a proposal that he should design scenes for *King Lear* at the Deutsches Theater. (1) Craig took a week to make his sketches. Yet again Reinhardt asked for changes, and was refused. Far from confessing defeat, he thereupon invited Craig to produce the *Oresteia* and then Sophocles' *Oedipus* in an adaptation by Hofmannsthal. But it was no good, and the negotiations fell through. 'He would make no compromise,' says the biographical note on Craig which appeared a few years later in *A Living Theatre*. (2)

Craig was invited to Holland to direct a production of *Everyman*. But that, too, came to nothing.

Then there followed a 'solemn farce'. Since *Much Ado About Nothing*, Craig had taken no hand in any London stage work, either as producer or as designer. But official theatrical circles in his own country were at last beginning to realize that he was not

Pour " Ie Roi Lear " 1908

only the son of Ellen Terry but an artist with a European reputation. . . . And in 1908, Herbert Beerbohm Tree asked him to design scenes for *Macbeth*. (3) Though not in the habit of restricting himself to *designing* a production, Craig agreed because he thought it would help him to raise money for *The Mask*. He made drawings, some of which were afterwards reproduced in *Towards a New Theatre*, and prepared models. This time it was an English scene-painter, Joseph Harker, who persuaded Tree that the designs were impracticable, and the contract was cancelled. The incident gave rise to a controversy over which torrents of ink were shed. Craig's opponents seized upon certain of his drawings, especially those for *Macbeth*, and declared that they could not be used; the tiny figures were so out of proportion to the towering walls that it was obvious no stage would be large enough for scenes on that scale.

From this it was easy to jump to the conclusion that Craig was only a dreamer – a jump made with alacrity by the American scene-designer and theatre historian Lee Simonson, a savage detractor of Craig, though industrious in his praises of Adolphe Appia. (4) Unfortunately for Lee Simonson, however, Craig had proved with his London and Moscow productions that he was quite able to take account of stage requirements and to adapt himself to theatres as they then were, even if he wished for something different. Incidentally, he answered Simonson long beforehand in a 'dialogue between a theatrical manager and an artist of the theatre', written in 1910 and published in *The Theatre Advancing*:

MANAGER: Really, you look at things in a strange way. Now come down to earth and tell me how we can realize your design upon the stage.

ARTIST: We cannot; I have told you so repeatedly, but you were so quick with your questions that you would not let me tell you something which saves the situation. That design, as I have just said, is made to give you a certain impression. When I make the same scene on the stage it is sure to be quite different in form and colour, but it will create the same impression on you as this design in front of you now.

MANAGER: Two things quite different will create the same impression? Are you joking?

ARTIST: No, I am not joking; but I will do so if you insist upon it.

MANAGER: No, tell me more; explain what you mean.

ARTIST: Well, a design for a scene on paper is one thing; a scene on the stage is another. The two have no connection with each other. Each depends on a hundred different ways and means of creating the same impression. Try to adapt the one to the other, and you get at best only a good translation. (5)

One more proposal of some importance came along before the first world war. Jacques Rouché, having founded the Théâtre des Arts in Paris, was eager to secure the collaboration of the man he regarded as 'one of the greatest innovators of our day'. (6) He had seen photographs of Craig's productions and reproductions of his designs, and was well acquainted with his ideas, which he had described in his book, *L'Art théâtral moderne*. Contact was established in 1910, through Piot, the painter. There were meetings and letters. The negotiations were prolonged and sometimes difficult; Craig laid down draconian conditions, both in artistic and in financial matters. (7) At last agreement was almost reached – when Craig suddenly returned the contract, unsigned. According to Rouché, the true reason for the breakdown of the negotiations lay in something Craig had said to him at one of their meetings: 'Allow me to close your theatre for five years, allow me to found a school for actors, a school for scene-designers, a school for costume-designers and stage carpenters. Otherwise, in a few weeks, I can achieve only the second-best, something mediocre that you could do without me.' (8) Was this simply a joke? By no means. Years ago, while preparing his London productions, Craig had already discovered the necessity of methodical work and the need to reject the impromptu. 'The tendency of the western theatre,' he had written in 1908, 'is to disregard the vital principles of the art: to invent or borrow with haste so-called reforms which may attract the Public, not those which are necessary to the health of the art.... Hastiness characterizes all things in the theatre of today; hasty reforms, hasty preparation, hasty ideas as hastily carried out.' (9) And so Craig was longing for a school of his own, the need for which was becoming more evident every year. At the end of 1909, shortly before he met Rouché, he wrote in his *Daybook I*:

> The stage needs a school, it needs many schools. Practical and technical schools – schools for the theory and for the experimental study of the Art of the Theatre. We are all too ignorant. For instance can anyone on the stage today tell us what is *Language* and where it comes from – what its history? Can anyone on the stage tell us what is *Light*? Whence it comes – what its power – No – yet these two things, Light and Language, are great and lesser parts of our material of the modern theatre.
> They are both great factors of our new theatre of tomorrow.
> Where is the school then?
> I want to sit and study week after week in the body of the Hall whilst someone who knows all about Language shall make some of his knowledge clear to me. (10)

*

At the beginning of 1907, Craig notes in his *Index*, 'Finding: Liberty and its price.' (11) Ten years earlier he had suddenly given up acting, and that first liberation had made it possible for him to turn to production and to work out his theories. In 1907, alone in Florence and on the verge of his parting with Isadora, he found a new kind of liberty, as a result of which he embarked upon a period of patient, solitary study which would enable him, or so he thought, to exert a more direct influence on the contemporary theatre. There is nothing fortuitous about his quotation from Flaubert in an essay of this period: 'The artist should be in his work like God in creation, invisible and all-powerful; he should be felt everywhere and seen nowhere. Art should be raised above personal affection and nervous susceptibility. It is time to give it the perfection of the physical sciences by means of a pitiless method.' (12)

At the same date he added: 'All came along this year – 1907: Screens, and SCENE, the *Über-marionette*, Black Figures, *The Mask*.' (13) During the next few years he supplemented his discoveries and tried to apply them, to put the finishing touches to some long-standing plans and carry them out with or without help; and the different projects overlapped, as can be seen from his *Daybooks*. The story of *The Mask* is interwoven with his experiments on his models and with the preparation of his production of *Hamlet*.

It would be possible to trace the course of Craig's work week by week or even day by day; but in doing so we should lose sight of the lines of force that ran through it. It therefore seems to me to be preferable to present not a strictly chronological account of his different activities, but a careful analysis of each experiment – *The Mask*, the 'Thousand Scenes in one Scene', the Moscow production of *Hamlet*, the School for the Art of the Theatre, and the projects for Bach's *St Matthew Passion* which were the culmination of seven years' study and experiment. The links between these various undertakings will come to light of their own accord.

*

In February 1945 the first number of an 'international review of dramatic art' appeared in France with the title *Masques*. Introducing it, Jacques Copeau said the title reminded him of the time when he was making his first investigations, the time when Craig was bringing out *The Mask*, almost unaided. 'It would be ungrateful to forget this,' wrote Copeau, 'and it would be presumptuous even to hope that *Masques* will be a more fully-equipped craftsman and a bolder pioneer than *The Mask*.' And he went on:

> For that magazine, which initiated us so nobly and guided us so helpfully is by no means out of date. Today, when we turn the pages inside its handsome vellum binding, we realize more clearly than ever that it linked up the theatre with all the great forms of art and tried to rescue it from every kind of rut. There is not an artist of our day whose entire universe has eluded his influence. (14)

Copeau's words are as true now as then.

As I said before, Craig had been thinking of the magazine since 1905. In May 1907 he began to work out his plans in detail. First of all he considered a trilingual publication, in English, German and Dutch. There was even a suggestion of a French edition. Translation difficulties and financial considerations obliged him to restrict his ambitions, and the first number of his 'monthly journal of the Art of the Theatre' came out in March 1908 in English alone. He started it with the very modest capital of £5. He now had to deal with printers and block-makers and see that the numbers appeared regularly. Craig kept *The Mask* going from 1908 to 1929 with no financial backing whatsoever; subscriptions and sales brought in barely enough to cover the cost of printing, postage and advertising.

Reading the first issue of *The Mask*, one would think it had been produced by a large, closely united team. True, the team was closely united, but it consisted of three people, or rather of two: Gino Ducci, a postman friend of Craig's, acted as *gerente responsabile*, and Dorothy Nevile Lees as editorial assistant. It was the latter who, with unflagging devotion, typed the articles, corrected the proofs, went to see the printers and other suppliers, supervised the block-making, jogged the memory of the subscribers, made translations from the Italian, wrote book-reviews, and ransacked libraries to find documents they did not know they possessed. (16) And then there was Craig himself. Officially he was only the 'art adviser' of the magazine, but in actual fact it was he who kept it alive. He not only guided its policy, but wrote innumerable articles and engraved countless woodblocks for it. '*The Mask* could only have been produced in Florence and with me as proprietor – with me there must be no *pause* between the thought and the act. The *pause* spoils all my work.' (17) *The Mask* was his very self.

Yet it was a fourth personage – J.S. – who signed the leading article in the first number, and who soon began to receive letters from England, Italy, France, Germany, and even Moscow, from where Craig sent him his impressions of the Russian theatre. This J.S., 'John Semar', was the official editor of *The Mask*; but no one ever managed to set eyes on him. For the good reason that he did not exist, except as a screen for Dorothy Nevile Lees and above all for Craig, who wrote most of the editorials and many other articles under this name. (18) However, John Semar was only one of the sixty or seventy pseudonyms (19) used by Craig in the magazine, in reversion to a practice he had begun with his first periodical, *The Page*. Craig had no funds to pay contributors, and he proved himself quite capable of providing almost entirely from his own pen the material needed for a magazine – first a monthly, later a quarterly. But his name could not possibly appear on every page; the readers would get sick of seeing it. Besides, he could put his ideas across all the more successfully if he managed to create the illusion that a large group of authoritative contributors, with himself as their unchallenged leader, was supporting him and working on the same lines as he. Even the name of the magazine was significant, for the mask was not only one of the symbols of the theatre, one of the principal elements of the drama, whose use Craig wished to revive; it also symbolized the struggle he was carrying on: he would be *masked* to confront his adversaries. (20) His campaign was a form of guerilla warfare where all must be secret – a fight 'to the death' in which the enemy must be ignorant of the numbers and quality of the attacking force. (21) Hence this vast number of fictitious identities, in which he obviously delighted; for without trying to deceive his enemies, he has always enjoyed luring them to their doom in his impish plots.

What was Craig's aim in founding *The Mask*? A good many theatrical journals were published in those days in England, Germany, Austria, Italy, France, Ireland and the United States.

But the great majority of them were edited by men who had neither a thorough knowledge of stage theory nor a practical experience of the theatre. Most of them were mere vehicles of information, dangerously eclectic, with no guiding idea. Craig did not want to provide propaganda for some half-hearted experiment or insincere reform. He wanted to establish a means of spreading the knowledge of the 'new movement' he had started and of his ideas about the theatre. 'After the practice, the theory' was *The Mask's* first slogan.

His guidance will be valuable, [wrote J.S. of Craig] in that he has himself practised what we shall preach, and we, preaching what he has practised and what others may add to that practice, shall by so doing attempt to show where lies the future of the Theatre. Moreover, in securing Mr Craig's guidance we may claim to have secured that of the head of a movement which has actually taken place, which is spreading far and wide in the European Theatre, and of which the Theory now needs to be definitely and clearly stated so that convictions may be strengthened, scattered forces united, and all move forward with stability and unity of purpose towards one object – the re-establishment in its original dignity of a beautiful and ancient Art. (22)

In his desire to work for a 'new Theatre' based on 'beauty' as the purpose of art, Craig rejected the customs that had caused the decline of the theatre and dismissed all the conventions wrongly declared to be 'traditions'. But this did not mean that he intended to break with the past, with ancient or remote forms of theatre. In the thick of what seemed to be his most revolutionary experiments he proclaimed that he stood by the traditions, but only the worth-while ones:

Here let me sketch my view past present and future of the Theatre and where my belief differs from those of modern stage workers. I believe effort should be made to *simplify* and I see effort being made to *complicate*. I believe that the very *material* of the theatre needs simplifying before we shall be able to create simpler works.
I do not wish to revert to an *old manner*, but I don't want to depart from *a noble tradition*. I wish to rebuild on *old truths* – which in art never grow to look old. (23)

And we have to understand this before we can grasp the meaning and purpose of *The Mask*, as described in the preliminary prospectus:

The object of the publication is to bring before an intelligent public many ancient and modern aspects of the Theatre's Art which have too long been disregarded or forgotten. Not to attempt to assist in the so-called reform of the modern Theatre – for reform is now too late; not to advance theories which have not been already tested, but to announce the existence of a vitality which already begins to reveal itself in a beautiful and definite form based upon an ancient and noble tradition. That which you find in *The Era* and *The Stage*, the two representative journals of the modern English Theatre, you will not find in *The Mask*. Something will be found in *The Mask* which will be found nowhere else. *The Mask* represents the theatre of the future, and as there are many persons living who are interested in the theatre of the future we believe we shall not lack readers. The Theatre of the Future necessarily embraces all that has to do with the theatre of the past, . . . Without an intimate and affectionate study of the theatre of the ancients it would be impossible for man to create a new theatre, and it is because of the contempt shown towards the ancient theatre by those who have started so-called 'new movements' in the theatre, that these movements have died shortly after they were brought forth. . . . (24)

Thus, *The Mask* was neither a purely theoretical magazine nor a journal of theatre history. Craig did not worry about balancing theory and history in careful proportions to suit everyone's taste. He conjured up the past (Commedia dell' Arte, Sacre Rappresentazioni, the spring festivals in Tuscany, etc.), reprinted ancient or unknown writings and engravings (Serlio, Riccoboni, Gozzi, etc.) and called attention to arts that had fallen into neglect (marionettes, etc.) for two reasons – to show how the European theatre had fallen off at the beginning of the twentieth century by contrast with the vitality it had possessed in earlier centuries and which was still displayed in certain far-off countries; and to prove that the theatre of the future was not revolutionary in its essence, but represented a natural development and flowering of traditions not forgotten or distorted. The articles in *The Mask* were often headed or followed by passages from Plato, Aristotle, Goethe, Flaubert,

Schlegel, Nietzsche, Lamb, Tolstoy, Shakespeare, Ruskin, Pater, La Bruyère, etc. Such quotations were very carefully chosen, to illustrate the beliefs and support the position of the new theatre and its pioneers.

While thus turning towards the past and the future, did *The Mask* ignore current events, and the efforts being made to restore the contemporary theatre to the dignity of an art? By no means. No theatrical developments were passed over in silence – neither the worst, which Craig and his 'contributors' attacked vehemently, nor the original, courageous experiments which came closest to Craig's ideals. To give only a few examples, *The Mask* discusses at different times the acting genius of Duse and Grasso, Stanislavsky's theatre, the revival of the Polish theatre initiated by Wyspiansky, and Hevesi's work at Budapest, and gives Yeats the opportunity to set forth his ideas himself. This intention to deal jointly with past, present and future, omitting none of the elements belonging to the art of the theatre, was demonstrated from the very beginning. The first number of *The Mask* includes, for instance, the opening section of one of Craig's most celebrated essays, 'The Artists of the Theatre of the Future', an article by Edward Hutton (25) on 'The Real Drama in Spain', a 'Note on Masks' by John Balance (i.e. Craig), a tribute by Craig to Eleonora Duse, and a reprint of one of the most important chapters from Serlio.

At the beginning of this century *The Mask* was unique in refraining from all attempt to promote any particular, limited theatrical undertaking and in championing a consistent ideal which encompassed all the elements of stage art. It was the first theatre magazine to have a deliberate *policy* and stick to it in defiance of all obstacles – the first magazine dedicated to a cause and upholding it in the teeth of prejudice and dogma. It served as the mouthpiece for Craig's thoughts and aspirations – for his resolve to lay the foundations of a new theatre the outline of which was growing steadily clearer, and to fight against degradation in all its forms – against realism and vulgarity, commercialism and the star system, the search for cheap effectiveness and the pursuit of selfish interests, cowardice and apathy. If he so often had recourse to paradox, it was because nothing must be neglected that might serve to shake theatre people and audiences out of their sluggish satisfaction with an apparent prosperity behind which the theatre was sinking into moral rack and ruin.

It is difficult to estimate the influence of *The Mask*, for many of the articles Craig wrote for it were reprinted later in his books, particularly in *On the Art of the Theatre* and *The Theatre Advancing*, and in this form they no doubt reached a wider circle of readers. But the magazine's files reveal an international audience. Subscriptions came from England, America, Spain, France, Germany, Finland, Italy, Austria, Canada, Russia and India, and the subscribers included Walter Crane, Lord Dunsany, Hugo von Hofmannsthal, Percy MacKaye, W. B. Yeats, Gaston Gallimard, Yvette Guilbert, Jacques Copeau, Jacques Rouché, Kenneth MacGowan, Louis Jouvet, James Joyce, Donald Oenslager, George Bernard Shaw, Toscanini, Malipiero and Berenson – to mention only the most famous. Tributes poured in: from Yvette Guilbert, 'This journal is at the same time instructor and guide, for while it teaches us of past things, it also directs our future efforts, and that is why *The Mask* is MY journal' (26); from Yeats, '*The Mask* always inspires me. . . it creates a vague vision of a new sort of joyous, overflowing dramatic art. No sort of criticism is any use to an artist but technical criticism, criticism at once technical and philosophical, and that is what *The Mask* gives one' (27); from Strindberg, an ardent reader, who notes in his *Briefe ans Intime Theater:* 'There is a whole literature on the theatrical revival, and first and foremost I would like to mention Gordon Craig's wonderful magazine, *The Mask*.' (28)

*

The second issue of *The Mask*, which appeared in April 1908, carried one of Craig's most famous essays, *The Actor and the Über-Marionette*. Of all his writings, this perhaps did most to create the myth that he was a Utopian dreamer with a contempt for the art of the theatre, and gave rise to the greatest number of misconceptions, misguided commentaries and biased interpretations. Written in Florence in March 1907, it calls for special study to take us beyond its surface paradoxes and help us to fit it into its place in the development of Craig's ideas and to appreciate the number and variety of its repercussions and the extent of its influence on the present-day theatre.

It is hardly necessary to point out, as a preliminary to this scrutiny, that Craig had been an actor himself, that he had been closely acquainted with the greatest actors of his day and had seen them at work; and that he had come into contact with the actor's egotism, met its resistance and the rebellions it caused. What he said about the actor in 1907 was the result of long experience followed by years of reflection.

Among Craig's unpublished manuscripts is one dating from 1898 (29) in which he set down views that have little in common with those he was to express later in *The Mask*. At that time, a few months after he gave up acting, he maintained that the play was to the actor as the human figure to the painter, and that it was therefore natural for the beauties of a play to be as carefully respected as those of the model. Acting should not try to copy reality or truth, but to suggest it. This, adds Craig, is a *creative art*, not to be defined in words – a universal language. In those days Craig still thought that a play should be directed by the leading actor. Two years later he became a producer himself, putting on *Dido and Aeneas*, followed by other productions and by plans and designs which, though never carried out, bear witness to his new angle of vision. Through this experience he discovered the essence of the art of the theatre, and before long he laid down its principles: the art of the theatre is not to be confused with acting, which is only one of its elements; the leading actor must not be the stage director, because the actor has to fit into his place and obey the instructions of the producer, who carries entire responsibility for the unity of the whole performance. From the moment he reached these conclusions, Craig began to meditate on the subject of the *über-marionette*.

And now, in the spring of 1908, the celebrated pronouncement was made for the first time: 'The actor must go, and in his place comes the inanimate figure – the *Über-marionette* we may call him, until he has won for himself a better name.' (30) These words were to be the cause of much misunderstanding, which has persisted until the present day. Some people even leapt to the conclusion that what Craig wanted was to drive the actor from the stage for ever and replace him by a wooden puppet. True, Craig rather invited such an interpretation by saying 'I believe in the time when we shall be able to create works of art in the Theatre without the use of the written play, without the use of actors.' (31)

To appreciate the full significance of *The Actor and the Über-marionette*, we must read it in connection with other essays published around the same time, including 'The Artists of the Theatre of the Future', 'To Madame Eleonora Duse' and 'A Note on Masks'. And we must bear in mind the whole implication of *The Mask* – that it is too late to reform the existing theatre, that its dignity can only be restored by creating it anew. Craig was no doubt prompted by the same thought in writing *The Actor and the Über-marionette* – that it was too late to reform the actor, he must be replaced by an actor of a new kind, the *Über-marionette*. It remained to define that mysterious being.

Craig began by a general criticism of the actor, especially the actor of his own day. He writes in 'To Madame Eleonora Duse';

> No one can seriously call an actor or actress an artist of the Theatre . . . the actor brings his own part up to a certain incomplete perfection. He knows his own lines, he knows how much emotion to pour into them, and having done this he thinks he has created a work of Art. He has not done so: he has been content with very much less than the least perfection – he is not an artist. . . (32)

Craig says the same thing in *The Actor and the Über-marionette:* 'Acting is not an art. It is therefore incorrect to speak of the actor as an artist.'(33) Art implies calculation, the planned use of materials that are under control; it has no room for what is fortuitous. But the actor is the slave of emotions which *possess* him and prevent him from exercising complete and permanent control over the movements of his body, the expression of his face, and his voice. Emotion is stronger than thought, and instinct than knowledge. Instead of mastering himself, instead of doing really creative work by means of carefully selected visible signs, the actor loses control of himself and his performance becomes merely 'a series of accidental confessions'. What Craig calls the egoism of the actor is simply this form of exhibitionism, where the actor reveals himself and never anything else. This is a danger to the audience, which, as emotion responds to emotion, ends by allowing itself to be hypnotized, losing all notion of the dramatic work and of the whole art of the theatre.

As well as servitude to the emotions there is servitude to literature. Even when the actor displays himself most unashamedly, and is in fact proud of himself for doing so, he is only interpreting words written by someone else, he is only an instrument, a medium between a work of literature and the public, between the author and the audience. There is nothing in all this to justify calling him an artist.

Craig's final bugbear is realism on the stage; his whole work and everything he has written are a reiterated protest against the clumsy, blatant, direct imitation of reality. The actor must not be content to record like a camera, to reproduce appearances, to copy nature instead of creating with the aid of nature. If he does he will be nothing but a mirror, and not even a faithful one. He wants to be natural, and thinks he is putting life into his part, when all he is doing is to mimic life. He thinks he has to 'impersonate' a character, and imagines that if he gives the impression of 'getting under the skin of the part' he has risen to the highest level of his art. According to Craig it would be better to aim at 'getting *out* of the skin of the part altogether'. At a time when the realists were advocating an art based on the complete identification of the actor with his role, Craig uncompromisingly condemns that type of acting. The actor, he says, must remain outside his role, in order to retain entire mastery over his powers and to control his instinct, his nature, by using his imagination and intelligence. And in this way Craig comes to the idea of the *über-marionette*.

One need only glance through *The Mask* to realize how important Craig found marionettes, their art, their history in all parts of the world, their technique. He formed his own collection of marionettes, including a great number of Javanese and Burmese figures; for a year he brought out a magazine on the subject; and he wrote a number of plays for marionettes. He knew that this art had fallen on bad times and that the puppets dangled in their booths bore little trace of their ancestral dignity; he knew the subject was not taken seriously – that it was greeted with the same contempt as a mention of masks or pantomime which, after being essential parts of the dramatic art of the ancients, were now regarded by the general public, and even by some 'enlightened' minds, as trifles fit only for entertaining children. Fortunately there were still some people who fully recognized the marionette's powers of expression. Craig quotes Anatole France:

> I have seen the marionettes of the rue Vivienne twice, and enjoyed them tremendously. I am infinitely grateful to them for taking the place of living actors. To speak frankly, I must say that actors spoil plays for me. Good actors, I mean. I could put up with the others! But fine artists, such as those at the Comédie Française, are more than I can bear! Their talent is too great. It hides everything else! One can see nothing but them. . . .

And again:

> I have already confessed that I love marionettes, and those of M. Signoret please me particularly. They are carved by artists and shown by poets. They have the naïve grace, the divine awkwardness of statues graciously pretending to be dolls, and one is enchanted to see these little idols acting plays. . . . These marionettes are like Egyptian hieroglyphics, that is, like something mysterious and pure, and when they perform a play by Shakespeare or Aristophanes I seem to see the poet's thoughts unrolling themselves in sacred characters on the walls of a temple. (34)

Anatole France speaks of marionettes as 'idols', and according to Craig the marionette is 'a descendant of the stone images of the old temples – a rather degenerate form of a god'. (35) Craig is reminded of ancient Egypt, with its animated statues, and the festivals of distant India, the country where he believes the marionette to have originated. He writes in lyrical phrases of these extraordinary beings, untouched by emotion, the impassive exponents of an art in which everything, including gesture and movement, is symbolical and which is on the same level as the true arts, released from the 'confession' of feelings. Here the artist controls his materials, obeys definite laws. Craig once defined marionettes as 'men without egoism'.

But this does not mean in the least that he intended marionettes to drive the actors from the stage. <u>He merely wanted to rid the stage of the actor's weaknesses. The *über-marionette* is the actor who has acquired some of the virtues of the marionette and thus released himself from servitude.</u>

> The *über-marionette* will not compete with life – rather will it go beyond it. Its ideal will not be the flesh and blood but rather the body in trance – it will aim to clothe itself with a death-like beauty while exhaling a living spirit. Several times in the course of this essay has a word or two about Death found its way on to the paper – called there by the incessant clamouring of 'Life! Life! Life!' which the realists keep up. (36)

And as some people had mistaken the real meaning of his essay, Craig explained in his preface to the 1925 edition of *On the Art of the Theatre* that 'The *Über-marionette* is the actor plus fire, minus egoism; the fire of the gods and demons, without the smoke and steam of mortality'. (37) His condemnation of realism as contrary to art carries with it the complete abolition of the realistic actor. In the revived art of the theatre, the actor must abstain from servile imitation of nature and from all attempt at impersonation.

But why the *über-marionette*, why not simply the marionette? Because the actor, as *über-marionette*, will retain one advantage over the marionette – he will be conscious of his gestures and movements. In this connection Craig says something whose implications have never been fully appreciated: 'Today [actors] *impersonate* and interpret; tomorrow they must *represent* and interpret; and the third day they must create. By this means style may return.' (38)

This concept of the actor and his role leads naturally to a new technique of acting. The actor must cease to express *himself* and begin to express something else; he must no longer *imitate*, he must *indicate*. Then his acting will become impersonal, he will lose his 'egoism' and use his body and voice as though they were materials rather than parts of himself. To this end a symbolical style of acting must be devised, based on the power of the creative imagination. The passions will no longer be displayed to us by means of mimicry which claims to be expressive when it is merely frenzied; but they will be brought clearly within our perception

There is an unmistakable connection between Craig's views on masks and his theory of the *über-marionette*, and it was not by chance that his 'Note on Masks' was published a month before *The Actor and the Über-marionette*. This was no sudden passion for masks on his part. He had used them in his production of *Dido and Aeneas*. In those early years of the twentieth century people were fond of delving into the past, the 'antiquarian spirit' was in fashion; but it was not Craig's intention to revive the Greek mask in the way that other men were complacently reconstructing what they believed to be the Elizabethan stage. The past inspired him, with the traditions it revealed, but he had not the least desire to copy it, or to load his stage with 'period' properties. He regarded masks simply as among the most important of these, and on 3 February 1909 he wrote in his *Daybook I*: 'I wish to remove *The Actor* with his *Personality* but to leave *the Chorus of Masked figures*.' (39) This may seem puzzling at the first glance, but on reflection it will be seen as the perfect summary of several of his governing ideas.

Craig set no store by the play of features that seemed so important to theatre people of that day. He loathed the absurd mimicry and exaggerated grimaces which aimed at making the stage characters seem 'true to life' – reducing the face to a mere instrument of conventional realism. It was logical that in the attempt to release the actor from his emotional shackles, Craig should strive to rid him of everything that contributed to his servitude and of all that helped him to surrender to it. To cover the actor's face with a mask would depersonalize him, make him 'un-natural'; it would compel him to pay attention to his movements, to rely on his physical means of expression, to re-create instead of reproducing. The mask is a safeguard against realism, a guarantee against the emotions. It turns a man into an *über-marionette*, it forces the actor to play in a symbolical style, having himself become a symbol:

. . . human facial expression is for the most part valueless. . . . Masks carry conviction when he who creates them is an artist, for the artist limits the statements which he places upon these masks. The face of the actor carries no such conviction: it is over-full of fleeting expression, frail, restless; disturbed and disturbing. . . . (40)

We may ask ourselves how this view of the actor fits in with the theories put forward two years previously in *The Art of the Theatre*. Is there a cleavage between the two essays, or is *The Actor and the Über-marionette* a continuation of *The Art of the Theatre*? This question can be readily answered: the theories set forth in 1907 form a logical sequel to the principles laid down in 1905, and carry them still further. By requiring the actor to strip himself of all egoism and learn to control himself, and by advocating the resumption of masks, Craig was making the actor into pliable material. By de-personalizing him, he was destroying the seeds of any possible resistance. *The Art of the Theatre* calls for the restoration of discipline in dramatic creation; *The Actor and the Über-marionette* shows the actor how to discipline himself. These two forms of discipline are inseparably linked; one cannot take effect without the other. The actor is both his own instrument and the instrument of the stage director, and this is necessary if the whole production is to have the unity without which it cannot be a work of art.

It is therefore true to say that the ideas expressed by Craig in this essay are much less paradoxical than his manner of expressing them; and one can understand the considerable influence it has had on the style of modern acting. Was that influence always direct? It is hard to tell. Craig was a prophet in the wilderness, foretelling developments and suggesting lines of investigation that did not attract attention until much later, and his ideas have affected some utterly dissimilar forms of theatrical activity. Everyone in France knows how much men like Jouvet and Barrault learnt from his writings. What is not so generally realized is that *The Actor and the Über-marionette*, paradoxical as it may seem (but here the paradox is a matter of historical fact) heralds at one and the same time the experiments made in the Russian theatre immediately after the first world war, the abstract experimental work of the *Bauhaus*, the methods of the German expressionists, and Brecht's ideas about the actor's technique.

Some fifteen years later than Craig – in 1921 – Tairov proclaimed that literature was the actor's enemy and that instead of presenting a mere commentary, the theatre should create independent works of art. Meyerhold, Annenkov and Eisenstein were bent on giving the actor entire mastery over his body, regarding physical expression as more important than elocution: hence Meyerhold's 'biomechanics', the idea that the actor must be trained as an acrobat. That was what led the Russian producers to borrow from the circus, not only its methods but even performers who were capable of physical feats denied to the stage actor.

> The art of the actor [wrote Annenkov in 1919] and the degree of perfection he reaches in his profession, are always relative. The art of the circus performer is perfect because it is absolute. If an acrobat makes the slightest miscalculation, if he has a second's weakness, he loses his balance, falls off the trapeze, his act is a failure, he is no longer an artist. The revolutionaries of the theatre will find in the circus performer and his self-mastery the seeds of a new form of theatre, of the new style. (41)

The perfection to which Annenkov alludes is that of the *über-marionette*, and it must be emphasized that for a time, during his first reflections on the *über-marionette*, Craig thought of using athletes and dancers, acrobats and artist's models. (42)

Despite considerable differences, the studies carried out by the *Bauhaus* group, and particularly by Oskar Schlemmer, had a certain affinity to Craig's ideas, which Schlemmer quotes in his important theoretical work, *Mensch und Kunstfigur*, written in 1924. (43) Through the use of masks and the transformation and de-personalization of the human body with the help of unwonted forms and materials, Schlemmer and other *Bauhaus* experimenters were working towards the incorporation of the *über-marionette* concept into the general idea of an abstract theatre, of which Craig had been one of the precursors. The *Bauhaus* group were plastic artists, and their work did not put Craig's own ideals into practice; but it represents a possible extension of his ideas.

We shall see in due course the close connection between Craig's principles and the expressionist style of stage production; but it is evident from the foregoing that the expressionist actor (44) may be regarded as the partial embodiment of the qualities of the *über-marionette*. As Kornfeld puts it, the expressionist actor strove to break away from reality and its attributes in order to become simply the *representative* of thought and destiny. He no longer sought to impersonate a character in a tragedy, to transform himself into that character. He used symbolical acting, movement and gesture to translate and accentuate his role, sometimes succeeding in conveying his meaning by a minimum of action. He did not imitate, he convinced.

The link between Craig's and Brecht's concepts of the actor remains to be considered. The two men were utterly unlike in their aims and in their means of expression. Craig was never for a moment concerned with the educational, epic or political aspects of the theatre. There is nevertheless a certain affinity between some of their principles. They both admired the stylized acting of the Asian theatres. They both rejected any appeal to the emotions, with the dangers entailed in identification and hypnotism. Both of them wanted to show, to explain, not to imitate. For Brecht, as for Craig, the actor must stand outside his role. Brecht's insistence on this may be equated to an adaptation of the *über-marionette* to critical and historical ends.

To lump together, in this list of 'inheritors' of Craig's ideas, the Russian constructivists, the advocates of abstract theatre, the German expressionists and Bertolt Brecht, may seem to be going rather too far. But the point is that Craig's real influence has not been confined to matters of style. Trends of thought follow one another, conflict, borrow methods and formulae from one another: that is the essence of the theatre, the internal dialectic of its history.

NOTES

1. The Edward Gordon Craig Collection at the Bibliothèque de l'Arsenal includes a large selection of Craig's sketches for *King Lear*.
2. *A Living Theatre*, op. cit., p. 70.
3. In 1907 Craig wrote his essay, 'The Artists of the Theatre of the Future', which was first published in *The Mask* (Vol. I, No. 1, March 1908, pp. 3–5; Vol. I, No. 3–4, May–June 1908, pp. 57–70) and reprinted in *On the Art of the Theatre*, op. cit., pp. 1–53. In the section 'On Scene and Movement' there is an important passage dealing with the scenery for *Macbeth*.
4. See Lee Simonson's two books, *The Stage is Set*, Harcourt, Brace and Company, New York, 1933 and *The Art of Scenic Design*, Harper and Bros, New York, 1950.
5. *The Theatre Advancing*, Constable, London, 1921, pp. 93–4.

6. Jacques Rouché, *L'Art théâtral moderne*, new edition, Bloud & Gay, Paris, 1924, p. 49.

7. On the subject of the negotiations between Craig and Rouché and their correspondence at the time, see Rose-Marie Mondouès, 'Jacques Rouché et Edward Gordon Craig', in the *Revue de la Société de l'Histoire du Théâtre*, III, 1958, pp. 313–19. In a manuscript opuscule preserved in his private collection (*Florence 1910. Paris. E.G.C.*), Craig noted down his artistic and financial conditions and which plays he thought of staging, according to what actors and which theatre were placed at his disposal. The list includes *Macbeth*, *King Lear*, *The Merchant of Venice*, *Much Ado About Nothing*, *The Tempest*, *A Midsummer Night's Dream*, *Faust*, *Peer Gynt*, *The Bluebird*, *Everyman*, some mysteries, and unspecified plays by Molière and the Greeks.

8. Quoted by Jacques Rouché in his Introduction to the first French edition of *On the Art of the Theatre* (*De l'Art du Théâtre*, N.R.F., Paris 1920, p. XVII).

9. *On the Art of the Theatre*, pp. 97 and 103. These passages are taken from Craig's article, 'Some Evil Tendencies of the Modern Theatre', which first appeared in *The Mask*, Vol. I, No. 8, October 1908, pp. 149–154.

10. *Daybook I. November 1908 to March 1910*, p. 187. Craig's *Daybooks* have never been published, and I have to thank him for giving me access to them and for allowing me to quote passages from them.

11. *Index to the Story of my Days*, op. cit., p. 297.

12. Quoted in 'The Actor and the Über-marionette', which was written in March 1907. See *On the Art of the Theatre*, op. cit., p. 77.

13. *Index to the Story of my Days*, p. 297.

14. Jacques Copeau, 'Renouvellement', in *Masques*, 'revue internationale d'art dramatique', Vol. I, February 1945, p. 3.

15. History of this publication : March 1908 to February 1909, Vol. I, monthly: 1909–10, Vol. II, quarterly (4 numbers): 1910–11, Vol. III, quarterly (4 numbers): 1911–12, Vol. IV, quarterly (4 numbers): 1912–13, Vol. V, quarterly (4 numbers): 1914–15, Vol. VI, 2 numbers. Suspended until 1918. 1918–19, Vol. VIII, 12 monthly leaflets. Suspended until 1923. 1923, Vol. IX, a single issue for the whole year: From January 1924 to October 1929, regular quarterly issues (Vols. X to XV). According to the printers' bills, the circulation was about 1000 copies.

16. Dorothy Nevile Lees has assembled a collection of books and documents relating to Craig, which is now in the Library of the British Institute in Florence. She has given me valuable information, and I should like to take this opportunity of offering her my warmest thanks.

17. E. G. Craig, *Daybook I*, manuscript already quoted, p. 117.

18. In 1924 Craig thought up a short biography of John Semar. The manuscript is now in the file, 'Mask 1926–7. MSS and copy', in the Gordon Craig Collection at the Bibliothèque de l'Arsenal, Paris. 'Semar' is the name of one of the Javanese marionettes in which Craig has always taken a great interest.

19. Craig was kind enough to give me a list of these, as follows: Stanislas

Lodochowskowski, Julius Oliver, Giulio Pirro, Samuel Prim, Charles Borrow, Carlo Lacchio, John Balance, Allen Carric, Adolf Furst, George Norman, John Semar, Jan van Holt, Jan Klassen, Edward Edwardovitch, Franz Hoffer, Louis Madrid, Felix Urban, Rudolf Schmerz, Anonymous, John Bull, G. C. Smith, O. P., V. Surgen, Ivan Ivanovitch, Britannicus, E. Gordon, You-No-Hoo, N or M, IM, Yu-No-Whoo, Yoo-No-Hoo, Chi lo Sa, François M. Florian, The Author of Films, William Marchpane, Giovanni Mezzogiorno, Henry Gay Calvin, Lilian Antler, Mable Dobson, Henry Phips, Georges Devoto, R. T. Vade, Benjamin Rossen, T. Kempees, J. H. Benton, ABC, CGE, QED, XYZ, A.B., CGS, Somers Bacon, G. B. Ambrose, John S. Rankin, Hadrian Jazz Gavotte, Edwin Witherspoon, Everard Plumbline, Antonio Galli, John Brownsmith, Drury Pervil, Fanny Hepworth, J. Moser Lewis, William McDougal, Marcel de Tours, Philip Polfreman, Loïs Lincoln, Scotson Umbridge.

It should be pointed out that Craig also used some of these names, including Julius Oliver, Giulio Pirro, Stanislas Lodochowskowski and Samuel Prim, to sign woodcuts.

Dorothy Nevile Lees, too, had pseudonyms: Pierre Rames, Conrad Tower, Anthony Scarlett, P.N., and sometimes John Semar.

20. See the article signed by the pseudonym John Balance, 'A Note on Masks', in *The Mask*, Vol. I, No. 1, March 1908, pp. 9–12.
21. See the typewritten notes in the file on 'The Mask 1932' (E. G. Graig Collection, Bibliothèque de l'Arsenal, Paris).
22. J.S., 'Editorial Notes', *The Mask*, Vol. I, No. 1, p. 23.
23. Gordon Craig, *Daybook I*, p. 77.
24. From the first prospectus announcing the publication of *The Mask*.
25. Although Craig's articles took up a good deal of *The Mask*, it was not confined to them and to reprints of old documents, but enlisted a number of outside contributors. Vol. I, for instance, included articles by Edward Hutton, J. Paul Cooper, Haldane Macfall, J. Martin Harvey and Leon Schiller – an acknowledged disciple of Gordon Craig, whose work as a producer had a considerable influence on the development of the modern Polish theatre.
26. 'A Letter from Madame Yvette Guilbert', printed on the back cover of *The Mask*, Vol. IV, No. 1, July 1911.
27. Printed on the inside back cover of *The Mask*, Vol. III, Nos. 10–12, April 1911, opp. p. 196.
28. Strindberg, *Briefe ans Intime Theater*, German edition, prepared by Emil Schering, 1921, George Müller Verlag, p. 111.
29. Untitled MS of 1898 (Gordon Craig Collection, Bibliothèque de l'Arsenal, Paris).
30. 'The Actor and the Über-marionette', in *On the Art of the Theatre*, p. 81.
31. 'The Artists of the Theatre of the Future', in *On the Art of the Theatre*, p. 53.
32. 'To Madame Eleonora Duse', *The Mask*, Vol. I, No. 1, March 1908, pp. 12–13
33. 'The Actor and the Über-marionette', in *On the Art of the Theatre*, p. 55.

34. 'A Note on Masks', *The Mask*, Vol. I, No. 1, March 1908, pp. 9–10.
35. 'The Actor and the Über-marionette', in *On the Art of the Theatre*, p. 82.
36. Ibid., pp. 84–5.
37. Written at Rapallo in 1924. See *On the Art of the Theatre*, pp. ix–x.
38. 'The Actor and the Über-marionette', p. 61.
39. *Daybook I*, p. 77.
40. 'A Note on Masks', *The Mask*, Vol. I, No. 1, March 1908, p. 10.
41. Annenkov, 'Le Joyeux Sanatorium', in *La Vie de l'Art*. Quoted by Boris Till, 'Recherches dans le théâtre russe, 1905–25', in *Spectacles, Cinquante Ans de Recherches*, op. cit., p. 10.
42. See Craig's manuscript, 'Über-Marions – Berlin 1905–1906' (Gordon Craig Collection, Bibliothèque de l'Arsenal, Paris).
43. This appeared in a French translation in *Spectacles, Cinquante Ans de Recherches*, op. cit., pp. 14–24. It was first published in German by Walter Gropius and Laszlo Moholy-Nagy in the fourth volume of the 'Bauhaus-bücher', *Die Bühne im Bauhaus* (1925), which remains the best source of information regarding the theatrical activities and principles of the *Bauhaus* group.
44. See my article, 'La Mise en scène et le décor expressionistes', in *Théâtre Populaire*, Paris, January 1957, No. 22, pp. 5–21.

1. Edward Gordon Craig at Corbeil, 1948

2. Craig at work on a wood-block (Florence, January 1913)

Designs for
Acis and Galatea,
1902

3A. Act II, Scene 1

3B. Act II, Scene 3

not. snow? —

proscenium

audiencehere

5. Scene I (photograph taken at rehearsal)

4. *Left*: *Bethlehem*, 1902: Two scene designs

The Vikings, 1903

6A. Design for
Act II

6B. Design for Act IV

7. *Venice Preserved*, 1904. Design for Act IV

8. *The Steps*, 1905

'First mood'

'Second mood'

9. *The Steps*
(continued)

'Third mood'

'Fourth mood'

10. Design for *Elektra*, 1905

11A. Design for *Elektra*, 1905

11B. Design for *Psyche*, (ballet), 1907

12. Etching for *Scene*: 'Hell', 1907

13. Etchings for *Scene*, 1907

To be looked at by artificial light.
EGC.

15. Design for *Hamlet*, Act III, Scene 2, 1904

14A. *Above left*: Design for *Hamlet*, Act III, Scene 4, 1899–1900
14B. *Below left*: Design for *Hamlet*, Act II, *circa* 1901

16. Design for Act I, Scene 2, 1910

Act I, Scene 1 (variant)

17. Models for *Hamlet*, 1909

Act I, Scene 2 (variant)

19. Claudius (N. O. Massalitinov) and Gertrude (O. L. Knipper)
18. *Above left*: Model for Act IV, Scene 4
Below left: Model for Act IV, Scene 5

20A. Ophelia (O. V. Gsovskaia) and Polonius (B. B. Luzhski)

21. *Right*: The last scene

20B. Laertes (R. V. Boleslavsky) and Hamlet (V. I. Katchalov)

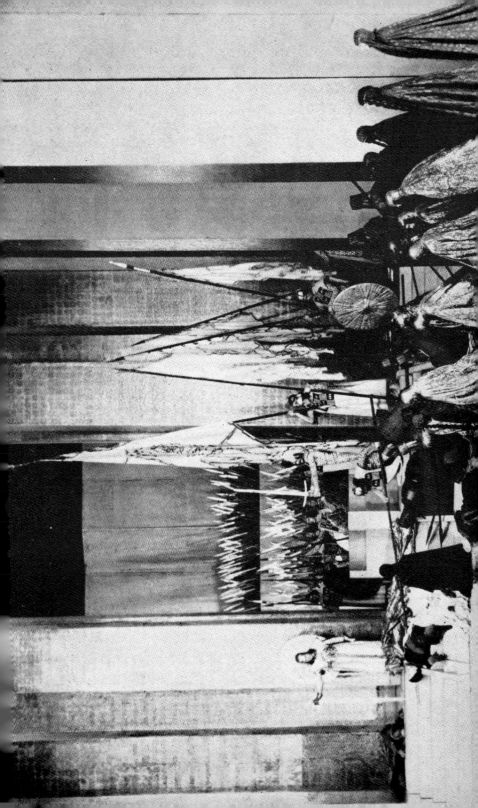

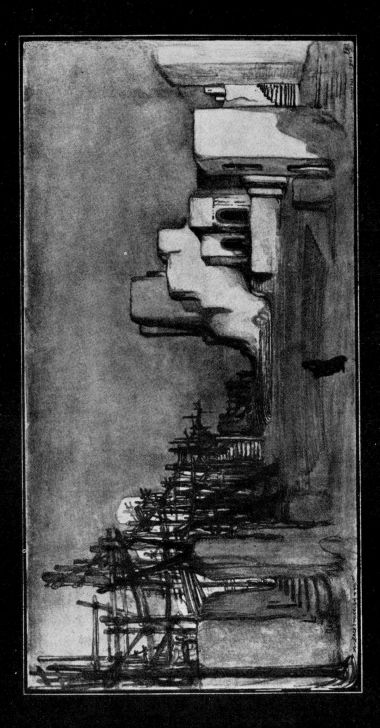

St Matthew Passion
(continued)

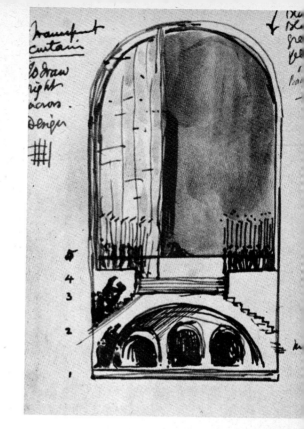

23A. Sketch, 29 May 1912

23B. Sketch, September
1913

24. Model (photograph)

VII

SCENE AND THE 'SCREENS'

Craig is not a rationalist. His principles were not arrived at by the kind of systematic reflection that results in a body of theory. He is intuitive, a visionary, guided by an ideal he perceives in flashes and seeks constantly to attain. Hence the 'prophetic' style in which he resembles Ruskin, the lyrical flights to be found in most of his writings, and the 'mystic' flavour that characterizes his work. The word may seem dangerous, but Craig has an almost religious concept of the theatre, he feels he has a 'mission'; and this makes it easier to understand why he has so often refused to take part in official theatrical activity and why he declined several tempting offers. He was looking towards a future full of mystery and revelation, working for a theatre which was not yet of this world and which lay beyond the frontiers of the theatre as usually conceived. But this did not prevent him from trying to give practical shape to his ideas then and there. In considering his work we have to distinguish between his dreams and his experimental research, between utopianism and exploration.

*

Among the clearest examples of this duality is one of Craig's major achievements, which belongs to the most productive period of his career – his etchings entitled *Movement*, the seeds of *The Thousand Scenes in one Scene*.

In *The Art of the Theatre*, Craig had proclaimed that movement lay at the origin of the theatre, that it was with movement, scene and voice that the artist of the future theatre would compose his masterpieces. What he chiefly admired most about Isadora Duncan was the expressive quality of her movements. In 1906 he made two *Studies for Movement* – a man battling through a snowstorm, and some figures climbing a flight of steps seen from the side. (1) In other words, movement was a central theme of his thoughts and projects.

In the last part of his essay, 'The Artists of the Theatre of the Future', where he lays down the general principles of the 'new art' he is aiming at, and considers through what phases it can be brought into being, we find the same procedure as in *The Actor and the Über-marionette*: 'In the beginning with you it was Impersonation; you passed on to Representation, and now you advance into Revelation.' (2) The art for which he is striving, an art which should reveal invisible things, will be reborn when architecture, music and movement are united in an ideal harmony. The first number of *The Mask* opens with this vision, in an article entitled 'Geometry' – a poetic manifesto rather than a methodical study – which concludes with the words: 'We will surround the people with symbols in silence; in silence we will reveal the Movement of Things. . . . this is the nature of our Art.' (3) Why the movement of things? Because in Craig's opinion the human body is not an instrument suitable for rendering movement.

The pronouncement just quoted was not the outcome of vague hypotheses; Craig had made what he considered to be an essential discovery, and he was now experimenting with it.

I have already mentioned the great importance Craig attached to Serlio's *Treatise on Perspective*. He was not in the least interested in copying its designs or following its suggestions; but the second volume, in particular, and the engravings that illustrate it were a source of inspiration to him, as is evidenced by the story of how his designs for *Movement* came into being. At the end of his copy of this second volume of the *Treatise*, Craig added eleven sheets of paper on which he jotted down the first notes for *Scene*, dated 1906 and 1907; (4) the most important of these, which form the starting-point of his concept, were written down on the very evening when he discovered how his scenes for *Rosmersholm* had been mutilated.

Certain illustrations of the *Treatise* were of particular interest to him: those on pages 19 and 20, where a chess-board pattern of lines is drawn in perspective on the ground, and no doubt the one facing page 24, which shows angular shapes, as it were walls all of the same height, intersecting at right angles. It occurred to him that each square on the chess-board might be raised or lowered by means of apparatus which would present it as the upper surface of a parallelepiped. The floor of the stage would thus become end-lessly variable, for the play of volumes would make it possible to construct staircases, platforms, seats, thick walls or wide spaces. Craig thus started with the idea of a stage which would be strong, yet mobile, complex yet simple in idea and effect. But he did not stop at that: he wanted the whole scene to be capable of movement in all directions. He invented vertical screens, each panel of which was equal in width to the side of the squares, and added a kind of ceiling constructed in the same way as the floor. The result was not so much a scene as a 'place', which could be infinitely varied by manipulating the relationship between its volumes. Some restrictions were, of course, imposed by the forms themselves, the simple square, the straight lines and rectangles; but Craig thought the judicious use of light would make it possible to soften certain angles and alter the appearance of the space. Endless possibilities were offered by forms and volumes he could move about at will, and by changes of light to create atmosphere.

What interested Craig in all this was not so much the construc-tion of movable architecture as the idea of movement in the abstract; he had devised an instrument which he thought would make it possible to develop the art of movement, and his discovery threw him into a strange state of exultation. He was beginning to work out a symphony of mobile forms, the principle of which he indicates in *Motion*, the preface to *A Portfolio of Etchings*, which he issued in Florence in 1908. (5) 'The Beginning . . . the Birth . . .' There are no definite forms. Nothing seems to bound the horizon, the ground is invisible, overhead is a void. Soon, in the centre, a single form stirs and slowly rises, like the beginning of a dream; and then a second and a third. And now, on the right, something is unfolding, without haste. Forms descend, mysteriously. The whole space is in motion, stirred by the inner life it receives from the light. Fearing, no doubt, that he will not be clearly understood, Craig tries to explain. Remember – he says in substance – remember Bach's *St Matthew Passion*. Does it not remind you of the sunrise, or of the way a tree grows? It begins almost imperceptibly, then gradually advances, serenely, unhurried, in absolute purity of form. It is as though a splendid tree were rising out of the ground, growing taller, and raising its countless branches towards the sky. That was what the *Passion* made him think of, and he wanted to express the same kind of progression in his *Movement*, in the music of the forms he set in motion. He wanted to frame laws similar to those which form the foundation of music, rules by which he could create works resembling the compositions of Bach and the early masters. It might not be possible to discover these by scientific inquiry, but he felt that his efforts would culminate in a discovery which would itself be scientific. He restricted himself almost entirely to vertical movement, and he realized that there was still a great deal to be done before the art of movement could come into being; he had simply discovered its fundamental elements, the actual source of what is now known as 'scenic kinetics'.

Together with these notes, Craig jotted down some rapid sketches. But he still had to put his vision into tangible shape. How was he to give plastic expression to something that defied capture? How could sketches, those dead, motionless things, express something that was all mobility and progression? At first he thought of trying wood-engraving. But in 1907 he had taken a further step in his career as a plastic artist by learning how to make etchings. Stephen Haweis had shown him how to prepare the copper plate and how to bite it in a bath of acid, and he very soon acquired great skill in the medium. During 1907–1908 he made a series of fifteen etchings, later reproduced in *Scene*, in which, by the interplay of forms and the distribution of shadows and oblique shafts of light, he conveyed the impression of fleeting movement and evanescent atmosphere caught in passing (Plates 12 and 13). These etchings were exhibited in Florence in 1908. Craig explains his idea in the preface to the catalogue, from which the following passages are taken:

> The most important thing is that movement, which is at the Root of this Art of Revelation, must be translated through Inanimate Forms. I speak here of movement in an actual, not in an imaginary sense.
> Impersonal movement in an actual sense exists in no modern art – nor can it justly be said to belong even in its imaginary sense to any other art.
> This appears to me to be corroborated to some extent by the other

two divisions of the Art of Revelation – by Architecture and by
Music. By Architecture, which not only in fancy but also in *actuality*
alone produces pure form: by Music which not only in the abstract
but in the *concrete* alone produces pure sound.

These fifteen designs therefore are studies for fifteen separate Motions
or moods of movement as translated through an instrument. Let me
attempt to make the thing clearer to you.

We have constructed an instrument. By means of this instrument the
artist is enabled to bring before the beholder a sense of the law which
controls our system – the law of Change. Movement will be for the
sake of Movement – ever attempting to create the perfect Balance,
even as in Music Sound is for the sake of Sound, ever attempting to
create the perfect Harmony.

The Imitation of Nature has no part in this art. The mood and the
thought of the artist passing through this Instrument shall raise by it
one mutable form after another, living only a moment; ceaselessly,
if imperceptibly, changing; arriving at last at its final and definite
state – only to fade – to re-form itself once again, and again – an
infinite progression. . . . (6)

Until quite recently I was under the delusion that in some way the
Theatre was connected with my vision. In me was a longing born of
an old affection that this should be so. But I know now that this art
about which I write and to which I have given my life, transcends the
Theatre. This has been made clearer to me only quite recently. My
aim – work – delight, remain the same in spite of this – only one thing is
changed – what before was Impossible now becomes Possible – . . . (7)

Thus, the art of movement which Craig's etchings sought to
adumbrate bore no relation to what was known as modern
dramatic art: it did not aim at interpretation, and the human
element was virtually excluded. Did this mean that it could have
no influence at all on the development of theatrical art, that it
could not be adapted for stage purposes? To answer these questions,
we must recall the principles of the new art: that it was to be a
single assembly of mobile forms and volumes; not one or more
stage settings but a single *scene*, a *place*, capable of infinite variation;
not a succession of stage pictures, but the 'movement of things' in
the abstract.

It is possible to look no further than the actual technical process
– the construction of a stage floor composed of mobile elements.

Many producers and architects have followed Craig in demanding a completely mobile stage – from Piscator to more recent stage planners, such as Werner Ruhnau, who suggests a stage made up of hexagonal surfaces mounted on apparatus by which they can be moved vertically, making it possible to build up the scene at will.

Another possibility is to concentrate on the mobility of the forms seen by the audience: one of the principal lines of research in the twentieth-century theatre has been directed towards completely harmonizing the movement of the objects on the stage with that of the actors, and these experiments form the basis of stage kinetics.

Craig himself derived from his 'discovery' a scene closely related to it. In this he felt he was restricting his aims, making something that would be comparatively easy to achieve. His 'Scene for the poetic drama' was a by-product of his ideal conception of an art of movement. (8)

*

In 1910 the painter Piot, then in Florence, went to see Gordon Craig at the request of Jacques Rouché, to discover whether it would be possible for Craig to do a production at the Théâtre des Arts. Reporting on his conversation with Craig, Piot wrote to Rouché:

> He showed me a stage design, the interest of which lay in the fact that he is trying to make the stage space infinitely changeable. . .
> . . . By means of a number of cubes which can shrink or expand, the cube of the stage becomes either square, oblong, or tall in proportion to its width – thus giving unlimited variety to the cubic volume of the stage, just as a painter selects a square, wide or tall canvas to suit his subject.
> The scenery is so greatly simplified that it takes its expression chiefly from changes in the lighting as it strikes a number of different shapes. In short, Craig's aim seems to be to achieve, by means of simplification, a musical ebb and flow of the scene, bringing it into the time-scheme so as to link it with the play. Up to now the scenery designed by painters, or self-styled painters, has consisted of motionless rags, dangling round the moving figures on the stage. Craig wants his

scenery to move like sound, to refine certain moments in the play just as music follows and heightens all its movements; *he wants it to advance with the play*. Or so it seemed to me from what he showed me. I don't know how far this idea can be put into practice; but the idea itself is first-class, and if it were carried out it would revolutionize the art of scene-designing; for there has always been an antagonism between the movement of the plot and the immobility of the scenery: if the scene could change in harmony with the development of the plot, this would provide an entirely new source of expression. . . .

In short, this man Craig has shown me an idea for scenery, and it's the first I ever saw put forward.

For we painters can never give you anything except *pictures*, better or worse; they will never be a real setting for the drama, and there is no *new idea* in what the Russians have shown us. That is successful, but it isn't an idea.

But whether Craig's dream can be carried out, or whether he has the strength of will to emerge from his dream, is something that can only be discovered by taking a chance on it. . . . (9)

A few months earlier Craig had written in his *Daybook I*: 'I wish to remove the *Pictorial Scene* but to leave in its place the *Architectonic Scene*.' (10)

The discovery recorded on the pages added to Serlio's treatise was a combination of long reflection and sudden inspiration. Craig now began a systematic search for ways of applying it. For many years he worked with models and experimented with lighting – from 1907 until 1923, the year of the publication of *Scene* (11). the book in which he summarized the principles of his discovery and suggested how it might be followed up. In September –October 1907 he was already building his first Model Stage for the purpose of experimenting with the 'Screens'. He had not yet perfected his lighting system, however. In 1909 he built another Model Stage and tested it with a project for the production of *The Merchant of Venice*. Two years later he designed a third stage, which was more portable and which he used in London (12) to demonstrate his invention, whose earliest applications were to take place in Ireland and at Moscow. After this he designed and constructed his famous *Model A*, begun in September 1913 and not completely finished until 1921: this, built with the help of

several assistants, in particular his son Teddy, was a complete
model of his device, which he continued to improve. The whole

Project 1908.

process was recorded in a manuscript book – the principles, the
materials (the screens and extra pieces) and the stage apparatus (a
table showing what coloured gelatine sheets had been used, and

what types of lamps and projectors and what resistances were employed). (13)

This device, for which he took out patents in the United Kingdom, the United States, France, Italy and Germany, has remained famous under the name of 'Screens', given to it by Craig when he wrote of it in public – in *The Mask* for May 1915. The screens are the basic material, while the underlying principle is expressed in the phrase *The Thousand Scenes in one Scene*. (14)

Craig was not inventing a new process of stage decoration, or a mechanical means of facilitating scene-shifting. He considered that each period in the history of the theatre had had its particular type of stage – the antique Greek and Roman theatre was dominated by the architectural unity of the scene, the church had been the favourite place for performances in medieval times, the *Commedia dell' Arte* had been performed on platforms set up in the street. Since the Renaissance, however, the Italian style of theatre had gradually been invaded by painted scenery which was destructive of unity and got in the way of the actor. Referring to his own invention in *Scene*, Craig claimed to have discovered the 'fifth scene'. (15) It was a device which satisfied both the need for unity and permanence and the desire for movement and change; it used a specific type of material, but one which offered a wide range of possibilities. Here we recognize the ideas underlying the etchings for *Movements*.

This 'fifth scene' consisted chiefly of screens composed of four, six, eight, ten or twelve leaves which could be folded either forwards or backwards. All the leaves of a screen were the same height, but they might be of different widths. They could be made of wooden frames covered with canvas, or of wooden panels, and certain accessories (steps, windows, pieces of furniture, etc.) could be used with them – chosen with the greatest care to avoid anything superfluous. Any space and any atmosphere could be suggested by an appropriate arrangement of the screens. If the angle of a screen were altered, the appearance of the stage would change at once. This was, therefore, a single scene, which could take on many different aspects. Craig compares his device to the human face. A face consists of two eyes, a forehead, a nose, a chin, a mouth and two cheeks, which add up to a definite pattern;

but its expression alters with any change in one of its features. It is the same with Craig's scene, which is not a series of separate pictures, but a series of different expressions passing over the same structure.

For the foremost characteristic of this scene is that it is an architectonic construction with a life of its own. It is a solid, three-dimensional unit which adapts itself to the actor's movements, a group of screens which stand up by themselves – they do not have to be hung from the flies, like old-fashioned scenery. They stand on the stage just as they are; they do not imitate nature, nor are they painted with realistic or decorative designs. They are monotone. Craig dismisses painting from the stage, for the theatre cannot and must not make use of any arts which are alien to it. He thus rejects any form of imitation, all sham. ' "A nice place," said a dear old friend to me on looking at the model of the scene I shall describe later – and I have always thought this was the best word to use – far better than scene – it is a place if it seem real – it is a scene if it seem false.' (16)

This invention, however, is both more and less than an architectural structure. It has to serve the play, its movement, the development of the plot. It must therefore be mobile, like the play itself: the screens can be moved about, folded and unfolded under the eyes of the audience, so that the transition from one scene to the next takes place gradually, like the changes in the play.

The screens were not the only element used by Craig, there was another, equally important: light, the effects of which he had carefully studied when experimenting with his models. The screens were not to be lighted in the same way as ordinary scenery; the scene would come to life, and attain its full expressive power, through light. The light travelled over it, animating it, creating atmosphere and transforming it. Light coloured the screens and gradually changed their aspect. Craig compares the union of scene and light to the union between two dancers or two singers who are in perfect accord, so that one can do nothing without the other. '. . . The relation of light to this scene is akin to that of the bow to the violin, or of the pen to the paper.' (17) But in establishing this relationship the actor must not be forgotten. Craig was not inventing an instrument for its own sake alone: '. . . any theory which attempts to state the uses of light in relation to scene without stating the use of light to the acting is valueless.' (18) And in a footnote to this, he explains:

> Actor and scene being one, they are to be kept as one before us, or we shall be looking at two things and so lose the value of both. Their value lies in being one.
> Being one, the Play, Actor, Scene, has to be kept before us and seen and heard as one – or we shall look from one to another and lose the whole. (19)

Seventeen years after writing *The Art of the Theatre*, Craig was still true to his principles, which *Scene* simply puts forward in fresh terms. *The Thousand Scenes in one Scene* was one among a number of means by which they could be applied. It considered the unity of scene, actor, light, colour and movement from the standpoint of expression.

Like Piot reporting to Jacques Rouché on his impressions of Craig's experimental work, Filiberto Scarpelli, the Florentine architect and author, wrote to Giovanni Grasso, the Sicilian actor, on 4 December 1913, describing a visit to the Arena Goldoni which he had made at Grasso's request:

> My dearest Giovanni,
> I went yesterday to Signor Craig at the Arena Goldoni.
> My impression? Craig is a prodigious man, if prodigious signifies the power of conjuring up from nothing, before your eyes, that which amazes you.
> And the elements of which Craig makes use for his creations are nothing or almost nothing: some screens and some electric lights.
> He sets upon the stage of his little theatre (no bigger than a child's marionette theatre) his tiny screens, and while you look on, with a rapid movement of the hands, arranges them in a certain way: a ray of electric light comes to strike between those simple rectangles of cardboard, and the miracle is accomplished: you behold a majestic scene: the sense of the small disappears absolutely; you forget the dimensions of the theatre, such is the scrupulous equilibrium of the lights and of the lines which Craig knows how to give to the scenes.
> Another slight movement of the screens (always before your eyes) and the scene changes and then changes again, without the lines and

the light effects ever recalling to you that which you have already seen. And thus one passes from the vision of a piazza, a street, an imposing portico to that of an audience-chamber, a prison or a subterranean dungeon. Craig is a great painter, a great architect, a great poet. He paints with light, he constructs with a few rectangles of cardboard, and with the harmony of his colours and of his lines he creates profound sensations, as only the fathers of poetry knew how to create. I am not exaggerating, dear Giovanni. The sight of some scenes for *Othello* gave me the thrill that only *the reading of Shakespeare* had been able to give me! We are far, very far, from the usual scenographic resources, be they even the best that can be remembered. . . (20)

Three years had elapsed between Piot's letter to Rouché and Scarpelli's to Grasso. In the meantime, Craig's screens had been set up on the stage of the Abbey Theatre, Dublin, and on that of the Moscow Arts Theatre.

*

We have already seen how enthusiastically Yeats had responded to Gordon Craig's first stage productions. The two men had formed a friendship based on their joint determination to regenerate the art of the theatre. An abundant correspondence shows that they kept in close touch. On 20 November 1902, Yeats writes to Craig to invite him to a reading of one of his plays; he speaks of the young Irish company he is directing, and of his wish to gain an audience among the real Irish people. (21) In another letter he asks Craig whether some of the characters in another of his plays ought to wear masks. (22) It is clear from Yeats's theoretical and critical writings that he found in Craig's work an inexhaustible source of inspiration. Yeats was trying to revive verse drama, he was fighting realism, with its imitation of everyday life. The stage setting, he thought, should be as artificial as the play, while possessing its own artistic reality which excluded recourse to false perspective and to painted light and shadow.

The Mask often published information about the work of the Abbey Theatre, and printed several things by Yeats, including his play *The Hour-Glass* (23) and the essay, 'The Tragic Theatre', (24) which forms the introduction to his *Plays for an Irish Theatre* (*Deirdre, The Green Helmet, On Baile's Strand, The King's Threshold, The Shadowy Waters, The Hour-Glass, Cathleen ni Houlihan*). This volume was published in 1911 (25) and was illustrated with four designs by Craig, one for *Deirdre*, one for *The Hour-Glass*, and two for *On Baile's Strand*. Most important of all, Yeats was the only person to whom Craig gave a set of model screens, to help him compose the scenes for his plays, and only to Yeats did he give permission to make use of his invention, at the Abbey Theatre.

On Saturday, 8 January 1910, Yeats wrote to Lady Gregory, and told her of a conversation he had had with Craig the previous evening: 'Craig dined with me last night and, after Binyon had gone, made drawings etc. and explained further his "place" or whatever one should call his invention. I am to see his model on Monday at 5 – I think I shall, if it seems right, order one for us (this will cost he says about £2 for material and about £4 for the man's time).' Yeats would have liked to use the scene for a forthcoming production of *Oedipus*, but Craig 'wants us to play about with his model first and master its effects'. Yeats goes on to say: 'I now think from what he told me that a certain modification will give us an entirely adequate open air scene. That we shall have a means of staging everything that is not naturalistic, and that out of his invention may grow a completely new method even for naturalistic plays.' (26)

During the summer of 1910, Yeats 'played about with' the small model Craig had given him, finding in it a scene capable of endless transformations and of the expression of every mood. He was amazed by its simplicity and by the variety and wealth of the effects to be drawn from it.

Henceforth, [he says] I can all but produce my play as I write it, moving hither and thither little figures of cardboard through gay or solemn light and shade, allowing the scene to give the words and the words the scene. I am very grateful, for he has banished a whole world that wearied me and was undignified and given me forms and lights upon which I can play as upon some stringed instrument. (27)

And on 12 January 1911, the screens made their first appearance on any stage, at the Abbey Theatre, for the first performance of *The Deliverer*, a play by Lady Gregory, and a revival of *The*

Hour-Glass. Lady Gregory's was a symbolical drama, set in Egypt and dealing ostensibly with Moses, but in reality with Parnell. The scene represented the outside of a temple. The screens were arranged obliquely and folded so as to suggest pillars. The light came from above and from the sides. For *The Hour-Glass* the ivory-coloured screens were arranged with the greatest simplicity, and properties were kept to a minimum – the Wise Man's chair, of the same colour as the screens, a missal, a bell, an hour-glass. The costumes, made from designs by Craig, were in harmony with the scene and stood out clearly against the neutral background.

The next day Yeats wrote off to tell his friends of the triumph his scene and costumes had scored with the audience. (28) A few days previously he had already, in a letter to the Press, declared what importance he himself attached to Craig's discovery:

The primary value of Mr Craig's invention is that it enables one to use light in a more natural and more beautiful way than ever before. We get rid of all the top hamper of the stage, all the hanging ropes and scenes which prevent the free play of light. It is now possible to substitute in the shading of one scene real light and shadow for painted light and shadow. Continually in the contemporary theatre, the painted shadow is out of relation to the direction of the light, and what is more to the point, one loses the extraordinary beauty of delicate light and shade. This means, however, an abolition of realism, for it makes scene-painting which is, of course, a matter of painted light and shade, impossible. One enters into a world of decorative effect which gives the actor a renewed importance. There is less to compete against him, for there is less detail, though there is more beauty. (29)

Some time later he wrote to Craig, 'Your work is always a great inspiration to me. Indeed I cannot imagine myself writing any play for the stage now, which I did not write for your screens.' (30)

*

On this occasion the programme of the Abbey Theatre contained an announcement that the method of stage decoration used for the present performance would shortly be seen in a production of *Hamlet* at the Moscow Arts Theatre.

NOTES

1. These two designs are reproduced in *Towards a New Theatre*, op. cit., facing pages 48 and 61.
2. *On the Art of the Theatre*, op. cit., p. 46.
3. 'Geometry', in *The Mask*, Vol. 1, No. 1, March 1908, pp. 1–2. This article is unsigned, but there can be no doubt as to the writer's identity.
4. Gordon Craig Collection, Bibliothèque de l'Arsenal, Paris.
5. *A Portfolio of Etchings*, Florence 1908. The preface, 'Motion', was also published in *The Mask*, Vol. I, No. 10, December 1908, pp. 185–6.
6. *Catalogue of Etchings being Designs for Motions, by Gordon Craig*, Florence, 1908, pp. 6–8.
7. Ibid., pp. 10–12.
8. See *Scene*, with a Foreword and an Introductory Poem by John Masefield, London, Humphrey Milford, Oxford University Press, 1923, p. 19.
9. Quoted by Rose-Marie Moudouès, 'Jacques Rouché et Edward Gordon Craig', op. cit., pp. 313–19. In referring to the work of the Russians, Piot was thinking chiefly of the pictorial scenery of Diaghilev's Russian Ballet.
10. *Daybook I*, p. 77, entry dated 3 February 1909.
11. Craig wrote *Scene* at Rapallo in March 1922. The original MS takes up forty-two pages of his manuscript volume, *E.G.C. MSS 7, 1914–1916–1920*.
12. Craig gave this demonstration on 18 September 1911 in his London studio. The *Daily News* published an article about it in its issue of 19 September, and *The Times* described the invention, on 23 September 1911, in an article reprinted by Craig in several of his exhibition catalogues (City of Manchester Art Gallery, 1912; City Art Gallery, Leeds, 1913, etc.) and in a number of *The Mask* which was largely devoted to his new invention (*The Mask*, Vol. VII, No. 2, May 1915; see pp. 156–7).
13. Unhappily, *Model A* itself is no longer extant; but I have been able to study the explanatory manuscript in the Gordon Craig Collection at the Bibliothèque de l'Arsenal (*Model A. MSS Book 14*).
14. 'Screens. The Thousand Scenes in One Scene – Some notes and facts relative to the "Scene" invented and patented by Edward Gordon Craig', in *The Mask*, Vol. VII, No. 2, May 1915, pp. 139–60. Chief among this group of contributions are a detailed description of Craig's device and a description of its artistic, technical and economic advantages.
15. *Scene*, op. cit., p. 18.
16. Ibid., p. 1, footnote 1.
17. Ibid., p. 25.
18. Ibid., p. 23.
19. Ibid., p. 23, footnote 2.

20. Letter printed in *The Mask*, Vol. VII, No. 2, pp. 159–60.
21. Gordon Craig Collection, Bibliothèque de l'Arsenal, Paris.
22. Ibid., Letter of 3 November 1911.
23. *The Mask*, Vol. V, No. 4, April 1913, pp. 327–46.
24. *The Mask*, Vol. III, No. 4–6, October 1910, pp. 77–81.
25. Published by A. H. Bullen, London and Stratford-upon-Avon.
26. *Letters of W. B. Yeats*, op. cit., p. 546.
27. W. B. Yeats, 'The Tragic Theatre', in *The Mask*, Vol. III, Nos. 4–6, October 1910, p. 81.
28. This letter is in the Gordon Craig Collection, Bibliothèque de l'Arsenal, Paris.
29. *Evening Telegraph*, 9 January 1911.
30. Letter of 29 July (1913), now in the Gordon Craig Collection, Bibliothèque de l'Arsenal, Paris.

VIII

THE MOSCOW *HAMLET*

In *The Art of the Theatre* (1905), Craig bluntly asserted that '*Hamlet* has not the nature of a stage representation' and that the other plays of Shakespeare, so vast and so complete when read, could not but lose heavily by stage treatment. Three years later he again declared that 'to represent *Hamlet* rightly is an impossibility'. (1) His research, his experiments, his discoveries, his yearning for an art of revelation, had all gone to confirm his opinion: like Goethe, he considered that 'Shakespeare belongs by rights to the history of poetry; in the history of the theatre he only appears casually'.

And yet few plays have filled such a prominent place in Craig's career as *Hamlet*. As a young actor, he played the part on tour and in London. *Hamlet* was the theme of the drawings in which the originality of his ideas was first revealed. He was for ever making new designs for the play (Plates 14B and 15). And during his months in Germany he was intending to produce it.

In the spring of 1908, while Craig was considering invitations from Berlin, Holland and London, Stanislavsky telegraphed, inviting him to Moscow. He replied:

Dear Stanislavsky,
I thank you for your telegram.
I do not wish to hurry you at all – but I am now making arrangements to visit certain other countries to produce a few plays, and should like to visit your city at the same time.
I have only a little time to devote to this kind of work and unless it is all done during one short *tournée* it is likely to be impossible this year. I also desire to reserve for certain towns certain productions. *King Lear* I have already arranged for. It would give me *great pleasure* to produce *Hamlet* for you. In no case could I produce any play which I have not studied for a long time.
Do you understand?
Yes – of course you do.

You say you have not yet decided your repertoire.

I hope you will not consider it rude on my part if I suggest that in my case the play chosen for me to produce should be selected if possible after consulting me.

It would give me pleasure and some satisfaction to receive a letter from you, if it is not asking too much from so busy a man.

Gordon Craig. (2)

This was the first step towards one of the most famous and passionately discussed productions in the history of the modern stage (Plates 16–21). Subsequent developments brought the producer to grips with one of the mightiest works in the repertory, led to a meeting between two of the men of the theatre who have had the strongest influence on present-day stage art, and set two completely different attitudes in confrontation. The experience was of decisive importance, and both parties drew their own conclusions from it.

Three years went by before the curtain rose on the first night of Edward Gordon Craig's production of *Hamlet* at the Moscow Arts Theatre, on 8 January 1912. They were years of intensive and sometimes difficult preparatory work.

*

It may seem surprising that Stanislavsky should have turned to Craig. But he too was searching for a new path. He was not satisfied with the formal realism of the Arts Theatre's first productions, and wanted to get further. He had of course been helped to do so by Chekhov's appearance on the scene; but he was still frequently disappointed by the results he achieved. Painting, sculpture, poetry and music were now eschewing mere imitation and striving to suggest things unseen, and the stage, he felt, must not lag behind. He first called in Meyerhold, who tried to set up a Studio Theatre on stylized lines, with experimental productions of Maeterlinck's *Mort de Tintagiles*, Hauptmann's *Schluck und Jau*, and so forth. At first Stanislavsky was thrilled and fascinated; but when the first production opened he realized that this was not the way to solve the problems of the Arts Theatre; it was no more than the skilful application of a theory that helped the actors to

conceal their shortcomings. These performers had no real technique, they were incapable of expressing the new drama, with its
subtleties. Increasingly convinced of the urgency of establishing
the actor's art on a firm foundation, Stanislavsky could not be
fobbed off with experiments in production methods. He made a
contribution of his own to the non-realistic theatre by producing
Knut Hamsun's *Drama of Life* and Leonid Andreiev's *The Life of
Man* in symbolic, stylized scenery, and the audience thought this
was a new direction for the theatre. Stanislavsky considered,
however, that in point of fact he had again lapsed into stereotypes
and the facility of the artificial. Despite his success he remained
dissatisfied, feeling that he had done nothing to enrich the art of
acting.

How was he to escape from the deadlock?

Isadora Duncan came to Moscow, and Stanislavsky became
enthusiastic about her. He discovered that like himself, she was
searching for the 'creative motor' which an actor must set going
before he begins his performance, if he is to express the inner life
of the character he is playing. It will be remembered that it was by
thinking along these lines that Stanislavsky arrived at his 'system'.
Whenever they met, Isadora talked to him about Craig, about his
personality, his ideas and dreams. The Arts Theatre seemed to be
the very place where those ideas could be applied, and Stanislavsky persuaded his fellow-directors to invite Craig.

Did this mean that Stanislavsky was abandoning the basic
principles of realism, set aside for the moment when he enlisted
Meyerhold and when he staged the two plays by Hamsun and
Andreiev? Not in the least. Shortly before Craig came to Moscow,
Stanislavsky wrote a report, 'Ten Years of Work in the Arts
Theatre,' in which he called for a return to the realistic traditions
upheld by Stchepkin, while avoiding stereotypes, and declared
that the Arts Theatre, having started with realism, had returned
to it enriched by effort and experience. And a few months later, on
5 February 1909, he wrote to Madame Gurevich, the critic and
theatrical historian:

Of course, we have returned to realism, to a deeper, more refined and
more psychological realism. Let us get a little stronger in it and we

shall once more continue on our quest. That is why we have invited Gordon Craig. After wandering about in search of new ways, we shall again return to realism for more strength. I do not doubt that every abstraction on the stage, such as impressionism, for instance, could be attained by way of a more refined and deeper realism. All other ways are false and dead. (3)

But there is a significant passage in his report on 'Ten Years of Work in the Arts Theatre' where Stanislavsky admits that the methods of acting worked out there have not proved satisfactory in dealing with Shakespeare's plays:

When adapted to plays aiming at powerful and moving effects, these methods were eclipsed by the visual side of the production, which was stronger and more convincing than the sentiments themselves. Thus it was with Shakespeare. The company was not yet ready to bring to life, sincerely and with simplicity, the great passions and lofty thoughts of a genius of world stature. (4)

He was probably remembering Nemirovich-Dantchenko's production of *Julius Caesar*, in which he himself had taken a hand. In preparation for this, Nemirovich-Dantchenko and the scene-designer, Simov, had gone to Rome to assemble as much historical data as possible. That was in 1903 – the year when Craig produced *Much Ado About Nothing* at the Imperial Theatre, and carefully refrained from travelling to Messina to measure the place up. . . .

*

On 1 November 1908 Craig arrived in Moscow. As described by Stanislavsky and by the actor Leonidov in their respective memoirs, it was a picturesque occasion. Craig, they say, was wearing a light overcoat, a wide-brimmed hat and a long woollen muffler. To enable him to face the Russian winter, they ransacked the theatre's wardrobe and lent him a fur coat, a fur hat and a pair of felt boots from a two-year-old production, *Woe from Wits*. This strange get-up appealed to his sense of humour and he wore it for the rest of his visit.

Craig was soon on friendly terms with everyone at the Arts

Theatre – with the directors, the managers and the company, which included Moskvin, Sulerjitsky, Katchalov, Balieff, Artëm, Olga Knipper, Maria Petrovna Lilina and Alice Koonen. He saw several productions – *The Blue Bird, Revizor, The Cherry Orchard, Three Sisters, The Wild Duck, An Enemy of the People, Brand* – and enjoyed *Uncle Vanya* most of all. The Arts Theatre was a theatre after his own heart. Not that he agreed with its director that realism was the best possible form of expression; but he admired the company and its standards of work, the intelligence of the actors and their devotion to their profession. As he wrote to 'John Semar', (5) the Arts Theatre was a live theatre where neither effort nor money was grudged, where a play might have hundreds of rehearsals, where a scene would be changed and changed until it gave satisfaction. The actors were not to be caught 'winking at the audience'. What they did, they did to perfection. Nothing was left to chance; everything was treated with a seriousness Craig felt to be dangerously lacking in the English theatre.

Craig had brought some sketches to Moscow, and a pocketful of photographs of the Arena Goldoni. He talked to everyone, following the drift of his own ideas and dreams. Alice Koonen consulted him about playing Portia. To Moskvin he showed his designs for several Shakespeare plays and his etchings for *Movement*, explaining that his scene would be suitable both for *Hamlet* and for *Peer Gynt*, and that he was seeking for a new 'country', a new race of actors. But it was with Stanislavsky he talked most of all, telling him of his search for an art of movement, speaking of the *Über-marionette* and of the need to create works of art with inanimate materials – stone, marble, bronze, canvas, paint. Stanislavsky was unresponsive to anything he deemed abstract, and regarded Craig's boldest theories as vague and contradictory. But he admired his designs for *Macbeth*, and agreed with him on some points. He too had come to hate traditional scenery and to wish for simplified backgrounds, and he approved when Craig declared that the actor's presence on the stage called for architectural construction instead of painted canvas and artificial perspective.

It was agreed that Craig should become a stage director at the Arts Theatre for a year and should stage *Hamlet*, as he had suggested. He was promised the working conditions he asked for; he was to have complete freedom, he was allotted three assistants, including Stanislavsky himself and Sulerjitsky, and allowed to take his pick of the actors and technical staff, stage-carpenters, scene-painters, electricians, etc. On 25 November he went back to Florence to work out his *mise en scène*.

*

In April 1909 Craig returned to Russia. He went first to St Petersburg, where the Arts Theatre company was then appearing, and afterwards to Moscow, where he remained until July. This was the beginning of a new phase in the preparation of *Hamlet*: the general conception of the play was now to be defined and its structure patiently analysed. Other questions were discussed as well, of course. For instance, Craig put before Stanislavsky his idea for a 'Platonic Theatre'. (6) He had a fervent enthusiasm for the *Symposium*, he saw in Socrates the finest example of a man who would not stoop to compromise or apostasy; and he suggested that Plato's dialogues should be delivered without interruption, in a specially designed open-air theatre, where people could come in whenever they liked and stay to listen for as long as they wished. He talked to Sulerjitsky about open-air theatres, and showed him photographs of the Arena Goldoni. Sulerjitsky was enthralled, and expressed astonishment when Stanislavsky displayed no interest in the idea and dismissed it as 'sentimental'. (7)

But it was *Hamlet* that led to the great discussions. Craig had brought a whole 'library' with him, and it soon became clear that there were many mistranslations in the Russian edition of the play.

For Craig, *Hamlet* was neither a historical play nor a romantic tragedy, but a symbolical drama embodying a clash of principles. He notes in his working copy that the main idea of the play, perhaps its only one, is the victory of Fire, Imagination, Beauty, Justice and Law over Water, Fact, Ugliness and Unlawfulness. But these are not left as so many abstract principles, they are contrasted in a tragedy that pits one man against the universe. (8) Hamlet stands alone in an evil world for which he has no sympathy, with which he feels no bond. That, Craig declared, was the key to the *mise en scène*.

Questioned about Hamlet by a journalist a month before the first performance, Craig replied:

> Have I any specially new ideas in regard to Hamlet as a character? No, I don't think so, except that I take an entirely commonsense view of the man and his motives. He simply succeeded in performing in two months a task that has been tried in every Court in Europe for centuries. He set out to cleanse social and official life of its moral grime and its degeneracy. He set about his task with direct purpose, and with the full enthusiasm of a young, virile and cruelly wronged man. His ideas were logical, and he reasoned and thought out every movement and act during that brief time of storm and stress that ended in tragedy. That is my idea of Hamlet. (9)

In other words he denied any would-be romantic interpretation of the character, and did not think him mad or even neurasthenic. He simplified the drama by stressing its fundamental contrasts; but at the same time he widened its spiritual scope – as noted by Stanislavsky, who makes an excellent summing-up of Craig's concept of the tragedy in *My Life in Art*. Hamlet is the victim of a purification rite. He has become different from other men because for a brief moment he has crossed the frontier of life and glimpsed the world beyond, where his father is in torment. After having this vision he looks at life with different eyes, trying to fathom its mysteries. Court etiquette, love, hatred, all take on a changed meaning for him, and he finds himself confronted by a tremendous task. Things would be comparatively simple if the whole problem could be solved by assassinating the usurper,

> but the crux of the matter lay not only in the murder of the King. In order to lighten the sufferings of his father it was necessary to cleanse the entire court of evil; it was necessary to carry fire and the sword throughout the whole kingdom, to destroy the harmful, to repulse old friends with rotten souls, like Rosencrantz and Guildenstern; to save the pure of soul like Ophelia from earthly ruin and immure her, safe at last, in a monastery. (10)

Hamlet thus appears to simple mortals, amid the trivialities of the Court and the humdrum events of ordinary life, as a kind of superman – and therefore, mad. As Craig points out in his notes for a speech to the actors, 'Madness is something which when it seems to succeed is called Heroic; when it seems to fail is called Folly.' (11) This view of the tragedy led him to set aside everything he felt to be subordinate; it determined not only his conception of the characters and their dealings with one another, but his ideas for scenery and lighting.

Craig now began to go through the play with Stanislavsky, scene by scene. They had with them two interpreters, Ursula Cox and Michael Lykiardopoulos, one of whom kept a record in English and the other in Russian. The importance of these conversations should not be exaggerated; according to Craig they were no more than a phase of the preparatory work. (12) But in the form in which they have come down to us they not only reveal many differences of opinion, but shed light on some of the basic ideas embodied in the production.

Craig considered one of the scenes holding the key to the interpretation of *Hamlet* to be Act I, Scene 2, where the King informs the Court of his intentions, sends off his messengers to the King of Norway, and urges Hamlet to forget his grief and look on him as a father. Craig took this scene as his starting-point in working out the meaning of the tragedy. Naturally, therefore, it was discussed at great length. Before entering into details, Craig was careful to lay down certain principles:

In this play I have found many parts which are not in the least important to the action, and I do not want the important to be lost on account of the unimportant. For example: in Hamlet's monologue in the second scene, Act I, beginning 'Seems, Madam! nay, it is; I know not seems' – in this monologue only the first two lines and, at the end of the monologue, the last two lines are important. These four lines express an important thought and must be spoken accordingly. All the rest of the monologue must be pronounced more as music, so that the thought becomes so much lost in the sounds that the audience simply *does not follow* the thought except in the above-mentioned four lines.... How this music is done will depend on the individuality of the actor.

I want all this to be in no way realistic. In the staging of this we must speak not so much of what *to do* as of what *not to do*. I think it is possible for the actors, without getting into stiff and unnatural poses, and without speaking with unnatural pauses and emphases, quietly to convey the thought and feeling.

More than anything in this work I am afraid of misunderstandings. We must have many discussions as to what Shakespeare wants in this play – not what he *wants to say*, not by any means, but what he wants as an artist.

This brings Craig to his general conception of the tragedy and of the stage treatment that results from that conception:

All the tragedy of Hamlet is his isolation. And the background of this isolation is the court, a world of pretence.
The only person to whom some ties still join him is his mother, who would like to answer him, only something does not let her.
And in this golden court, this world of show, there must not be various different individualities, as there would be in a realistic play. No, here everything melts into a single mass. Separate faces, as in the old masters of painting, must be coloured with one brush, with one paint.

The King's vulgarity and falsehood must be made evident through his monologue. Shakespeare is painting in broad strokes here. He has to be interpreted with a certain roughness of manner, and Craig warns Stanislavsky that if he treats Shakespeare as he treated Chekhov, too many superfluous details will crowd in.

The court, as shown in this second scene of the play, must be seen by the audience through Hamlet's eyes, he being the central figure in a tragedy conceived as a monodrama.

Stanislavsky: I understand what you say about monodrama. Let us try by every means to make the public understand that it is looking at the play with the eyes of Hamlet; that the King, the Queen and the Court are not shown on the stage as they really are, but as they appear to Hamlet to be. And I think that in the scenes where Hamlet is on the stage we can do this.

Such, then, were the general principles by which Craig was guided in working on this important scene. And when the play was produced, it was indeed through Hamlet's eyes that the audience saw the court, shown as a vile, luxurious world. The stage was divided into two parts; at the back, the King and Queen sat on a high throne, and from their shoulders a huge golden cloak fell down, its folds spreading over the entire width of the stage. Holes were cut in this gigantic cloak, and through them emerged the heads of courtiers, also dressed in gold, their submissive faces turned towards the sovereign. The lights were dimmed, and the rays of projectors glided over the surface of this degenerate world, striking sinister, menacing glints from the gold cloth. In the foreground sat the black-garbed figure of Hamlet, lost in thought. The whole scene, whose mystic impression appealed greatly to Stanislavsky, was rendered still more expressive by 'piercing fanfares of brass instruments with unbelievable dissonances, which proclaimed to the whole world the criminal greatness and hypocrisy of the King who rose to the throne'. (13) When the time came for the King, the Queen and their attendants to leave the stage, a curtain fell, leaving Hamlet alone in front of it: 'O, that this too too solid flesh would melt, Thaw and resolve itself into a dew!...'

Craig and Stanislavsky pursued their discussion. When Hamlet was on the stage it would be possible to show the world of the tragedy as it appeared to him; but what was to be done, asked Stanislavsky, when Hamlet was not there? To which Craig replied that he would like him to be there the whole time, constantly before the eyes of the audience.

Craig: I want the public to feel the connection between what is going forward on the stage and Hamlet. So that the public should feel as keenly as possible all the horror of Hamlet's position.
Stanislavsky: I would suggest that in the scenes in which Hamlet does not take part we should show the characters not as with the eyes of Hamlet, but realistically, such as they actually are.
Craig: I am afraid that in following out the idea of seeing everything through the eyes of Hamlet we may be pedantically consistent in the execution of this idea. But on the other hand to make the characters realistic is also dangerous. They can at once lose all their symbolism, and then the play may lose very much. . .

Craig came to consider that in the scene between Polonius and Laertes, the hypocrisy of Polonius ought to be emphasized, either by having Ophelia present or by bringing in a sturdy workman to serve as counterpoint to this perverted universe. Stanislavsky replied, 'We have already tried that method, and Meyerhold bases his whole theory on that kind of thing; but we have not achieved any positive results.' Craig was driven to take refuge in the general principles of his art ('I think that as a matter of fact one could act *Hamlet* without the text, but I don't suppose anyone would like it'), and the gulf that separated him from Stanislavsky immediately became apparent:

> *Stanislavsky:* If you preach your ideas all at once you will repulse the public and so hinder the carrying out of your theories in life. Things can only be done very gradually. Christ made the same mistake – he demanded all at once, for which reason people to this day do not understand him.
>
> *Craig:* I don't believe at all in doing things gradually. You can *think* if you like for 2000 years, but you must show what you have thought out *all* at once, and quite clearly and definitely.

While working on *Hamlet* Craig was still meditating upon an art which should strive to go beyond the mere interpretation of written words. He thought the words might be set aside and the tragedy expressed entirely by the actors' movements, enhanced by music. This, observed Stanislavsky, would no longer be Shakespeare's play, but a new art with the theme of *Hamlet* as its starting-point; the idea rather appealed to him:

> *Stanislavsky:* I should be glad to try something of this sort with you some time. Something without words, as I myself hate words.
>
> *Craig:* We should hate not words, but ourselves who make use of words, of this kind of art.

Unfortunately, Stanislavsky did not think that actors capable of carrying out such an experiment were to be found in his company. A few, perhaps, could do it – Knipper, Lilina, Moskvin, himself. But it would be more prudent to divide up the work. For the moment they were dealing with *Hamlet*, and they might consider new forms of art as a side-line. . . . Meanwhile they returned to Shakespeare's play and the analysis of Act I, Scene 2.

This scene depended on the King, who, said Craig, should call
to mind a supra-terrestrial being. Stanislavsky suggested that the
actor should first try to find a realistic mode of expression, and
proceed from there to the abstract idea. Craig accepted this, and
went on to speak of Hamlet himself. The actors must understand
that Hamlet is a spirit sunk in matter, or rather a spirit entirely
surrounded by matter. They must also grasp the fact that Hamlet
is not the weakling he is usually shown to be, but a force. Stanislavsky, who considered that the actor must bring his character to
life from within himself, put in at this point:

> For our purposes it would be better not to speak to the actors of the
> intention of the stage-manager to make a strong Hamlet. Going
> through the whole play psychologically, laying stress on certain
> points in the psychological development, you can arrange these
> points in such harmony and proportion that a strong Hamlet must
> necessarily be produced. . . Otherwise, if you simply tell the actor of
> your intention, he will at once come on the stage with expanded
> chest and strong, theatrical voice.
> *Craig:* Oh! That is awful! You have an even worse opinion of actors
> than I have.
> *Stanislavsky:* I have not at all a bad opinion of actors. There are simply
> stage habits from which it is not so easy to free oneself.

According to Craig, Hamlet's strength is one of the keys to the
play. The prince's tragedy is not due to some kind of weakness, of
uncertain origin, which prevents him from taking action. The
problem, for him, is to decide how he is to avenge himself justly
and for the welfare of Denmark. He is impersonal – therein lies
his tragedy.

As has already been pointed out, Craig felt an affinity with
Hamlet; and for him, the play symbolized his own struggle with
the contemporary theatre:

> I want that between Hamlet and all the rest of the world there should
> not be one single point of agreement, not the smallest hope as to the
> possibility of a reconciliation. I could see in Hamlet the history of the
> theatre. In Hamlet all that is living in the theatre is struggling with
> those dead customs that want to crush the theatre.

It must also be remembered that Craig saw the future history of the theatre as an advance from impersonation and interpretation to representation, and from representation to creation. With *Hamlet* he was in the phase of *representation*. Hence the following statement, in which he departs from the psychological discussion and describes the general style he wishes to impart to his *mise en scène:*

> I should like to play to begin without a curtain – in fact to have no curtain at all. So that the public on coming into the auditorium should have time before the beginning of the play to take in *these new lines*, and this, for them, new appearance of the stage. It would be good also if each scene began by people in special costumes, coming onto the stage, arranging the scenery, seeing to the light and so on; in this way making the audience feel that this is a *performance*.

In confrontation with Stanislavsky, who still adhered rigidly to the principles of 'realistic illusion', Craig was suggesting a performance based on stylization and recognized as such. This was no doubt the fundamental reason for their failure to agree. It was also Craig's contribution to the future Russian theatre, to the work of Meyerhold, Tairov and Vakhtangov. In Craig's production of *Hamlet* two of the Arts Theatre's young students, Vakhtangov and Serafina Bierman, were among the courtiers who looked out from the vast folds of the golden cloak in Scene 2. 'The two young people *understood* (perhaps even better than did Stanislavsky) my aims for a Theatre to serve drama greatly, and they were most faithful and remembered and carried on the ideas I gave and thus they became famous and made famous their theatres.' (14)

*

A week later Stanislavsky and Craig began discussing Act I, Scene 3, between Laertes, Polonius and Ophelia. (15) If this discussion is considered in isolation Craig's ideas may seem paradoxical; but taken in conjunction with the talks about the previous scene they will be found to fit into a general conception of the tragedy which, though surprising at times, is perfectly consistent.

In Craig's opinion, Act I, Scene 3 was unimportant, and should be played lightly, so as not to hold the attention unnecessarily. He admired the Italians for the mastery with which they slip through passages which contain nothing essential – speaking the lines without stress. They do them as lightly and agreeably as if they were playing ball, he said, adding that this saves the audience from unnecessary strain, so that they are able to react more strongly to important passages.

In this scene Polonius, Laertes and Ophelia are perceived to be linked by a bond of stupidity and servility.

Craig: The scene takes place in the family of Polonius. I want this family to be distinct from all that has gone before. Laertes, in the essence, nothing but a little Polonius.

Stanislavsky: In what way must this family be different? It must be unsympathetic?

Craig: Yes; the family is unbusinesslike – stupid.

Stanislavsky: And Ophelia?

Craig: I am afraid so. She must be stupid and beautiful at the same time. There's the difficulty.

Stanislavsky: She must be a negative type, or a decided one?

Craig: I should rather say she must be indefinite.

Stanislavsky: Are you not afraid that the public, which is accustomed to see Ophelia as a sympathetic character, when it sees her stupid and unpleasant will say that the theatre has disfigured Ophelia? Must we not be a little careful?

Craig: Yes. I know.

Stanislavsky: Perhaps on the stage it would be more tactful to make her on the whole sympathetic and nice, but in some places to show her stupid. Would *that* do?

Craig: Ye-es. But I think that she, and the whole family, especially in this scene, are awfully worthless. And only when she begins to go mad does she become more definite. All the advice which Laertes and her father give Ophelia shows their extraordinary lowness of character.

Craig's interpretation was not that of Stanislavsky nor that of the critic Bielinsky, and Stanislavsky was afraid the public would think it mistaken. But Craig cared nothing for preconceived ideas. A year later he wrote in his *Daybook II:* 'Shakespeare all the world over, not in England alone, has become the property of every one and we who would play him, we actors and *régisseurs*, are not allowed to interpret him in our own way, but are expected to interpret him in a hundred ways to suit the "tastes" of the hundred different "owners" of Shakespeare.' (16) Craig claims the right to show the play as he sees it; and as though to cut short a discussion which threatened to end in a deadlock, he answered Stanislavsky's query 'But how does Shakespeare look at Ophelia?' by saying 'I think, as I do.' Moreover, while the Russian critic Bielinsky sees Ophelia as 'a somewhat middle-class creature, but gentle, capable even of dying, but incapable of any sort of protest or active measure', (17) Samuel Johnson considered, according to Craig, that 'from the very beginning, from her childhood, she is rather stupid'. (18)

This astonishes Stanislavsky, who protests:

Stanislavsky: If Hamlet throws over a fool it is not interesting, but if he has so gone off into the clouds that he throws up a beautiful, pure girl – then there is a tragedy.
Craig: I don't see it. She is a miserable little creature.
Stanislavsky: But why did he love her?
Craig: He loved only his imagination. An imaginary woman.

This left the problem of how the character was to be acted. Craig saw no action in this scene, nothing but conversation. So there should be as little movement as possible: '. . . Do you not see Ophelia here with various affectations, crying without any special internal emotion – but standing in one place without unnecessary movements, not moving?'

Stanislavsky could think of no actress capable of playing the part in this way. It would need genius. Craig counters this with a question that illustrates his conception clearly:

Craig: Which of your actresses has the most *sense of humour*?
Stanislavsky: I think Mrs Lilina; it seems so to me.
Craig: I think she could solve this problem.

The actress is to interpret Ophelia by holding aloof from her, not by reconstructing her from inside. Humour was a characteristic of the *Über-marionette*, too. Once again the contrast between Craig and Stanislavsky rose to the surface:

> *Craig:* In Shakespeare there are no feelings or moods whatever which one must read between the lines. He is too clear. In modern plays the mood generally makes itself felt not so much by the words themselves, as by what there is between the lines; but in Shakespeare it makes itself felt before all and entirely by the actual words.
> *Stanislavsky:* Yes, but one must know how to make the words heard.
> *Craig:* It is to that end that I give such simple scenery. And I should like the movements also to be simple and few in number.

And Craig concludes by describing the style of acting he considers necessary in a production of *Hamlet*:

> ... I should like the actors to understand that the performing of Shakespeare does not demand great variation of pose or movement. Shakespeare's ideas are in the words. To translate them into movement, into acting, is only possible on one condition, that there should be as little as possible of this acting and movement.

*

Despite their differences, however, Stanislavsky's belief in Craig was unimpaired. In May 1909 he wrote to Madame Gurevich:

> Not only have we not grown disappointed in Craig, but we are now convinced that he is a man of genius. The entire theatre has been placed at his disposal, and I myself, as his closest assistant, have put myself entirely at his command, and I am proud of it. It will take a long time before even a few people begin to understand Craig, for he is half a century ahead of us all. He is a fine poet and a wonderful artist – a producer of the most refined taste and knowledge. (20)

While Stanislavsky set to work on his production of Turgenev's *A Month in the Country*, in which he applied his 'system' for the first time, (21) Craig returned to Florence, to his studio in the Arena Goldoni, where he settled down to make his models for the *Hamlet* scenes, using his screens, working out his *mise en scène* as he went along. On 5 September he wrote to Stanislavsky as follows:

... I hope your carpenters or mechanics will find some means of being able to make the screens turn easily so that a single leaf at a time can move with the least pressure.

I think that they ought to be making some experiments now with that, for my object in designing this scene is that it shall be able to pass from one shape to another with great ease and that is where your mechanics can greatly assist me.

I believe I have for the last scene of all something that is beautiful, bringing a feeling of the immensity of the creation when compared with the life or death of a single man.

The more I read *Hamlet* over the more I see your figure. *I cannot believe for one moment that anything more than the simplest rendering of this character can ever reach those heights which Shakespeare seems to touch,* and the nearest to those heights that I have seen in the acting in your theatre is your performance in *Onkel Wanja*, and it was this fact which I could not quite express to you in Moscow.

How can there be anything higher or grander than the simplicity with which you treat your roles in the modern plays?

I mean *your* personal acting.

Does not the thought in *Hamlet* develop itself and find its words through precisely the same process as the thought in Tchekov's plays? If there are passages in *Hamlet* in which the words are less simple than in Chekhov, surely there are other passages which are the very essence of simplicity. Because the words are less colloquial are they less simple? It would be horrible if it were so. It would mean that Shakespeare was not a great artist.

How much I would like to see you as *Hamlet* I cannot possibly tell you. I can conceive no more ideal thing on the stage and each time that I think of the play being performed in Moscow I am grieved to think of what the stage will lose without your presence. I am sure Kachalov will be very good indeed and that everyone in Moscow will think so. But I have a deep down conviction which I cannot change that the whole of Europe would be moved and set thinking if they could witness your performance of this part. (22)

Craig worked in a state of exhilaration in Florence, but there were times when he felt that all *mise en scène* was a futile waste of effort. In the last twenty years he had acquired an exhaustive knowledge of stage techniques, and now he wanted to go further, to lay the foundations of the new art of his dreams. This work on

Hamlet, based on ideas he had left behind him, was a waste of time, he felt. The important thing was to learn more, to make fresh discoveries, and he was more than ever obsessed by the thought of a school: 'A college! . . . Masters . . .' (23)

But perhaps *Hamlet* would be a stepping-stone towards the art of his dreams. He went on working.

*

On 28 February 1910 Craig was back in Moscow, and the work was soon in full swing. A large model stage was prepared, with a miniature replica of the lighting system to be used in the production. Craig explained how the screens were to be arranged; there was not to be a succession of scenes, but a single one with a multiplicity of aspects: since there was to be no curtain, the architecture of this scene would be in harmony with that of the auditorium, of which it would form a kind of extension. Arrangements of screens, steps and a very few properties would suggest the place and above all create the atmosphere of each scene with the help of lighting, which Craig used in two ways – by the use of moving projectors to pick out a surface, round an angle, or create a kind of tragic shuddering at moments of climax; and in diffused splashes to colour certain bright or sombre portions of the scene. The light was not intended to give an illusion of reality, but to heighten the tragic expression. (24) Sometimes it fell from above, sometimes it seemed to spring up from the stage, at other times it swept right across it. Instead of a curtain at the end of each scene or act, there would be darkness. Light would be projected onto the gold costumes, making them sparkle into life and sometimes, as the wearers moved, producing the effect of a flowing wave. All this was shown in the rehearsals with the model, attended by Stanislavsky, Sulerjitsky and Mardjanov, the last of whom was responsible for the making of the screens.

During his previous visit to Moscow Craig had held a theoretical discussion with Stanislavsky on each scene, on the characters and on the relations between them. They now passed to the actual course of proceedings on the stage. The chief actors watched as Craig indicated their movements by pushing small wood and cardboard figures, which he had made himself, about the model scene with a long stick. He also explained the tone to be adopted. This was often difficult, as it had to be done through an interpreter. Craig wanted the actors to work as though this were a game, without allowing themselves to be paralysed by thinking too much. Faithful to his idealistic conception, he kept telling them that the tragedy of *Hamlet* represented 'the triumph of love' – that Hamlet succeeded in his aim, not through determination, physical strength, wealth or social position, but through the force of his ideal. (25)

These rehearsals took place in the mornings; in the afternoon Craig busied himself with the costumes. In designing them he had very soon departed from his original models (which included the Bayeux tapestry, the Ravenna mosaics, and Viollet le Duc). Working with the dressmakers, he selected heavy materials that would fall into sculpturesque folds, and tested them over and over again.

By the time Craig left Moscow, on 4 May, everything had been settled. It was left to Stanislavsky, Sulerjitsky and their assistants to carry out the decisions reached. . . .

*

Stanislavsky fell seriously ill, work on *Hamlet* was interrupted, and as a result the date of the first performance had to be considerably postponed.

When the work was at last resumed, difficulties began to arise, both in finance and in the matter of acting.

In a letter dated 21 June – 4 July 1910, Stanislavsky writes to Craig about the financial and technical difficulties encountered by the Arts Theatre in making the costumes:

You desire a simple, natural cut, that will give a simple, natural, beautiful sculpturesque line and good sculptural folds that can be well lighted on the stage and will harmonize with the simplicity of the lines of the screens. But everything that is exquisitely simple is always difficult to find. We have tried all the cuts and all the fashions that you gave us, and a lot of our own. But these thin, fine shop stuffs cannot express anything at all. All the costumes hang like dressing gowns or shirts. There is scarcely any difference between them, they are all like each other, and not one of these cuts, as we have got them on our models, has that simple, artistic *cachet* that should show on every real work of art. All these costumes when worn by supernumeraries seem shabby, uninteresting and quite the opposite of exquisite, although all the cuts and drawings have been carefully studied and their essential part fully understood. In some cases we used our own imagination, we made use of different accidental ideas. But in spite of all that, the costumes are shabby, uninteresting. I tried to rake up my memory, I reread carefully all that concerned these costumes and their time, and finally I came to the conclusion that a great many of the cuts you have selected are intended to be made out of very thick and dense materials, that give on the drawings such beautiful and deep folds. (26)

Craig had asked for just such heavy materials as long ago as 10 May 1909, at a working session with Stanislavsky and Suler-jitsky! (27)

So far as the lighting was concerned, all seemed to be well. A group of visible projectors had been hung in front of the pros-cenium arch, above the front rows of stalls. Special apparatus had been ordered, and Stanislavsky had even sent Mardjanov to Berlin with letters of introduction; *Hamlet* would certainly have the benefit of the newest and best stage lighting. (28)

But the screens were a problem. 'What a tremendous distance there is,' Stanislavsky observes in *My Life in Art*, 'between the dream of an artist or a stage director and its realization upon the stage!' Unlike the general run of Craig's detractors, he does not, however, accuse him of having impracticable ideas. He blames the stage equipment, which was still coarse and primitive in comparison with technical advances in other spheres. (29) With our present-day materials and stage machinery, the construction and manipulation of the screens would no longer raise insoluble problems.

Craig, with his detestation of painted scenery and artificiality, would have liked the screens to be made of some natural material, so iron, copper and other metals had been tried. But the weight of such scenes would have required the installation of special electri-cal apparatus. They therefore tried wood and then cork; but with no better results. And Craig had had to resign himself to canvas stretched over wooden frames.

Craig wanted the screens to move before the eyes of the audience, the scene changing in this way without lowering the curtain. This proved impossible and a curtain had to be used after all. But 'what oneness and unison the Craigian manner of shifting the screens would have given to the whole performance!' (30)

The problem of the acting was even more complicated. On 5 March 1910, Craig and Stanislavsky had had a long talk about the art of the actor, during which Stanislavsky had described, in its general lines, what he called his 'system', the ideas he was then hammering into shape. Writing next day in his *Daybook I*, Craig observed that there was certainly something interesting in it all, a theory of acting derived from stage practice and one which deserved attention and respect; but he added that he had put forward some objections, and any reader of his work can imagine what these would be. Craig admired Stanislavsky as an actor, but could not accept his system as a general method. Stanislavsky would do his best to get the actors to interpret Craig's symbolical vision of *Hamlet*, even if he did not entirely approve of it; but in a letter to Craig he says he thinks the best way of achieving this will be to apply his own system: '. . . Kachalov has begun to be interested in the part of Hamlet. In Petersburg I worked a little with him and afterwards in Moscow we went with Mardjanov over his whole part, marked it according to your indications and to my system that you do not yet like, but that answers better than anything to your purpose.' (31) However, Stanislavsky had not yet finished working out his theory, and was meeting with considerable resistance from his own actors.

In such circumstances, how could the acting be expected to come up to Craig's standards? At the end of December 1911, when he returned to Moscow for the final rehearsals and to put the finishing touches to the lighting, he could only register disagreement. He would have none of the usual 'theatrical' style of acting, and he was equally hostile to the direct and prosaic expression of feeling. And what did he see here? The same thing as Stanislavsky, who writes: 'There was no noble simplicity, no grand assurance, no masterly restraint. There were no sonorous voices and beautiful speech, harmonic movement and plastics. But there was that which we feared most of all – either the usual theatrical pathos or the other pole, a very tiresome, heavy and prosaic living over of the parts.' (32) Stanislavsky discovered yet again that while he had managed to devise a style of speaking which would do well enough for contemporary plays, as soon as verse was attempted the actors fell out of step with him and lapsed into declamation.

In an attempt to clear up the difficulty, Stanislavsky acted some passages from his own roles before Craig, using different methods – the conventional French manner, the German, the Italian, the Russian declamatory, the Russian realistic, the impressionistic method. None of this was to Craig's liking.

> With all his strength he protested on the one hand against the old conventionality of the theatre, and on the other hand he would not accept the humdrum naturalness and simplicity which robbed my interpretations of all poetry. Craig wanted perfection, the ideal, that is, simple, strong, deep, uplifting, artistic and beautiful expression of living human emotion. (33)

*

But at last the day came: on 8 January 1912 the curtain of the Arts Theatre rose for the first performance of *Hamlet*. It was a great success. The audience called for Craig after the Play Scene, and at the end of the performance he had to come before the curtain again, with Stanislavsky and Kachalov.

Nevertheless there were vigorous protests in some of the Russian papers: *Golos Moskvy* referred to sterilizing stylization and *Utro Rossii*'s reviewer found the screens dull. But *Ryetsh* praised the taste demonstrated throughout the production, the Moscow University paper spoke of felicitous innovations, and the foremost Moscow newspaper, *Russkoye Slovo*, called it 'the most tremendous event in present-day stage art'.

The Times sent a special correspondent, who described the work of his exiled compatriot as follows:

> . . . Every scene in the *Hamlet* has for its foundation an arrangement of screens which rise to the full height of the proscenium and consist of plain panels, devoid of any decoration. Only two colours are used – a neutral cream shade and gold. . . .

Mr Craig has the singular power of carrying the spiritual significance of words and dramatic situations beyond the actor to the scene in which he moves. By the simplest of means he is able in some mysterious way to evoke almost any sensation of time or space, the scenes even in themselves suggesting variations of human emotions. . . .

. . . the production is a remarkable triumph for Mr Craig, and it is impossible to say how wide an effect such a completely realized success of his theories may have on the theatre of Europe. . . . (34)

Craig and Stanislavsky were less enthusiastic. The production had not fulfilled their hopes. Yet Stanislavsky, whose admiration for Craig had never flagged even at the most difficult moments of their work together, gives warm praise in his memoirs to the beauty of *Hamlet*, its 'unforgettable' scenes, such as the Court Scene in Act I, the scene of the players' arrival, the Play Scene, the 'mousetrap', and the final scene.

The arrival of the players, in their brilliant costumes, their theatrical entry to the sound of flutes, oboes, piccolos and drums, symbolized for Craig, seeing them through Hamlet's eyes, everything that was joyful in the art of the theatre. When they appear, the Prince recovers the zest that had been his before his father's death; amid all the grief and perversion of court life, he experiences a few moments of the marvellous, exhilarating happiness that art can confer.

Craig's art broke forth in its full splendour in the Play Scene. As in the Court Scene in Act I, the stage was divided into two parts, front and back of the trap. The front portion was arranged as a stage for the 'players', flanked by two great pillars. At the back was a raised throne where the King and Queen took their seats, with a row of courtiers on either side. The King, the Queen and their suite were all dressed in gold; they looked like bronze statues in the dim light, swept from time to time by the ray of a projector which lighted on one or another of the costumes so that it shimmered with a sinister gleam. The actors, in their gaudy clothes, stood in a blaze of light, with their backs to the audience, performing the murder of Gonzago, while Hamlet and Horatio kept watch from behind the pillars. The King began to tremble, Hamlet bounded forward like a tiger and, amid the general turmoil, rushed after the murderer, who ran across the forestage in the full blaze of the lights. The King's guilt was made manifest to all.

In the final scene, against a background of spears and banners with the gold screens behind them, Fortinbras approached

> like an archangel, mounting the throne at whose foot lay the bodies of the King and Queen; the solemn and triumphant sounds of a soul-gripping funeral march; the slowly descending, gigantic banners that covered the black body of Hamlet with their white folds, showing only the dead and happy face of the great cleanser of the earth who had at last found the secrets of life on earth in the arms of death. So did Craig picture the Court that had become Hamlet's Golgotha. (35)

But this beauty was not enough to content Stanislavsky; he was dissatisfied. In the first place with himself, because he had not been able to show Craig and his work as he wanted to show him: the Arts Theatre had failed to carry out the ideas of an admired guest. In the second place because he had hoped that this production would serve to guide him in his own research, whereas it had merely added to his perplexities. They had tried to make the *mise en scène* of *Hamlet* as simple as possible; yet it seemed to him to be grandiose and affected, the last thing Craig had wanted. Again, Stanislavsky, when trying to devise a style of acting suitable for Shakespeare, had decided – contrary to Craig's opinion – that his own 'system' was better for the purpose than any other method. He was now forced to recognize that it had failed.

> The actors of the Arts Theatre who had learnt to a certain extent the methods of the new inner technique, used them with some degree of success in the plays of our modern repertoire which were near to their own lives. Apparently it still lay before us to go through the same work and to find analogical methods and means for plays in the heroic and the grand style. When *Hamlet* was first produced by us, our Theatre had not yet begun its quest in that direction. (36)

So he reverted to psychological realism, without having discovered the solution of the 'Shakespeare problem'. The production of *Hamlet* did not change the current of his own thoughts, but it was to have a lasting influence on all those who tried to go further than he.

Craig, who left Moscow on 28 January 1912, was not satisfied either. In 1926, when Johannes Poulsen invited him to Copenhagen, asking him to design the scenes and costumes for Ibsen's *Pretenders* and to co-operate in the *mise en scène*, he agreed, but told Poulsen: 'Remember it is almost 15 years since I did any work inside a theatre. The experience in Moscow decided me to wait until I should possess my own theatre. . . .' (37)

And when anyone asks Craig nowadays which of his productions he considers to have been the best and most complete, it is those of 1900–1903 that he mentions, not *Hamlet*. In *Hamlet* his intentions were not accurately carried out. For technical reasons a number of scenes were altered, particularly that of Ophelia's burial, and some of his stage directions were changed. As for the acting, it of course fell short of the perfection he was aiming at.

Why did he elect to stage *Hamlet* at the Arts Theatre, despite his conviction that it was impossible? From a desire to rise to a challenge, to work again on a stage, to please his friends, to accept Stanislavsky's invitation?

I chose *Hamlet* as it is of all modern plays the most inspired, the most literary, the most dramatic, the most picturesque. As a mixture of literature, drama and picture represents our modern idea of the Art of the Theatre it is therefore the most representative example of *modern* theatrical art. Added to these reasons I chose it because I had long known the figure of Hamlet, had acted the role myself, and wished once more to test my theory that the Shakespearean play does not naturally belong to our art of the theatre. (38)

His previous opinion had now been confirmed. More than ever he felt it necessary to pursue the search for the art at which he was aiming and to establish his school. When he produced *Hamlet* in Moscow he hoped the Arts Theatre might help him towards this. He even wrote to Stanislavsky, on 20 February 1911:

Will you give me my school in Florence?
If you will do so:
I will give you and demonstrate to you within a year

(1) the principles of movement of the human body –

(2) within two years I will give you and demonstrate to you the principles of movement on the scene of single figures and of massed groups of figures –

(3) and within three years I will give you the whole principle governing action, scene and voice;

(4) after that I will give you the principles of improvisation or spontaneous acting with and without words.

Will you do this for me that I may do this for you? (39)

Craig's innumerable ideas about his proposed school doubtless influenced Stanislavsky in founding his Moscow Arts Theatre Studios, the first of which was set up in 1911, with Sulerjitsky as its director.

As for Craig, he still had no school – for the time being.

His vision of *Hamlet* found expression in the woodcuts he made for an edition of the play, now being planned by Count Kessler.(40)

He went on with his research work, as before, in his studio at the Arena Goldoni, where his school would come into existence at long last.

NOTES

1. See the essay, 'Shakespeare's Plays', in *The Mask*, Vol. I, No. 7, September 1908, pp. 142–3 – reprinted in *On the Art of the Theatre*, op. cit., pp. 281–5.

2. Unpublished letter, now in the Museum of the Moscow Arts Theatre.

3. Quoted by David Magarshak, *Stanislavsky. A Life*, London, MacGibbon & Kee, 1950, p. 294.

4. Quoted by Nina Gourfinkel, *Constantin Stanislavski*, Collection 'Le Théâtre et les Jours', L'Arche, Paris, 1955, p. 126.

5. Letter published in *The Mask*, Vol. I, No. 11, January 1909, pp. 221–2, under the heading 'The Theatre in Germany, Holland, Russia and England – A Series of Letters from Gordon Craig', and reprinted in *On the Art of the Theatre*, op. cit., pp. 125–36.

6. *Daybook I.*

7. *Daybook I*, p. 139.

8. *Hamlet*, E.G.C.'s annotated copy. Gordon Craig Collection, Bibliothèque de l'Arsenal, Paris.

9. The *Evening Standard*, 6 December 1911.

10. Stanislavsky, *My Life in Art*, translated by J. J. Robbins, Geoffrey Bles, London, Theatre Arts Books, New York, Fourth edition, 1945, p. 514.

11. See 'Hamlet in Moscow. Notes for a short Address to the Actors of the Moscow Arts Theatre, by Gordon Craig', *The Mask*, Vol. VII, No. 2, May 1915, pp. 109–15.

12. The Gordon Craig Collection at the Bibliothèque de l'Arsenal contains the stenographic record of the talks between Craig and Stanislavsky on the following scenes: Act I, Scene 2 (St Petersburg, 16 April 1909); Act I, Scene 3 (24 April 1909); Act III, Scene 2. It is from this record that I have quoted the passages, hitherto unpublished, from the discussion of Act I, Scene 2.

13. Stanislavsky, *My Life in Art*, p. 515. The incidental music for *Hamlet* was composed by Ilia Sats.

14. This note, together with a sketch for Act I, Scene 2, is in the Gordon Craig Collection at the Bibliothèque de l'Arsenal.

15. The Russian stenographic record of this discussion (on Act I, Scene 3), which took place on 24 April 1909, was published in the *Annuaire du Théâtre Artistique de Moscou*, Vol. I (1944).

16. *Daybook II, March 1910 to December 1911* E.G.C., p. 15. Gordon Craig's private collection.

17. According to Stanislavsky, in conversation with Craig.

18. According to Craig.

19. Ophelia was not played by Stanislavsky's wife, Lilina, but by a young actress, O. V. Gzovskaya.

20. Quoted by David Magarshak, *Stanislavsky. A Life*, pp. 294–5.

21. Space forbids any description of Stanislavsky's 'system' here. It is excellently described by Nina Gourfinkel in her book on Stanislavsky, op. cit.

22. Unpublished letter, now in the Museum of the Moscow Arts Theatre. The role of Hamlet was played by Katchalov, not Stanislavsky.

23. *Daybook I*, 18 September 1909.

24. *Hamlet*, E.G.C.'s annotated copy, 1909, Gordon Craig Collection, Bibliothèque de l'Arsenal, Paris.

25. A summary of Craig's observations to the actors in his *Daybook II*.

26. Letter in the Gordon Craig Collection, Bibliothèque de l'Arsenal, Paris.

27. The stenographic record (in indirect speech) of this discussion is in the Gordon Craig Collection, Bibliothèque de l'Arsenal.

28. See Stanislavsky's letter to Craig, 21 June – 4 July 1910.

29. Stanislavsky, *My Life in Art*, pp. 519 et seq.

30. Ibid., p. 522.

31. Stanislavsky's letter to Craig, 21 June – 4 July 1910, already quoted.

32. Stanislavsky, *My Life in Art*, p. 522.

33. Ibid., p. 523.

34. *The Times*, 9 January 1912.

35. Stanislavsky, *My Life in Art*, p. 517.

36. Ibid., p. 524.

37. Letter of 29 August 1926, quoted by Craig in *A Production, being thirty-two*

collotype plates of designs projected or realised for The Pretenders *of Henrik Ibsen. And produced at the Royal Theatre Copenhagen 1926, by Edward Gordon Craig,* Oxford University Press, London, Humphrey Milford, 1930, p. 5.

38. Gordon Craig, in *City of Manchester Art Gallery. Exhibition of drawings and models for Hamlet, Macbeth, The Vikings and other plays, by Edward Gordon Craig,* 1912, op. cit., p. 22.

39. Letter now in the Museum of the Moscow Arts Theatre.

40. It was at the beginning of February 1912, when Craig went through Paris on his way back from Moscow, that Count Kessler suggested the idea of this edition of *Hamlet* to him.

IX

THE SCHOOL

Craig spent the summer of 1911 in London. On 16 July, six months before the first performance of *Hamlet*, his friends and admirers arranged a dinner in his honour at the Café Royal. The members of the committee which sent out the invitations included Lady Gregory, Max Beerbohm, Walter Crane, Martin Harvey, William Rothenstein, H. G. Wells, W. B. Yeats and James Pryde. Some two hundred of Craig's supporters thronged to this dinner; writers, painters and musicians formed the majority, there were not many theatre people.

The chairman was William Rothenstein, who had been one of Craig's earliest champions. Messages were read (1) from Yvette Guilbert, Granville Barker, the Hungarian stage director Alexander Hevesi, Jan C. de Vos, stage manager of the Dutch State Theatre at Amsterdam, and the American theatre historian Percy MacKaye. The Moscow Arts Theatre was represented by its Secretary, Michael Lykiardopoulos, who expressed the Theatre's pride at having been the first to offer Craig an opportunity of carrying out his ideas. Stanislavsky sent a personal message of congratulation and good wishes from Moscow. At last Craig was gaining recognition as a prophet, not only in foreign countries but in his own, where his fame was spreading rapidly. In September an exhibition of his designs, chiefly for *Macbeth*, was held at the Leicester Galleries. He gave lectures to explain the intention of his screens and the way they should be used. At the end of the year, Heinemann published his most famous book, *On the Art of the Theatre*, comprising the two dialogues – the first from *The Art of the Theatre*, the second from *The Mask* – and the most important of the essays he had published in *The Mask*. But more than ever, his school was in the forefront of Craig's thoughts. He spoke of it in interviews (*The Observer* of 23 July, the *Evening Times* of 8 August, the *Daily Mail* of 30 August, the *Weekly Scotsman* of 28 October) and wrote a long article about it, setting forth his plans, in the October number of the *English Review*. (2)

As soon as he got back from Moscow after the opening of *Hamlet*, Craig decided to form an International Committee including members from England (Ellen Terry, Walter Crane, Laurence Binyon, E. K. Chambers, J. L. Garvin, Augustus John, Gilbert Murray, Ralph Vaughan Williams, etc.), Ireland (W. B. Yeats, Lord Dunsany), Hungary (Alexander Hevesi), Russia (Baltruschaitis, Sergius Poliakoff, etc.), Germany (Count Kessler, Henry Van de Velde), Italy (Salvini, Count Carlo Placci, etc.), Japan, Holland, Finland and France (Yvette Guilbert, Sarah Bernhardt, Jacques Doucet, Jacques Rouché, etc.) He still had to raise funds with which to pay for premises, equipment and salaries. After approaching a number of people he succeeded, thanks to the untiring and effective help of Elena Meo, in persuading a wealthy patron of the arts, Lord Howard de Walden, to promise a subsidy of £5,000 for the first year and £2,500 a year for the three succeeding years. On 27 February 1913 – Ellen Terry's birthday – Craig announced the foundation of his school. It was not to be in London, as had been planned at first, but in Florence, where the Arena Goldoni provided an ideal experimental stage. For the school was not to confine itself to theoretical teaching; Craig wanted to create a working laboratory exercising a living influence in the present and laying down firm foundations for future workers to build upon.

The theatre was sick. Its workers were impelled by self-interest rather than by the love of art. So-called reforms were never thorough. A half-hearted pursuit of cheap effects was to be found everywhere, with one production after another resorting to a confused jumble of so-called innovations. Before there had been time to test a theory, some half-baked application of it would be thrust before an easily dazzled public. The theatre was a game, of course, but it was a serious game, the rules of which should be learnt and punctiliously obeyed; like all art, it was a branch of sport – and it needed sportsmen.

It needed craftsmen too, for it was meant for the people. It needed 'constructors – builders – craftsmen'. The tours organized by the famous impresarios of Russia and Germany might produce

'Napoleonic' triumphs, but it was not 'conquerors' that were needed, and the theatre must build on none but sure foundations.

Sportsmen and *craftsmen* (3) were what Craig wanted for his School. Its purpose was to develop creative ability, not the faculty of imitation. It would be a place for painstaking research, removed from the disturbing presence of the public, not subjected to the pressure of everyday theatrical activity. The School for the Art of the Theatre would provide opportunity for trying out ideas and making experiments of all kinds, the results of which would be passed on to the theatres of Europe and America.

In accordance with the theories upheld in *The Mask*, the School would not confine itself to any one branch of the art of the theatre (scene, costume, acting), but would embrace them all. Nor would it restrict its interest to any particular type of play: melodrama, mime, farce, would all receive attention. The School would study the past – the great source of tradition – the present, with its demand for immediate improvements, and the future, which would witness the birth of the new theatre.

In March 1913 a prospectus (4) was sent out, describing the organization of the School. At the beginning of this prospectus is a quotation from Nietzsche's *The Will to Power*, where he declares that the most desirable thing under all circumstances is discipline, which makes the soldier and the scholar efficient. The true scholar should have the true soldier's capacity to obey and yet to be ready at any moment to take the lead.

Craig soon drew up rules to ensure this strict discipline, and every student admitted to the School undertook to obey them. (5) No student must work outside the School except by special permission of the Director. Every student must keep a book in which to enter notes and comments on each day's work. There must be strict obedience to the authorities, without hesitation or argument. Students must be persevering, hard-working, obedient and absolutely discreet. No student must talk about the School's work to outsiders. ' "I do not know" is the one reply to make to the inquisitive, and for relations the best answer is, "When results are to be seen you shall be the first to see them." '

Craig intended to retain complete authority over the School:

The School is under the sole direction of Mr Edward Gordon Craig. It will aim at doing, and revealing the means of doing, what is left undone by the modern Theatre. It will aim at infusing the life of imagination into every Art and Craft connected with the stage, so that fresh vigour will be given to the creative powers of those actively connected with the drama.

It will consist of two separate bodies of earnest and thorough workers who, inspired by Mr Craig and building with him upon the foundations of his past work, will strive by means of experiment and research to rediscover and re-create some of the elemental principles of beauty, in a department of the art-world from which at present they are conspicuously absent.

The School was thus to comprise two divisions, differently composed and with different aims and activities. The First Division was to consist of fifteen or twenty salaried experimental workers (architects, painters, musicians, electricians, photographers, carpenters, model makers, etc.) selected by Craig himself; they would work with him, study his methods, and act as his assistants in his *mises en scène*. From them would be chosen the staff for teaching the Second Division.

This Second Division, not included in the original plan, would consist of about thirty paying students, who must have received a good general education. Those who showed special aptitude and talent would move up later to the higher Division. There would be a wide range of subjects for study – movement, gymnastics, voice training, music, speech, drawing, scene designing and painting, costume designing and making, modelling, fencing, dancing, mimodrama, improvisation, stage-managing, lighting, history of the theatre, marionette designing, making and performing, model making, and the Italian language.

This list of subjects is revealing. For instance, it may seem surprising to find no mention of acting, or of the psychological study of roles. Did this mean that Craig had given up all idea of training actors, and intended to create only a kind of allegorical theatre? The fact was that, like Ellen Terry, he considered that 'acting' could not be taught. All that could be done was to teach students the basic techniques of the dramatic performance – movement and diction: how to get from one side of the stage to the other, how to use arms, legs, torso and facial muscles with expression.

> . . . You can even be taught how to move your soul – or rather, how to allow your soul to move you – but this is still not acting. That comes under the heading of movement. Then you can be taught how to produce your voice so that it reaches to every part of the building and into the soul of the listener. You can be taught how not to speak; but all this is not acting, it is speaking. (6)

As we have seen from the beginning, Craig attached the utmost importance to movement, with which he considered the theatre had originated. He wanted the students at his School to make a thorough study of different kinds of movement – the movements of the human body, the movement of trees, wind, water, fishes, reptiles, birds – analysing and comparing them, noting resemblances and differences, and deducing principles from them. In discovering the principles of the movement of beings and of things, which is harmony, man would discover a new language and the laws governing it and could thus, with nature as his point of departure, rediscover the forgotten laws of perfect artistic expression.

Hence the importance of mime in the curriculum at the Arena Goldoni. Once a week, said Craig, he would send out some of his students into different parts of the town. When they came back, a few hours later, they would tell him what they had seen, and each of them would mime some 'dramatic' incident that had made an impression on him. 'Here you have an opportunity for the employment both of creative and mimetic talent. You see, I have a very firm faith in mimodrama, and I intend to offer my pupils all scope for its cultivation and display. . . .' (7)

Craig declared emphatically that he did not want to turn his pupils into parrots, but to help them to develop their powers of creative invention by building on their imagination and intelligence. This was why improvisation took such a prominent place in the curriculum. Since writing *The Actor and the Über-marionette* Craig had discovered the Italian theatre and studied its history. *The Mask* had published numerous studies of this subject, including a series of articles by Dr Michele Scherillo on the Commedia dell'

Arte – pure dramatic creation, a fount of invention, a theatre completely untrammelled by literature. In a period when improvisation was universally despised, Craig brought a reminder of Riccoboni's assertion that the actor who improvised was a finer artist than he who played a part which he had learnt by heart. This art, like everything that looks easy, required patient, methodical study; the actor must bring to it imagination, intelligence and a resourceful tongue. The study of the art of improvisation was more than ever necessary, for it would help towards the regeneration of the theatre. Craig's advocacy of improvisation was by no means inconsistent with the theories he had expressed in *The Actor and the Über-marionette*, for the actor who improvises is no longer an imitator, he becomes a creator. (8)

Another feature of the School's programme was the attention devoted to handicrafts – modelling, scene-painting, and the making of costumes, marionettes and models. Craig omitted none of the theatre's practical requirements, no branch of its craftsmanship, for he thought that through these, likewise, forgotten techniques could be brought to light and revived, that they could give occasion for experimenting with methods and processes. Though first and foremost an art, the theatre was none the less a craft, and neglect of this aspect could result in nothing better than second-rate amateurishness.

Lastly, Craig attached particular importance to the history of the theatre. His pupils were to work like archaeologists, studying all types of theatre including those of past centuries and of distant countries, and all forms of theatre architecture, the aspects and rules of which they would analyse by constructing models. Without becoming obsessed with the past, or resorting to mere imitation, they must seek out any traditions that still had something to offer.

The history and techniques of the theatre figured prominently in *The Mask* from the outset, and even more so after the first world war. Craig also thought the School should have as part of its working equipment a museum, to which he would present his collection of books, documents and rare items – masks from the Congo and Liberia, Burmese and Javanese marionettes, masks from India, Java and Japan, documents of the greatest rarity, early editions of Terence and Ruzzante, of Andreini, Vecellio and Riccoboni, Gherardi and Furtenbach, etc.

*

At the end of March 1913 Craig went back to Florence, where his first assistants came from England to join him at the beginning of April. He did not intend to take paying pupils for the first year. The stage of the Arena Goldoni was fully equipped, but everything else had to be organized. In the rest of the building they set up workshops for carpentry, wood-carving, photography, mechanics, and installed the library. Two months later a mixed Anglo-Italian team of about twenty members – designers, model-makers, joiners, electricians, etc. – began a programme of studies interrupted on Sundays by expeditions into the Tuscan countryside in a black-and-yellow stage coach which Craig had bought for a song so as to provide his assistants with opportunities for shared leisure.

Many visitors came to see what was being done, including Frans Mijnssen, the Dutch writer and critic, the Russian actor Leonidov, André Gide, Lugné-Poe and Suzanne Després. Yeats was tempted to join the young artists working under his friend's leadership, but Craig discouraged this suggestion:

My school is not for the likes of you, I fear. You could learn nothing there. What you've learnt you've learnt already – and how much you have learnt about the theatre is positively appalling. Now we shall learn from you about fairies and red dogs. My school will lead me and all of us in a place right out of the theatre – right out and sprawl us on some queer shore . . . (9)

On 9 August 1913 Craig wrote to Jacques Doucet to tell him how things were going, and sent him a copy of *A Living Theatre* and some photographs of the School. The work would take a long time, but it was wonderful to have made a start. The experimental work was benefiting considerably by being done in the open air; this was the best way of getting rid of the stifling class-room atmosphere and freshened the pupils' minds at the same time as giving them a feeling of adventure. The first term's work had

consisted chiefly of putting things in order, and it was preferable
to go on at a natural pace, better too slowly than too hastily.

If, and when, you come, [Craig continues] you must also let us take
you for a ride in our coach. It is as elegant as any coach that ever drove
down the Champs Elysées, and it is a miracle that it fell into my hands.
I do not think that another School in the world possesses a coach.
They would say it was a luxury; but considering the price we paid
for it, and the joy the men and women get out of it, I consider that
it was a necessity. Another thing which I do not think that any other
School possesses is an open-air theatre of such surprising beauty; but
its full beauty can only be known when you enter it.
The noise of the street is left behind, and the quiet combined with the
steady curves and the light from above has a quality that I am inclined
to call mystic. I have no idea what 'mysticism' may be, and there is
too much nonsense written about it today, but if to experience
beauty and not merely to *see* it is Mysticism, then this place can be
called the most mystic of places. . . .
To have done that in so fabulous an age as this, when Hippogriffs sit
at counters and Basilisks bask in the Champs Elysées – while Chimaeras
sit in circles in the Chambers of Deputies of the different Nations . . .
To have done this against these preposterous and almost ludicrous
odds – will at all events have been amusing.
                    Yours cordially,
                    Gordon Craig. (10)

In 1914 Craig and his assistants built a model for his 'Platonic
Theatre' project and added to the one he had given to Yeats. Then
they made *Model A*, with its miniature stage, its own screens and
extra pieces (doors, steps, windows, tables, thrones, etc.). Nocentini
constructed the model, Caprile and Palai carved the extra pieces,
Brown planned and installed the lighting system. The various
models were photographed; show-cases were made for the
museum, and its treasures catalogued; new lighting equipment
was invented and tested; and an exhibition of Craig's designs was
arranged in London, the proceeds to go into the School funds.(11)
Most important of all, Craig was working on his plans for the
mise en scène of Bach's *St Matthew Passion*, while his assistants
constructed a model from the designs he had made for it.

                    *

To produce Bach's *Passion* – Craig had dreamt of this ever since August 1900, when Martin Shaw had introduced him to the music ('He would play this music, which enchanted me so much, and explain as he played, and I would draw as I fancied on the white wall') – he drew in black and red chalk, and the drawing spread till it was as large as a fresco. (12) In the following year he made his first design on paper – an amphitheatre in some Mediterranean town, the left side of which is a tangle of planks and baulks of timber (Plate 22). In April 1906 he went with Isadora Duncan to hear Bach's *St John Passion* in the Koepelkirk at Amsterdam. What moved him was not so much the subject as the music, which seemed to him 'to be more than all the great sermons of the world by priests, by saints or by writers'. (13) On 29 January 1907, back again at Amsterdam, he went alone among an immense crowd to listen to the *St Matthew Passion*, given by soloists, choirs and orchestra. This time he felt that 'something might be added' to the work in the way of dramatic representation. 'But that "something" was to be very, very little – nothing like one of those Reinhardt performances, with everybody shouting and waving their arms in the air and people catching hold of a man and dragging him away and putting him on a cross. All that would be simply futile.' (14) What Craig meant was a grand but simple performance, to be presented every Easter in a church kept specially for the purpose, 'given under my direction each year until I could no longer do it, and I could pass it to the right person. . . .'

From that time onward, Craig began to assemble material – reproductions of paintings and frescoes by Leonardo da Vinci, Pietro Lorenzetti, Andrea del Castagno, Benozzo Gozzoli, Rembrandt and Fra Angelico, photographs of church interiors, sketches of masks, etc., from which he drew ideas for his architectural designs.

But more than by all this, his work was influenced by a little-known Romanesque church in Ticino, San Nicolao de Giornico, which had some curious architectural features. In August 1910 Craig made some sketches of its interior. This had a chancel raised above a crypt with three aisles which led out from the nave and at a slightly lower level. A double stairway spanned the mouth of the crypt and led up to the altar. The place was a revelation to

Craig; he had never seen a church built in this way. The chancel, the crypt and the floor of the church surely symbolized the Christian universe – heaven, hell and the earth. It was an arrangement reminiscent of the stage for the mystery plays, with its 'mansions'. For Craig, San Nicolao was the most mystic, most human and most beautiful of theatres.

In the spring of 1912 Craig was in Paris, beginning work on his *Hamlet* woodcuts for Kessler's projected edition. On 13 April Maillol came to see him, accompanied by Maurice Denis, the painter, and looked with admiration at his designs, engravings and screens. Next day, Craig visited Maillol in his studio at Marly. They went out together for a walk in the park, where Louis XIV's château once stood, and looked at the scanty traces of its open-air theatre. This, Craig thought, might be a good place to perform the *Passion*. A few days later, Kessler introduced him to Countess Grehfühle, who offered to raise the money to present the *Passion* in Paris. The first thing was to find the right place. They went to look at a number of theatres, and at the Grand-Palais, the vast central space of which would have been wonderful for the purpose. Meanwhile, Craig made a few small designs. The first of these, dated 29 May, was directly inspired by the chancel of San Nicolao (Plate 23A): it showed an upper level, which could be closed by a curtain, a crypt with three aisles, and a double staircase like a bridge. Another sketch, of 31 May, shows that Craig is gradually freeing himself from his memories of Giornico, but retains the stairway and the two levels. Wholly bent on the idea of giving the *Passion* in the Grand-Palais, he was already drawing plans for arranging the space, (15) and it was now, perhaps in order to have all his time free, that he gave up the idea of working with Jacques Rouché.

But there was to be no performance of the *Passion* at the Grand-Palais; like so many others, the project came to nothing. At the beginning of 1913 Craig opened his School and there, with his assistants, he returned to the task. In September he made a design for the structure which almost satisfied him (Plate 23B), and from that he went on to the final model, which was completed in July 1914 (Plate 24).

Craig's purpose in the *St Matthew Passion* was not to illustrate each successive episode in the historical tragedy, but to reveal the symbolism in the work and bring out its contrasting aspects. This meant that the movements of individuals and crowds must be kept to a minimum and that there must be no showy lighting effects; discretion must be the guiding consideration throughout. Craig was also interested in bringing out the relations between Christ, 'the only heroic figure', and his disciples.

This model for Bach's *Passion* was twelve feet tall. Unfortunately it was broken up during the war, when the Arena Goldoni was requisitioned; but photographs of it have survived. (16) Though never used, it was one of Craig's most accomplished works.

Taking the architecture of the church at Giornico as his inspiration, Craig departed from the Italian-style stage and chose another, directly connected with the auditorium, like the chancel with the nave of a church. He set up a permanent stage structure on two principal levels, the lower stage, or 'crypt' to be used for the 'terrestrial' parts of the drama and the upper stage, or 'chancel' for the 'celestial' parts. (17) But he moved away from the church architecture, in the same way that, he thought, Bach had begun by taking his theme from the Church and had afterwards gone beyond it. Craig's final structure had nothing Romanesque about it; the 'crypt' had no vaulted ceiling and no pillars with capitals; these had been replaced by square columns and a lattice. The upper 'chancel' was no longer enclosed in itself; Craig added several levels, culminating in a broad stairway with steep-sloping walls on either side, which led up into space.

Striving, in his search for an art of movement, to create an impression comparable to that produced by the gradual progression of Bach's music in the *Passion*, Craig discovered a new solution, a permanent structure comprising many different 'places'. This structure was the forerunner of all the countless experiments and achievements in stage architecture that took place later on in theatres all over America and Europe. It was after seeing the *Matthew Passion* model that Jacques Copeau and Jouvet constructed the stage of the Vieux-Colombier, in 1919. There again, Craig was a pioneer.

*

August 1914. War broke out. Lord Howard de Walden cut off the School's supplies. Many of Craig's pupils were called up. The School had to close. Such was the end of an enterprise that had only just begun, and on which Craig had set his greatest hopes. He had looked forward to the arrival of students with State fellowships, who would have gone back to their own countries to pass on what they learnt at the School, and even to open branches of it. . . . Now, all that remained of the experiment was some memories, some photographs, the vision of a stage-coach bowling along the Tuscan lanes. These, and some principles that would henceforth be drawn upon by everyone, from Copeau to Piscator, who attempted to make the theatre into a disciplined art once more.

On 3 August 1915 Craig noted that the war which had been going on for the last twelve months was said to be costing England a million pounds a day. Being neither a strategist, an economist nor a politician, he could only assume that France, Russia and Germany were each spending the same amount of money. In one year, one thousand four hundred and sixty million pounds had been spent on destruction! How much could have been constructed, with such a sum!

In December 1916 the Italian military authorities requisitioned the Arena Goldoni. Today it is a cinema. . . .

NOTES

1. William Rothenstein's speech is among the messages reprinted in *A Living Theatre*, op. cit., pp. 58–67.
2. Edward Gordon Craig, 'Thoroughness in the Theatre. The only way to get it', in *The English Review*, October 1911, pp. 494–504. This article was reprinted in Craig's book, *The Theatre Advancing*.
3. See the article 'What my School needs – Sportsmen and Craftsmen', in *A Living Theatre*, pp. 51–6.
4. *School for the Art of the Theatre*. Founded 1913. London Offices: 7 John Street, Adelphi, London.
5. These rules were printed as a little 12-page booklet: *Rules, School for the Art of the Theatre*.
6. Edward Gordon Craig, 'Thoroughness in the Theatre', in *The English Review*, p. 503 and in *The Theatre Advancing*, London, 1921, p. 227.

7. The *Daily Telegraph*, 27 February 1913.

8. See the article signed 'J.S.' and entitled 'The Commedia dell' Arte or Professional Comedy', in *The Mask*, Vol. III, Nos. 7–9, pp. 99–100. J. S. = John Semar = Gordon Craig.

9. Quoted by Joseph Hone in *W. B. Yeats, 1865–1939*. London, Macmillan, 1942, p. 252.

10. This letter belongs to the Bibliothèque d'Art et d'Archéologie (Fondation Jacques Doucet) of the University of Paris.

11. This exhibition was held from 6 to 25 July 1914. See *A Catalogue of some designs by Edward Gordon Graig, exhibited privately at 7 John Street Adelphi by the members of the School for the Art of the Theatre.*

12. Gordon Craig, *Index to the Story of my Days*, op. cit., p. 231 and p. 235.

13. Ibid., p. 287.

14. Ibid., pp. 298–9.

15. The designs mentioned here and the plan for the arrangement of the Grand-Palais are included in Craig's first book of notes for the *St Matthew Passion – 1912 E.G.C. Paris, Florence 1913–1914 – Notebook 26* (Gordon Craig Collection, Bibliothèque de l'Arsenal, Paris).

16. Another slightly smaller model, constructed in 1914, was also destroyed when the Arena Goldoni was requisitioned in 1916.

17. Craig meant to use the two stages sometimes simultaneously and sometimes separately, probably using a curtain as shown in his 1912 design.

X

CRAIG AND APPIA

There has been a lot of talk about the relationship between the work of Gordon Craig and that of Adolphe Appia. Critics addicted to making 'historical discoveries' have inevitably flung themselves into the game of comparing dates and have drawn from it the conclusion that one man was influenced by the other. Others have contrasted Craig's 'paradoxes' and Appia's 'meditations', which simply shows that those concerned are more interested in displays of personality than in tracing the currents which contribute to the development of an art.

One evening in 1904, in Berlin, after one of Isadora Duncan's performances, Dr Thode asked Craig whether he knew Appia's work. No, Craig had never heard of Appia. In 1908, in Florence, Craig's friend Placci showed him reproductions of three of Appia's designs for Wagner operas; Craig was struck with admiration and realized that Appia's art had something akin to his own. So in the following year he asked his friend Fritz Endel how he could get in touch with Appia. The reply was that Appia was dead. At the end of 1911, Craig was in Moscow for the final rehearsals of *Hamlet*, and went to a dinner party given by Prince Wolkonsky, when the conversation turned to theatre and dance. The Prince spoke enthusiastically about Dalcroze and his eurhythmics, and also about Appia – who, it transpired, was still very much alive. Wolkonsky sent for a dozen photographs of designs by Appia, which Craig thought 'divine'. This, he considered, was certainly 'the foremost stage decorator of Europe'. (1) 'I must see him,' he wrote in his *Daybook II* on 27 December, 'for I feel his work and mine are closely united'.

The two men met in February 1914 at Zurich, where both were taking part in the Theatre Exhibition at the Kunstgewerbemuseum. By this time Craig had a number of productions and much experimental work behind him, he had published several books and

innumerable essays, and he was pursuing his researches at the
Arena Goldoni with the help of his assistants. Appia had written
two books – *La Mise en scène du Drame Wagnérien*, published by
Léon Chailley in Paris in 1895, and *Die Musik und die Inszenierung*,
published at Munich in 1899 – which, though dealing chiefly with
the problems of staging Wagner's operas, nevertheless proposed
various reforms of interest to the theatre in general, a number of
essays, some of which had appeared in magazines, and unpublished
notes for *mises en scène*. He had been concerned mainly with two
problems: that of Wagner's operas, for which he had made
many revolutionary designs, and that of Dalcroze's eurhythmics
and the movement of the human body in space (he had planned
espaces rythmiques for the Dalcroze Institute at Geneva). His, too,
had been the influence directly responsible for the construction of
the Hellerau Institute, near Dresden, where there was no division
between audience and performers and the architecture of the
stage could be altered at will by the use of a few movable pieces –
steps, slopes, platforms and hangings. Appia had several times
written about the presentation of plays, the most important of
these studies having been written in 1900 and published four years
later in *La Revue*; (2) but he had not yet made any designs for the
prose theatre. His only practical work had been done for a private
performance at the Comtesse de Béarn's house in Paris in 1903
(extracts from Byron's *Manfred* in Schumann's setting and from
Bizet's *Carmen*), for Dalcroze at Geneva (the *espaces rythmiques*),
and for Gluck's *Orphée* at Hellerau (1912–13).

Craig went to the station to meet Appia when he arrived at
Zurich. Appia did not know a word of English and Craig could
not hold a conversation in French. But they managed to get along
with the help of a little German, and above all by drawing. This
exchange of ideas was enthralling for them both; Craig noted its
main points in his *Daybook III*:

Yesterday Appia and I had our first talk. It was *very good*, very enjoy-
able.
Today our second talk, and it was *exciting*.
He spoke much of Wagner and of Hellerau and Jaques-Dalcroze.
Yesterday – less today.

I let him talk – although I told him that for me the *human* body in movement seemed to signify less and less.

Today he spoke of Wagner and the Art of Theatre. I had to say that Wagner hated the Theatre and used it as a Prostitute is used.

This made him divinely angry.

I tried to show him, without saying so, that he was searching for – for what I believe I have found –

The true and sole *Material* for the Art of the Theatre, *Light* – and through light *Movement*.

The veils of *music* and *the human form* made mist for his eyes and he could not see through.

I thought I caught him trying once or twice to push the veils aside, but he laughed on . . .

A fine man – seeing very clearly – many things.

One weakness (his strength perhaps) that first he 'needed' Wagner to hang upon – now he 'needs' Dalcroze.

Last night he saw the marionettes here (he says for the first time), and was amazed.

Well then – let's believe that they will lead him somewhere away from Dalcroze and Wagner . . .

Appia's laughing and strong disagreement with me on these points – how bracing it is – I have not been so braced for years. And what a fine fellow he is – a funny fat little body – a fine built head – built up also by hair and beard and a strong and vivid eye. The only *Man* I have yet met in the world around the theatre – for he is not quite in it, he flutters round it – rightly he fears the unrest which entering the theatre would bring him – but he fears and therein is he weaker if wiser than our old stage carpenter who descends into Hell and is unharmed.

The two men assessed both what they had in common and the differences between them, as may be seen from the following story related by Appia's assistant, Jean Mercier:

Craig wrote his name on the table-cloth and next to it that of Appia. He drew a circle around Appia on which he wrote the word 'music.' Admirable symbol of the truth! These two pioneers of contemporary dramatic art rested their reforms on the same base – the actor. But Craig was free in his reform; the reform of Appia was dominated and directed by a major force – music. Hence the circle which circumscribed and limited the name of Appia, while that of Craig had a freedom which spread to the limits of the cloth! (3)

In spite – or perhaps because – of this division, a deep friendship grew up between the two artists, based on mutual admiration. The Englishman regarded the Swiss as first and foremost a *stage designer* of genius. The encounter between their two personalities, their respective ideals, at Zurich, was the starting-point of a lengthy correspondence. Appia, writes Craig, is 'the *only one* in the whole western theatre whom I remember continually with that strange joy which is desperate and tragic because of your peculiar *powerlessness and power*.' And he goes on:

> You, my dear, are the very noblest expression in the modern theatre – *to me* you are: and I say that without any needless bowing of the knee. And to me there is far more vivid life and drama in one of your great studies for scenes than in any thing else known to me in our theatre of Europe.
> There are other rather wonderful powers in a few men and women – but none *speak* as your designs do.
> None speak *just so*. You know what I mean. (4)

For Appia, Craig was an artist whose creative force and power of suggestion filled him with admiration, and a friend to whom he could speak of his next book, *L'Œuvre d'Art Vivant* (5) and of the exhibitions where their work hung side by side:

> . . . everything you write to me interests and charms me; it comes from you. . . that is to say from a *dual* world; ours and yours. Mine, my own personal one, lies entirely elsewhere. And I am *delighted* that you should have my *Elysian Fields* (6) to remain always, intimately, apart from all snobbishness, close, very close to you, Craig.
> . . . In the depths of our souls we have *the same vibration and the same desire*; only expressed differently, owing to our different temperaments and our very different circumstances. What matter! We are together, for always. That is enough. (7)

It would never have occurred to Appia that Craig might have copied him, or even derived inspiration from him. In October 1915, when Carl van Vechten published a sensational article (8) purporting to show that Craig's ideas were taken from Appia and that but for Appia Craig would never have been heard of, nor perhaps would Stanislavsky (!), the two friends saw through it, though at first they were taken aback. Finally Appia informed van Vechten, in a polite but curt letter, that he could not accept the sole credit for a reform to which a number of others had contributed. (9)

It was true that Appia's first theoretical writings had been published before those of Craig, who was ten years his junior; but neither man was acquainted with the work of the other, and Craig's earliest revolutionary designs were made in 1899–1900, long before he had seen Appia's first project.

The fact is that Craig and Appia are the two strongest personalities in the idealistic movement which was striving to regenerate the theatre by transforming its aesthetic attitude.

What they had in common, and what they disagreed about, may be briefly summed up as follows:

Both protested against the enslavement of the theatre and wished to restore it to the status of a self-contained art. They disliked realism and all its methods – photographic imitation, trompe-l'œil, artificial perspective and sham. They declared that suggestion, evocation, symbolical representation, were far better than a slavish reproduction of reality. When working on a play or libretto, they did not feel bound by the author's stage directions, which they considered to be meant for the reader; they drew their inspiration entirely from the work itself.

Neither of them believed in the Gesamtkunstwerk, Wagner's idea of a supreme artistic theatre created by the union or fusion of several arts. Both declared that there must be harmony between the various means of stage expression – actors, scene, lighting, etc. – and wanted a three-dimensional stage world.

Lastly, both were working to establish a theatre whose main lines they already perceived: for Craig, it was to be a self-contained art, freed from literature; for Appia, it was to be a collective manifestation, 'with or without spectators'.

The differences between them, however, were fundamental.

Appia had studied music, but had no experience of acting, whereas Craig had begun as an actor. Appia's reflections were based on Wagner's operas, although his collaboration with Dalcroze had opened his eyes to other ideas. Craig's point of departure was his practical experience as actor and stage director.

Appia's writings are the result of methodical reflection, they are logical rather than intuitive; he demonstrates. Craig describes a vision and aims at convincing the reader then and there, even at the risk of annoying him: he shakes theatre people out of their torpor.

Appia's graphic work consists of only about a hundred scene designs and 'rhythmic spaces'. Craig's, even apart from his countless woodcuts and his numerous etchings and illustrations, comprises an enormous number of designs for scenes, costumes and properties and of technical drawings.

But the most deeply-rooted contrasts between Craig and Appia relate to matters of theory. Craig never proposed that his 'new theatre' should break away from the finer traditions, the most living elements in the classical or oriental forms of theatre. Whereas for Appia, though he frequently refers to the antique theatre, for example, the history of the theatre is of quite subsidiary interest.

As already pointed out, Craig and Appia both stress the need to harmonize the means of dramatic expression. But while Appia begins with music, as the 'living duration' which is to determine the form of the spectacle, and lays down a strict order of precedence beginning with the actor and going on, by way of space and lighting, to colour, Craig places all these elements on the same level and uses them all as materials contributing to the unity of the performance. Appia's order of priority leads to functionalism. Craig desires harmony for the sake of complete expression. Consequently, he deals with all the components of a performance on an equal footing, offering, for instance, a general theory of acting; whereas Appia never puts forward definite views on what acting should be.

Both men stress the importance of *movement*; but the author of *L'Œuvre d'art vivant* is thinking chiefly of the movement of the actor's body, which for him is the chief factor in the performance, and is only incidentally concerned with the movement of the other elements on the stage. Whereas the author of *On the Art of the Theatre* is seeking for *an art of pure movement* in which a constant succession of forms would be revealed; he does not regard the human body as the prime element in the theatre, but considers that movement extends as much to things as to human beings. Hence his conception of a scene with multiple aspects, which has no place in Appia's ideas.

In this rough-and-ready summing up there is one important point to be emphasized. Craig and Appia were both working towards a transformation of theatre architecture which would bring stage and auditorium into closer relationship. Appia was dreaming of an interior space capable of modification, a real 'cathedral of the future'. In 1905, when he wrote the introduction to *The Art of the Theatre*, Craig thought that the actual form of the building would probably be entirely changed. He sees a great building to seat many thousands of people, with at one end 'a platform of heroic size', (10) but he does not seem to connect the renovation of the theatre with the creation of any predetermined form of architecture. He may advocate doing away with boxes and sloping the floor of the auditorium, but at other times he accepts many forms of theatre as possible, just as he considers that *Hamlet* can be staged in twenty different ways. At the beginning of his career he admired the Bayreuth Festspielhaus; in 1914 he made a drawing of a theatre with a ring-shaped stage, (11) and in 1922 he advocated an entirely transformable theatre, in which the stage director could establish whatever relationship he wished between stage and auditorium and adapt his general structure to the requirements of the play. In fact Craig looked upon theatrical architecture from the point of view of its value as an instrument rather than from that of strict form.

We thus see that a study of the relations between Craig and Appia cannot confine itself to comparing their drawings and declaring that those of the former are dominated by vertical lines while those of the latter show a preference for superimposed horizontal planes. It is a pity Carl van Vechten did not take the trouble to look into the matter more closely before propounding his captivating theory.

NOTES

1. Craig, in a footnote added to the 1911 Preface of *On the Art of the Theatre*. See *On the Art of the Theatre*, op. cit., p. vii.

2. Adolphe Appia, 'Comment réformer notre mise en scène', in *La Revue*, Paris, Vol. 3, 1904, 1 June, pp. 342–9.

3. Jean Mercier, 'Adolphe Appia. The Rebirth of Dramatic Art', in *Theatre Arts Monthly*, August 1932, p. 628.

4. Letter from Craig to Appia, 'Rome, Via Margutta, 22 February 1917'. Appia Foundation, Collection Suisse du Théâtre, Berne.

5. *L'Œuvre d'Art Vivant*, by Adolphe Appia, was published in 1921 (Editions Atar, Geneva and Paris).

6. This was one of Appia's finest and most celebrated designs, made for Gluck's *Orphée*.

7. Letter from Appia to Craig, 'Glérolles. 26–5–17'. Gordon Craig Collection, Bibliothèque de l'Arsenal, Paris.

8. 'Adolphe Appia and Gordon Craig', in *The Forum*, New York, Vol. 54, October 1915, pp. 483–7.

9. Letter dated 8 February 1916, a copy of which is in the Gordon Craig Collection, Bibliothèque de l'Arsenal, Paris.

10. Introduction to *The Art of the Theatre*, Foulis, Edinburgh and London, 1905, p. 14. This introduction, entitled 'One Word about the Theatre as it was, as it is and as it will be', was not reprinted in *On the Art of the Theatre*.

11. This sketch is in the manuscript volume MSS 7. 1914–1916–1920.

XI

A LONG GAME OF PATIENCE

With the 1914 war there began for Craig what he once called 'a long game of patience', which is still going on today.

He went on writing, published a number of books, made drafts of others, filled an endless number of notebooks and manuscript books with all kinds of material – ideas suggested by performances he saw, technical notes and so forth. His work was seen in many exhibitions. His influence steadily increased. His advice was asked and his collaboration invited on all sides. He had become the 'prophet' of the modern theatre. But he seldom took part in any official theatrical activity, and none of the productions to which he did contribute embodied any novel principles. He still hoped to be given a theatre, or funds with which to reopen his School. But nothing came. So he began to concentrate on the history of the theatre, as a source of exciting discoveries and an antidote to disappointment.

Travelling about, Craig was able to estimate the size of his audience, and became more and more aware of his role of 'guide' in the development of the theatre – delighted when its debt to him was recognized, but growing depressed, suspicious and vexed when he found himself being stolen from without acknowledgement.

On 25 August 1915, shortly before visiting Florence, Copeau wrote to Jouvet: 'Craig, the only man whose theories are valuable, is incomplete for lack of a stage.' (1) This state of things occasionally inclined Craig towards misanthropy; he sometimes felt isolated, and thought longingly of the work he might have done with companions such as Isadora Duncan or Adolphe Appia. (2) Still, he never gave up hope. In 1907 he had dedicated *The Artists of the Theatre of the Future* to 'the single courageous individuality in the world of the theatre who will some day master and remould it.' (3) Now he transferred his hopes to the younger generation and to those who would come after them.

It is not possible to follow Craig's life year by year and month by month, from 1914 to the present day, or even to mention all his many changes of residence – including a move from Florence to Rome, where Elena Meo and their two children, Nelly and Teddy, joined him, (4) from Rome to Rapallo, where he was the neighbour of his old friend Max Beerbohm, and from Rapallo to Genoa. Since 1931 he has lived chiefly in France – at Saint-Germain-en-Laye, Paris, Corbeil, Le Cannet, Tourrettes-sur-Loup and Vence, where he settled in 1951. We must be satisfied with a glance at essential facts, at Craig's most important ideas and achievements.

*

The first world war interrupted the publication of *The Mask*. An issue appeared in July 1914 and another in May 1915; after that there were no more for several years. But the suspension of the magazine did not cut off all Craig's important contacts, to judge by such as have been recorded.

In 1913, Jacques Copeau founded the Théâtre du Vieux-Colombier in Paris. His chief anxiety was to make the stage as practical as possible; his idea was to have a set of cubes which could be arranged in a great variety of ways. He was also hoping to add a school of acting, a kind of laboratory, as an indispensable contribution to the art of the theatre.

Copeau was one of the few Frenchmen who had heard of Craig and his ideas, having read Jacques Rouché's *L'Art Théâtral Moderne*, which included a general description of those ideas, and *On the Art of the Theatre* itself. He wrote to Craig on 5 August 1915, saying he would like to publish a selection of his writings and designs with the *Nouvelle Revue Française*. He added that he was preparing a study of Craig's work for a magazine he intended to bring out after the war and would therefore be glad to establish closer relations with him, more especially as he realized that a greater familiarity with Craig's theories would be of great advantage to the Théâtre du Vieux-Colombier. (5)

A few days later Craig replied, (6) asking for fuller particulars of Copeau's work in the theatre and more information about the projected magazine. He explained that Rouché held the French-language rights of *On the Art of the Theatre*, so that no French translation could be brought out except by arrangement with him. He said he was gratified that Copeau should associate his name with the Vieux-Colombier's activities, as it was a rare thing, in the theatre, for one artist to express gratitude to another! And he hoped Copeau would come to Florence.

Copeau came, and the visit had a decisive influence on him. He got to know the town, not only its monuments and museums but also its workshops and booths, where the purest traditions of craftsmanship were still perpetuated. Above all, he got to know Gordon Craig, his Arena Goldoni, and his collection of rare documents.

> I breathed in the atmosphere of that sanctuary of beauty. I sat in the sun on the stone steps, where a young catalpa tree was growing. I felt, mounting within me, the thrilling thought of the disinterested work that could be done in that profound quiet, and my memory went back to some words it is my intention to act upon: 'There is only one solution for all this if you want to bring *joie de vivre* back into art. You must welcome these young people.' (7)

Copeau improved his acquaintance with Craig's ideas by poring over a set of *The Mask*. Craig displayed his models, his *Model A*, his screens, and even offered to cede the French patent of the screens to Copeau, who wrote to Jouvet:

> ... it is exactly what we need for our stage. It's quite beautiful, marvellously limpid, and 'made for us'. Right up our street. We have found out certain things for ourselves. But here it all is, complete, in colour. One might perhaps be able to improve a few details in the course of working with this material, but as it stands, it satisfies *all our needs*. ... [Craig] also showed me a lighting system which gives admirable results and seems marvellously simple and practical in the model. It remains to be seen if it would be equally so on the spot. It does away entirely with footlights and battens. ... (8)

Copeau never used the screens, but he was influenced by the principle of the single scene, and even more by the model of the stage structure for Bach's *St Matthew Passion*. If we compare the interior of the Vieux-Colombier as it was in 1913 with Copeau's productions in New York in 1917, 1918 and 1919 (*Pelléas et Mélisande*) and with the stage architecture of the Vieux-Colombier in its 1919 form, we see ample proof that Craig's structure had helped to steer Copeau in the direction of an architectural stage, meant to be to the theatre what the chancel is to a church. Copeau's structure lacks the grandeur of Craig's model, of course, and reveals his lingering affection for the *tréteau*, which had never interested Craig; but the relationship between the two is none the less evident: Copeau's is a permanent architectural construction, with different levels connected by steps and an unbroken transition from auditorium to stage.

When Copeau left Florence he was richer than when he arrived; his ideals were reinforced and he had a host of ideas to adapt to his own plans and needs.

As for Craig, he sought refuge from the state of suspense induced by the war, by delving deeper into the history of the English, French, Spanish and Italian theatres. In 1914 he had discovered Nicola Sabbattini's *Pratica di fabbricar scene e macchine ne' teatri*, Dorothy Nevile Lees having given him a copy of the extremely rare second edition of 1638. The question of *periaktoi* and revolving scenery interested him particularly. In 1916 he added some items by Ferdinando Galli-Bibiena to his collection, and these formed the starting-point of a considerable store of information and documents relating to the celebrated family of scenographers which flourished in Italy in the seventeenth and eighteenth centuries. A few years later, in 1925, he prepared a thick and extremely detailed volume on *The Bibiena Family, 1625-1812*, which has never been published.

But there was one branch of theatrical art that interested Craig more than any other during these years: marionettes. He was familiar with their history and technical aspects, and had thought a great deal on the subject. In 1918 he brought out a little magazine, *The Marionette*, which appeared monthly for a year. In this, as well as his own articles – many of which were signed 'Tom Fool' – he published lavishly illustrated studies by Corrado Ricci and other Italian experts, and reprinted extracts from old English or foreign authors, such as Dickens, Théophile Gautier and George Sand. Neither did he neglect the marionettes of Japan or those of Java – a large collection of which he had bought in 1913 – or the shadow figures of Egypt and North Africa. In 1916, moreover, he began to write his own *Drama for Fools*, a long series of plays for marionettes, of which the following were printed in the magazine: *The Gordian Knot, Mr Fish and Mrs Bones, The Three Men of Gotham, The Tune the Old Cow Died of* and *Romeo and Juliet*. The characters introduced include Shakespeare, Bacon, Max Reinhardt – who takes one or two shrewd knocks – and three witches, identified as Madame de Staël, Miss Milbanke and Mrs Harriet Beecher Stowe.

Despite every conceivable difficulty, including the shortage of money, *The Mask* made its reappearance in 1918, as a regular monthly leaflet. Then came another interruption, lasting until 1923, when Craig managed to bring out one number. Quarterly publication began again in 1924 and was kept up until the end of 1929. The magazine's ideals were unchanged, its aims were frequently reasserted and the old spirit of 'rebellion' still permeated it; theatrical history, however, began in course of time to take up the lion's share of the space.

Craig also published several books. In 1919 a volume of essays and articles, *The Theatre Advancing*, appeared in the United States, to be followed two years later by an English edition to which a long and important preface had been added. In 1920, after several years' delay due to the war, the first French edition of *On the Art of the Theatre* was published (9): *De l'Art du Théâtre*, N.R.F., Paris, with an introduction by Jacques Rouché. Meanwhile, Craig was preparing a big book on the Italian theatre from 1500 to 1900, which has never been published; his intention was to show England what Italy had done for its theatre. In 1923, sixteen years of research found expression in *Scene*, the book in which Craig gives his views on the history of theatre architecture and introduces his famous screens. The volume also contains reproductions of the series of etchings made in 1907 to express Craig's aspiration towards an art of movement. In 1924 came *Nothing or the Bookplate*, a vivid recollection of the period when Craig produced the majority of his *ex-libris*, and *Woodcuts and Some Words*, where he describes his experience as a wood-engraver. These were followed in 1925 by another volume of essays, *Books and Theatres*, which showed Craig, the artist of the theatre, side by side with Craig, the scholar and historian.

True to his custom of pursuing several activities at once, Craig was still making wood-engravings. Indeed, some of his most celebrated woodcuts were produced during these years, including, in 1920, the scene of the Storm in *King Lear*, where horizontal and diagonal lines contrast with curves and balance one another in a kind of stylized whirlwind, while the human figures, reduced to black silhouettes, intensify the drama of their surroundings. Four years later, Craig constructed a model of this scene in metal, making the changes required by stage conditions and rendered possible by the technical resources of lighting. The model was exhibited at the British Empire Exhibition at Wembley (British Drama League section). In his letter introducing it to Geoffrey Whitworth, the Secretary of the B.D.L., (10) Craig points out that he has not used a revolving stage or a cyclorama, as he considers that these huge, heavy pieces of mechanism have never so far been any real help to the actors.

*

In 1922 an International Theatre Exhibition was held at the Stedelijk Museum, Amsterdam. The work of Craig and Appia was given the place of honour, and the organizers of the exhibition, in which all important trends in the modern theatre were represented, invited Craig to come and open it. (11)

Many requests to work in theatres continued to reach him. Between the end of the war and 1925 he was invited to Paris, where Jacques Rouché wanted him to design and produce a ballet at the Opera, and to London, where Sybil Thorndike suggested he should stage *Macbeth*. Malipiero asked him to produce one of his operas, and La Scala at Milan wished him to do *Pelléas et Mélisande*. But in each case after negotiations, he abstained.

Nevertheless, on 1 October 1926 Craig went to Copenhagen, whence Johannes Poulsen, the actor who was at the head of the Royal Theatre, had written on 12 August, inviting him to design scenes for Ibsen's *Pretenders* – which was to be put on to mark the stage jubilee of Poulsen and his brother Emile – and to help with the *mise en scène*. The circumstances, the tone of Poulsen's letter and the play itself all contributed to induce him to accept the invitation, although he had done no work on a stage since *Hamlet*.

The equipment of the Royal Theatre had been brought up to date by Adolf Linnebach, a great admirer of Craig and one of the foremost specialists in the matter at that time. Once again, Craig found that his ideas had been bearing fruit.

He had been asked to 'help' Johannes Poulsen, but when it came to it, he directly inspired the whole production. He found the play difficult, involved, and inclined to drag in places; but the characters fascinated him. As in the case of *The Vikings*, he broke out of the historical framework and set himself to bring the poetic world of the play to life on the stage. 'When producing great drama, I have never been concerned in any attempt to show the spectators an exact view of any historical period of architecture. I always feel that all the great plays have an order of architecture of their own, an architecture which is more or less theatrical, unreal as the play.' (12)

In this production a permanent stage construction was used, with a great variety of extra pieces, and Craig had his first full-scale experience of the projection of scenes. This he employed not as a means of descriptive illusion, but as a method of suggestion and evocation.

The event was a great success. After the first performance the actors sent Craig a message of thanks and good wishes. Johannes Poulsen himself was the first to recognize the European theatre's debt to Craig:

. . . In every country in Europe there have been men who have carried out ideas suggested by Gordon Craig. Not only Reinhardt and Jessner in Germany, and Stanislavsky in Russia, but also Gémier and Copeau in France, Lindbergh in Sweden, Schanche in Norway, Johannes Poulsen in Denmark, and so on all through Europe. Only from England has he always been excluded because of the huge conservatism of the English theatre.

... the fate of such a man is always to be utilized by others to their profit and not his. The European theatre and even the American film has had success and earned money on his ideas while he himself has had to walk about in his old grey suit, with empty pockets. He has always, just like Socrates, been poor, but while others have filled their own little pockets, Gordon Craig has written his name in ineffaceable types on the sky of the European mind. (13)

The Pretenders was Craig's last important work for the stage. In 1928 he collaborated in another production – *Macbeth*, presented at the Knickerbocker Theatre, New York, by Tyler the impresario, with Douglas Ross as the director; but he does not think this was of any great value. Tyler asked him to design the scenes, and Ross spent three weeks at Genoa, going through the play with him and gleaning ideas. Craig made a lot of designs for scenes and many suggestions for the *mise en scène*, and the show (14) drew publicity from the use of his name; it ran for seven and a half months, with 230 performances, a considerable success for the United States in those days. But Craig had always despised that sort of composite work, and it appealed chiefly to his sense of the ridiculous. A number of his designs are signed 'C.p.b.' – not a new pseudonym this time, but simply short for 'Craig pot-boiler.'

*

In 1907 Craig had invented his 'Black Figures' – wood-carved silhouettes resembling Chinese shadow puppets; when they were printed, their white lines indicated stylized features and the folds of garments. In Moscow he had experimented a great deal with engraving and printing the small figures he made and used to show the actors how they were to move. These little personages, together with the Black Figures, were the starting-point of the illustrations for Count Kessler's edition of *Hamlet*, Craig did the woodcuts between 1912 and 1929. The work suffered many interruptions, but in December 1929 the Cranach Press published the German version, translated by Gerhardt Hauptmann and illustrated by Craig with seventy-five wood-engravings. (15) Craig's designs derived from his ideas for the Moscow production and consisted of black forms against a white background, showing the characters in a more stylized manner than any of his earlier woodcuts.

Shortly after this, Craig published two books in quick succession

Hamlet – engraving 1929.

– one on Henry Irving (1930), in which he presented a portrait of the actor who had come nearest to his ideal of the *über-marionette*, and the other on Ellen Terry.

As though to make things easier for theatrical historians, Craig also wrote a short book, *Fourteen Notes*, (16) in which he briefly compared the work and historical role of the leading figures in the modern theatre – Antoine, Appia, Stanislavsky, Reinhardt and himself. It was at this time, in 1931, when he seemed to be looking back over his shoulder, summing himself up and paying his debt to those who had chiefly helped him, that he made his last visit to England. Afterwards he settled in France, and though he travelled widely in Europe he was never to set foot in his own country again.

*

In October 1934 the Convegno Volta – held in Rome for a week each year by the Accademia Reale – dealt with the theatre, and assembled its most prominent representatives from all over the world – dramatists, producers, architects and so forth.

Craig was invited to speak. At first he refused, since he did not see how such a meeting could serve the theatre. As for making a speech, he would be delighted, if the (non-existent) British Minister of Fine Arts would instruct him to report the progress made by the theatre in his native land. . . .

Finally, yielding to insistence, he agreed to attend the Convegno on condition that he did not go as the representative of any country and was not asked to speak. During the week he met some old friends and some new acquaintances, including Yeats, Maeterlinck, Tairov, Amaglobelli, Joseph Gregor, Pirandello, Marinetti and Gropius. The central problem discussed was the theatre for the masses, which prompted Craig to make some obervations and suggestions. He pointed out that while such a theatre, holding fifteen or twenty thousand spectators, could be used for some of the works of Goethe, Shakespeare, Wagner, Schiller and Hugo, it would be utterly unsuitable for Chekhov, Mozart, Strindberg or Ibsen (with the possible exception of *Peer Gynt*). Instead of one huge theatre, why not build a group of theatres of different shapes and sizes, ranging from an auditorium to hold thousands of people, to a little one with 250 seats? In a 'cultural centre' of this kind it would be possible to present drama, opera and ballet, and it could also include restaurants, swimming-pools, Turkish baths, smokerooms and a library. This was another of the ideas thrown out casually by Craig (17) which is now being followed up. The new Lincoln Center for the Performing Arts, in New York, constitutes at least a partial fulfilment of it.

*

In the following spring, Craig paid a five-week visit to Moscow (27 March to 5 May) at the official invitation of the Soviet theatre. He was eagerly welcomed by his admirers, many of whom were influential figures. Meyerhold, Tairov and Amaglobelli, the director of the Mali Theatre, met him at the station. He visited the theatre museum and the exhibition dealing with Russian theatrical activity since the Revolution. He met Stanislavsky, Nemirovitch-Dantchenko and Alice Koonen again, and made a number of new friends, including the producer Zavadski, Obrastzov, the marionettist, and Sergei Eisenstein, who already knew his books and acknowledged a great debt to his ideas. He also met three foreign theatre men who happened to be in Moscow at this time: the Chinese actor Mei Lan-fang, Erwin Piscator and Bertolt Brecht.

In Moscow Craig found that the theatre was full of vitality and well provided with eager workers. He saw many productions which testified to their creative powers, including *Twelfth Night* at the Second Art Theatre, *Turandot* in Vakhtangov's presentation, Meyerhold's *Revizor* and Vishnevsky's *Optimistic Tragedy*, the last-named produced by Tairov at the Kamerny Theatre with a remarkable transformable scene by Ryndin. But what he admired most of all was *King Lear* at the Jewish State Theatre, produced, in a Yiddish translation, by Serge Radlov, with scenes and costumes by a young designer, Alexandre Tyshler and with Michoels as Lear. This he considered the most 'Shakespearean' production he had ever seen – a mixture of comedy and tragedy, melodramatic in its underlying tone and fantastic in its movements, highly coloured, yet as clear-cut and precise as a picture in black and white. Incidentally, Radlov and Michoels regarded Craig as their master.

*

On his way back from Moscow Craig stopped at Warsaw, where he met another friend and disciple, Leon Schiller, the Polish producer, and at Vienna, where he found Hoffmann, the architect. Then he returned to Italy, whence he soon moved to France.

After this he gave his time to writing articles and to making woodcuts for a projected Cranach Press edition of *Robinson Crusoe*. In 1938 the Habima Company invited him to produce a play at Tel Aviv, but the war prevented this. Craig spent the war years in Paris, making countless notes and working on his theatre collection. After being the first – at the beginning of the century – to speak of the need for a revival of mime, he had the satisfaction of presiding over a performance given by Etienne Decroux (who taught mime to Marcel Marceau) and his company at the Maison de la Chimie in Paris, on 27 June 1945. He was an assiduous visitor to the Paris theatres, where his friends included Christian Bérard,

Louis Jouvet and Jean-Louis Barrault; and he even had dreams of reviving *The Mask*.

One day he decided to move to the South of France, back to the Mediterranean climate he had always found so conducive to good work. There, surrounded by books and papers, he wrote his memoirs, *Index to the Story of My Days 1872–1907*, which came out in 1957. And there he worked until his death on 29 July 1966 at the age of 94, arranging, adding to and correcting his manuscripts, annotating the books he read, and taking an intense interest in all living forms of theatre and every aspect of the world around him.

NOTES

1. Letter from Jacques Copeau to Louis Jouvet, written from 'Le Limon par La Ferté-sous Jouarre (S.-et-M.)' and dated 25 August 1915. Published in 'Quatre lettres de Jacques Copeau à Louis Jouvet', *Cahiers de la Compagnie Madeleine Renaud – Jean-Louis Barrault*, Vol. I, No. 2, Paris, Julliard, 1953, p. 104.
2. See *Daybook 1931–1932–1933*.
3. Gordon Craig, 'The Artists of the Theatre of the Future', in *On the Art of the Theatre*, op. cit., p. 1.
4. Craig's son, Edward Anthony Craig (a scene-designer for theatre and films, and the author of books on theatre history and on designing for the cinema, known by the name of Edward Carrick) helped him in his work from 1917 to 1928 and very soon became his only assistant. He made translations from Italian into English, constructed models in wood, plaster and metal, undertook research for articles in *The Mask*, photographed Craig's woodcuts, prepared woodblocks for cutting, helped to draw up catalogues, searched for books and manuscripts, etc. His father taught him wood-engraving, and some of his woodcuts, of which Craig thought highly, were used in *The Mask*. Edward Craig was kind enough to reply very fully to the questions I asked him about his father's life and work, and I should like to take this opportunity of expressing my gratitude for his help.
5. Letter from Jacques Copeau to Gordon Craig, 5 August 1915. Gordon Craig Collection, Bibliothèque de l'Arsenal, Paris.
6. Letter from Gordon Craig to Jacques Copeau, 11 August 1915. Gordon Craig Collection, Bibliothèque de l'Arsenal, Paris.
7. Jacques Copeau, *Cahiers du Vieux-Colombier*, II, 'L'Ecole du Vieux-Colombier', November 1921, Paris, N.R.F., p. 16.
8. Letter from Jacques Copeau to Louis Jouvet, 10 October 1915, quoted by Maurice Kurtz in *Jacques Copeau, Biographie d'un théâtre*, translated from the

American by Claude Cezan, with a prefatory letter from Jacques Copeau, Paris, Nagel, 1950, p. 61.

9. *De L'Art du Théâtre*, N.R.F., Paris, with an introduction by Jacques Rouché.

10. Letter from Craig to Geoffrey Whitworth, 12 February 1924. Gordon Craig Collection, Bibliothèque de l'Arsenal, Paris.

11. This exhibition was afterwards transferred to the Victoria and Albert Museum, London (3 June to 16 July 1922), to Manchester (October 1922), to Glasgow (22 December 1922 to 3 February 1923) and Bradford (June–July 1923).

12. Edward Gordon Craig, *A Production, being thirty-two collotype plates of designs projected or realised for* The Pretenders *of Henrik Ibsen and produced at the Royal Theatre, Copenhagen 1926, by Edward Gordon Craig*, Oxford University Press, 1930, p. 16. This book is an excellent source of information on the production of *The Pretenders*.

13. Quoted by Enid Rose, *Gordon Craig and the Theatre*, op. cit., pp. 192–3.

14. The programme, Macbeth. *Annual presentation of famous masterpieces. Season of 1928–29. Designment by Gordon Craig*, includes an article on Craig by Percy MacKaye, extracts from a letter written by Craig to the actress who played Lady Macbeth, and a letter from Craig to Boleslavski, an ex-member of the Moscow Art Theatre, who had become Director of the American Laboratory Theater.

15. William Shakespeare, *Die Tragische Geschichte von Hamlet, Prinzen von Daenemark*, Weimar, Cranach Presse. The English edition came out in 1930: *The Tragedie of Hamlet, Prince of Denmark*, edited by J. Dover Wilson, Weimar, Cranach Press.

16. E. G. Craig, *Fourteen Notes*, Seattle, University of Washington Bookstore, 1931.

17. In his manuscript, *Technical Notes*, *E.G.C.*, MSS 15, pp. 164–5 Gordon Craig Collection, Bibliothèque de l'Arsenal, Paris.

XII

CRAIG AND THE MODERN THEATRE

Craig's personality, ideas and achievements have always given rise to vehement and conflicting opinions. But since his influence, whether one likes it or not, is to be found everywhere, it may be as well to try, as objectively as possible, to define his position in the history of the modern theatre.

*

Before the words 'pioneer' and 'prophet' came to be generally applied to him, Craig was a *rebel*. He rebelled against the decadence and confusion that characterized the theatre in the Victorian age. His reaction was that of an idealist, a disciple of Ruskin, an artist in quest of 'beauty in the absolute', with an aristocratic conception of art which contrasted with the ugliness of the prevailing bourgeois style.

But Craig was never – as has been too frequently asserted – a pure aesthete, indifferent to the theatre public. He never regarded research as an end in itself, and though he aspired to perfection he was not a believer in 'art for art's sake'. As early as 1905 he declared that the theatre must be given back to the people, for whom it was really intended:

The theatre was for the people, and always should be for the people. The poets would make the theatre for a select community of dilettanti. They would put difficult psychological thoughts before the public, expressed in difficult words, and would make for this public something which is impossible for them to understand and unnecessary for them to know; whereas the theatre must show them sights, show them life, show them beauty, and not speak in difficult sentences. And the reason why the theatre is being kept back today is because the poet is pulling one way, saying they should only be given words, using the theatre and all its crafts as a medium for those words; and the people are pulling the other way, saying they desire to see the sights, realistic-ally or poetically shown, not turned into literature. So far most of the brainy people are on the side of the poets; they have got the upper hand. Still the plays in the theatres are, artistically, failures; the theatre itself is a failure artistically and commercially, and the secret of this failure is the battle between the poet and the people. (1)

Though he castigated the contemporary theatre, Craig had no desire to set up as a *reformer*. He disliked the word, which he associated with the followers of certain vague systems or with the representatives of some particular branch of theatrical art, who wanted to improve it simply in terms of their own speciality:

Rather than a 'reformer', I should be more truly described, in relation to the theatre, as one who would put things in order.
I do not know if it is yet widely enough realized that 'putting in order' is the peculiar task of the artist, whereas it is the spirit of the reformer to destroy; and that this putting in order, with the consequent elimina-tion of what is valueless, is the artist's essential work. (2)

What Craig was trying to do was to *restore* the theatre to its former dignity. The beginning of the new century was a period of 'aesthetic revolutions', and Craig shared the attitude of the inno-vating painters, musicians and architects who began by challenging the prevailing academic concepts and methods, and then felt their way back to the specific laws and methods of their respective arts, attempting to restore them to their original purity. Craig, for his part, set himself to discover the laws peculiar to the theatre. He studied past or distant forms of his art and derived from them traditions which still had life and could be used as a basis for innovation. It was by this dual process of restoration and innovation that he hoped to establish a new, independent art of the theatre.

*

Craig's major premise was that neither the play nor the acting alone constituted the art of the theatre, but that this lay in the whole presentation. Some people thereupon jumped to the conclusion that he esteemed one or another of the visual elements in the performance – the scenery, the costumes or the lighting – above all the rest. He answered this charge in 1905 by saying: 'Does anyone think scenery is interesting to me, or that costumes amuse me, or that I consider the wig-maker more important than the actor or vice versa? None of these things interest me in themselves, but only as material for me to invest with life by means of the art which may be in me.'(3)

This shows Craig in agreement with the post-impressionist painters in their definition of artistic creation. (4) The painter disposes his canvas exactly as he chooses. He uses and controls inanimate materials, lines, forms and colours. By submitting these materials to his own creative action he transforms them into means of expression which can act jointly and severally upon the feelings of the beholder. Similarly, Craig's intention was to *compose* the dramatic performance, selecting what elements he wished and treating them like materials to be built up into a consistent, expressive structure in which none of them would surrender any of its own qualities. This would give maximum effectiveness to the production, for it would be effective in each of its components and also as a whole which, as we know, represents much more than the sum of its parts.

The other principles laid down by Craig, with regard to acting, scenery and lighting, are merely the corollaries of this major premise. If the performance were to be raised to the status of a work of art, its component elements must not be used to ape reality, but to transcend it. Systematic description must therefore be abandoned in favour of suggestion conveyed by the careful selection of elements, in many cases of a symbolical character. The principles I have thus briefly outlined were fully set forth by Craig in his writings and applied in his designs. And they transformed the theatre.

*

Craig's ideas spread throughout Europe and America – though his name was sometimes dropped from them – and exercised a far-reaching influence.

Craig has never confined his attention to one particular form of theatre or to one single stage technique. His interest in *mise en scène*, acting, scenery, costume and lighting, mime and marionettes has been twofold – that of the stage director and that of the writer – so that his teachings have had a wide circulation in all branches of the theatrical profession.

For a variety of reasons into which we need not enter here, Craig has made very few productions, so that his ideas have never become set in one hard-and-fast mould. After 1914 he was cast on his own resources – a man of forty-two whose official activities in the theatre had virtually come to an end. Some people maintained that he was unappreciated, others called him a dreamer in an ivory tower; and he became a figure of legend. Strange though it may seem, his very isolation helped to spread his ideas, which were all the more valued because he himself was almost inaccessible. He towered above the mêlée, an inspiration and a guide.

It is difficult to define the exact nature of Craig's influence and its limits. His aims have not been completely achieved by any present-day man of the theatre, but many principles he was the first to put forward are now generally applied and taken as a matter of course. Craig has more unconscious followers than avowed disciples.

Apart from matters of style, Craig's ideas have directly influenced the theatre's working methods. It is true that the modern theatre affords no example of the artist he hoped to see, a combination of playwright, producer and designer. But since the publication of *On the Art of the Theatre*, the producer's role as creator and co-ordinator has steadily grown in importance, ensuring the harmonious presentation which was Craig's foremost aim, while a close co-operation has developed among those responsible for the artistic aspects of the performance. We need only think of the team-work of Reinhardt and Stern, Jessner and Pirchan, Jouvet and Berard, Vilar and Gischia, Planchon and Allio. We need only remember Baty, Pitoëff, Brook, Visconti and the grandsons of Richard Wagner, all of whom have been both producers and designers, after the pattern of the 'stage director' described in *The Art of the Theatre*. But it was no doubt Brecht, though the aims he attributed to the theatre were entirely different from those of

Craig, who came closest, in the strict sense, to Craig's 'artist of the theatre', inasmuch as he produced his own plays and ensured the homogeneity of the Berliner Ensemble by instituting genuinely collective work.

The aesthetical history of the twentieth-century theatre is characterized first and foremost by a re-examination of forms that were found to be obsolete, by a revolt against realism and a search for new methods. Only the methods often differed and led in opposite directions. Craig did not start any of the movements that developed, but there have been very few that did not owe something to him.

This is most obvious among the scene-designers. Turning the pages of any book on modern scenery we find numbers of 'Craigish' designs, with the architectural construction, the combinations of horizontal lines, the areas of light and shadow, which are familiar from *Towards a New Theatre*. How many designs by Orlik, Strnad, Bel Geddes, Robert Edmond Jones or Bragaglia lead straight back to Craig's drawings! And Josef Svoboda's mobile panels for a recent production of *Hamlet* at Prague were strongly reminiscent of the Moscow production. Craig showed stage designers how to escape from the constricting clutches of realism and create scenes that played their part in the drama. He showed them the power of suggestion possessed by light and colour and the expressive potential of materials – which, though people are too much inclined to forget the fact, Craig was the first to use as a dynamic element in the performance.

Other theatre men, such as the leaders of the expressionist movement, have seen in Craig the promoter of an art where all elements of the performance are required to contribute to the 'revelation' of the drama and the elucidation of its symbolism.

One of Craig's dreams was a theatre where words and 'visions', sounds and colours, dance and music would combine to make a feast for eyes and ears. So it is not surprising that the promoters of 'total theatre' should have regarded him as their master and should still be able to reconcile their theories with his principles.

Lastly, there have been those who have taken as their guide Craig's ideal of an art of representation going further than the theatre as we know it. Craig spoke of the possibility of an 'art of movement', of mobile forms evolving in space. Basing themselves on this idea, one of the boldest and most controversial of those he has propounded, the partisans of 'abstract theatre' developed their experiments, which have resulted in driving nature from the stage and dehumanizing the actor.

As we see, Craig's influence is not restricted to one single style. He paved the way for experiments which are still going on. He did not inspire a new school of playwriting, but he contributed to a radical transformation of the theatre in its aesthetic aspects. He has been a liberator and an awakener, a provocation and an inspiration.

NOTES

1. Gordon Craig, introduction to *The Art of the Theatre*, op. cit., 1905, pp. 11–12.
2. Gordon Craig, 'Art or Imitation? A Plea for an Enquiry after the missing Laws of the Art', in *The Theatre Advancing*, London, 1921, op. cit., p. 163.
3. Gordon Craig, introduction to *The Art of the Theatre* (1905), p. 15.
4. See Barnard Hewitt, 'Gordon Craig and Post-impressionism', in *The Quarterly Journal of Speech*, Vol. XXX, No. 1, January–February 1944.

INDEX